On Edge

The life
&
climbs
of
Henry Barber

On Edge

The life & climbs of Henry Barber

Chip Lee

With
David Roberts
and
Kenneth Andrasko

Appalachian Mountain Club,
Boston, Massachusetts

To My Parents

Editing Supervisor, Arlyn S. Powell, Jr.
Production, Michael Cirone and Betsey Tryon

Contents

	Publisher's Preface	ix
	Preface	xiii
	Prologue	xx
1	Collecting Cards	1
2	Western Adventures	22
3	England and Emergence	49
4	"Hot Henry's Here"	76
5	At the Feet of the Master	101
6	Celluloid Heroes	136
7	Beauty and Death	165
8	Mountains Like Brave Fellows	186
9	Frozen Faces	208
10	The Dream of Kilimanjaro	238
	Glossary	283

Publisher's Preface

Those readers who are familiar with mountaineering, either through participation at some level or because they enjoy the literature on the subject, may find this preface unnecessary. It is intended, rather, for readers approaching this fascinating sport for the first time.

There are a number of terms and concepts associated with mountaineering, as there are with any other sport or activity. These concepts are explored more fully in the text and are defined in a glossary at the back of the book, but it will be helpful to introduce some of them here.

There are four major sub-areas of the sport, all of which Henry Barber has participated in. The best-known is called *expeditionary mountaineering*. It is what the general public usually thinks of when the sport is mentioned — an expedition mounted to some out-of-the-way and often exotic corner of the world, involving days, if not weeks, of cold, danger, and hardship before some remote peak is ascended. A second sub-area, growing out of the first to some extent, is *rock climbing* — the ascent of cliffs, pinnacles, boulders (and even, as we have seen in the press lately, of the walls of buildings) using a number of mountaineering and gymnastic techniques. Rock climbing is subdivided into bouldering, crag climbing, and big wall climbing, the three referring to increasingly major undertakings using increasing amounts of equipment. The third sub-area of mountaineering is *ice climbing*, the ascent of near-vertical frozen waterfalls and ice walls in winter using specialized techniques and equipment developed for this purpose. *Alpine* mountaineering is the ascent of peaks or large faces requiring both rock and ice climbing, as in the Alps.

A *route* is the line of ascent up the mountain or cliff or ice wall. The first person (or, as is usually the case, team) to climb a given route is credited with its *first ascent*. The ascent is often then described in mountaineering literature, and the names of the climbers go in the record book, so to speak. On rock and ice routes, more numerous and usually less taxing than full-fledged mountains, the leader of the first ascent party traditionally names the route.

There can be innumerable routes on the same cliff face. The better known ones are often described in climbing guidebooks to an area. Such guidebooks use a system that rates the climbs according to difficulty. Systems vary from area to area and country to country. In this book, as in the United States, the *Yosemite Decimal System* is the main one used. It rates climbs on a scale of 5.1 to 5.9 in terms of technical difficulty. As even harder climbs have evolved in the decades since the Yosemite Decimal system was invented, additional ratings, such as 5.10, 5.11, and 5.12 have been added, often subdivided into *a-d* grades.

Most climbing involves equipment used to protect the climbers, primarily ropes and mechanical devices that connect the climbers to the ropes and the ropes to the surface being climbed. When this equipment is used to produce artificial anchors that the rope is clipped through, it falls under the general category of *protection*, for obvious reasons. *Aid climbing* results when the protection pieces or the rope supports the climber's weight directly during very difficult climbing.

The opposite of aid climbing is *free climbing*, where the climber ascends without the direct aid of such devices as ropes, pitons, nuts, or bolts, although all may be used purely as a safeguard against falling. The first climber to ascend a route unaided — even a route previously climbed with aid — is credited with a *first free ascent*.

An important part of roped free or aid climbing is the concept of partnership. One person must be anchored in a secure position holding the rope if another is to climb safely; in case of a fall by the climber, his partner must arrest it. In climbing parlance, the *leader* climbs while his *second belays, or protects*, him. To climb alone is to *solo* — and to climb a route unaided and alone for the first time is to achieve a *first solo ascent*.

The recent popularity of free and solo climbing, as will be explained in the book, has something to do with the climber's desire to test himself, to face danger, to conquer fear as well as the mountain. *Exposure*, or the distance one may fall, is one rough measure of the danger involved. The word is also sometimes used in a more general sense — being in a very exposed position on a hard climb is roughly equivalent to being out on a very narrow limb. Another concept having to do with danger is *commitment*; when one is committed to a particular move or route, one has passed the point of no return. It is difficult, if not impossible, to turn back or climb back down the pitch, so the climb must be completed, or there will be dire consequences.

An even more nebulous idea, but one that is at the heart of this book, is that of *ethics*. A climber's ethics have to do with the personal style in which he faces a climb — its danger and his own natural fear. Attention shifts to the process and quality of the way one climbs, and not simply whether the climb was successful. Ethics in this sense is an obsession of Henry Barber's. Let us get on to his story now.

— Arlyn S. Powell, Jr.

Preface

CHIP LEE WAS A STUDENT OF MINE at Hampshire College. Already a good climber at eighteen, he had spent his recent years in the thrall of a friend who could without exaggeration be called a climbing genius: Henry Barber. The age gap was insignificant between Henry and Chip, but it might as well have been a father-son relationship. By the time Chip arrived at college, the climbing world was abuzz with rumors that "Hot" Henry was probably the best rock climber in the country — and perhaps, those who had seen him solo dared speculate, the best in the world.

There was a strong gang of climbers at Hampshire, in part because the Outdoors Program which Ed Ward and I directed put the kind of emphasis on highly-skilled wilderness activities that you just couldn't get away with in most colleges. When I'd come to Hampshire in its opening year, I'd been handed a vague mandate to "do something like what Outward Bound does." I'd taught at Colorado Outward Bound and knew better than to imitate their way of doing things. I had some passionate pedagogical beliefs — in the importance of "experiential learning," and in the complementary value of intellectualizing one's prowlings through the woods. And some personal passions: in my twenties nothing had been more important in life than climbing — for its own sake, because it was crazy and antisocial and immensely satisfying.

Hampshire had spewed forth from the academically conservative soil of the Connecticut Valley in western Massachusetts as a geyser of late-1960's idealism. It would take the college most of a decade to decide it really wanted to be another Amherst after all. In those halcyon early years I managed to pull off some wacky "experiments." I marched students who had read Thoreau along windy Cape Cod beaches in November, and got them to visit the house in Maine where, during an alcoholic Christmas, Robert Lowell had tried to strangle Jean Stafford (both wrote brilliantly about it). I taught a course in expedition literature that had students bivouacking in a giant maple tree, improvising a raft to cross the Connecticut, and hunting "yetis" in the woods on campus. I bamboozled other professors into accepting personal journals of blister-plagued assaults on the Appalachian Trail as bona fide evidence of academic progress. Most of the climbers at Hampshire loved it. The zenith of my crusade was the Division III work (read, roughly, "senior thesis") of Jon Krakauer. Despite steeply arched eyebrows and a tantrum or two in the Dean's Office, Jon managed to present as his self-certifying artifact a fine new route on Alaska's Moose's Tooth. Not journals, essays, philosophical ruminations *about* the climb, but the climb itself.

Chip Lee, however, was having none of this. He climbed, as I had in my own college days, strictly on his own time. None of this "hippie-dippy" relevance for him: he wanted a good, old-fashioned, basic schooling, and he commuted regularly to Smith and Amherst to take advantage of Hampshire's exchange system and steep himself in solid classics. He was wont to hang out with drinking buddies who chewed tobacco, appraised women from a dorm balcony rather than stir-frying vegetables with them, and called men his father's age "sir." In prep school he'd lettered in lacrosse and football. I'm quite sure he'd never touched a Frisbee in his life.

Chip came to me rather shyly one day to ask whether I'd superintend his Division II studies (read ... never mind: we never quite figured what it meant ourselves). He wanted to write short stories. I said fine. Chip was the kind of student who turned in his papers on time, was willing to rewrite them numerous times, and listened when I proscribed split infinitives. He was not a natural writer, but he was the hardest-working one I'd seen at Hampshire.

We had our first falling out over a short story he wrote about climbing. He'd tried to foist off on me a quite preposterous saga of a young hard man who goes up to some cliff in New

Hampshire with his buddy, starts soloing up the moderate lower stretches of an eventually difficult route, and pulls loose a block and falls twenty meters, nearly taking his startled friend with him, to what climbers jocularly call the "deck." That much was barely plausible, I thought, if handled well. But Chip would have it that, like cartoon figures popping back to normality after being flattened by a steam roller, his hero would get up, brush himself off, smoke a quick cigarette, and immediately insist on tackling another climb.

I argued with him about motivation, realism, machismo. Chip was uncharacteristically obtuse. Finally I pointed out that anybody who'd been lucky enough to survive a twenty-meter ground fall would head at once for a bar or a sauna rather than aiming, dazed and bleeding, for another horse.

Chip told me, with an air of authority completely at odds with the deference I'd come to expect, that I was wrong. The hero was himself; the whole thing, as I should have known, had really happened. I blustered and spluttered some more about motivation and credibility, then burst out, "Why didn't you tell Ed and me?"

Chip went on — sheepishly, to his credit — to confess that he knew how Ed and I worried about accidents, and he didn't want us to vex ourselves unnecessarily, and . . . he had even gone so far as to swear all his climbing friends to secrecy. Now he tried to swear me to secrecy, since he apparently feared Ed's supervisory wrath even more than my own.

It was a glimpse for me — unwelcome, of course — of what it must be like to become what young climbers unabashedly refer to as "an old fart." When I was twenty-one, I had tried to disguise from the older climbers who were my college mentors the fact that my best friend and I were about to set off on a two-man, forty-day expedition to an unclimbed ridge on a difficult mountain in Alaska. We knew they'd disapprove; we knew they were in some vague but irrelevant sense "right;" and we knew we had to do it.

I broke my vow and told Ed, and we sat around deploring the recklessness of youth, but I think both of us gained a perverse respect for Chip at that moment. Perhaps he did for me, as well. We started talking about Division III, and gradually the plan for what, years later, this book represents shaped itself in his head.

Chip wanted to write a biography of Henry Barber. Worse, Henry acquiesced. Both thought it was eminently publishable. A number of professorial alarms went off in my head, all at once. *We* know who Henry Barber is, but in this country where a reserve linebacker for the Atlanta Falcons is better known than Yvon Chouinard, what kind of public could be expected to give a damn about Henry Barber? How could Chip write about someone he hero-worshipped? In a dozen ways, he seemed too close to his subject. And despite "reality," there *were* all kinds of things wrong with Chip's account of his near-miss at Cathedral Ledge. He was too close to climbing, too, I thought.

But he couldn't be talked out of it. And I began to think, 'Well, maybe it's a good idea, after all.' A broad public could perhaps be made to care about the young man who was a virtuoso on hard rock, one of the best in history — if it could be taught who Henry Barber was. I didn't know Henry well, but I sensed that he was an interesting — difficult, vain, complicated — person. But could Chip do it?

We made a deal and called it Chip's Division III. Four "publishable" chapters, by the end of the year. I breathed a sigh of relief, as professors always do after working out compromises with hopelessly ambitious students. Let's get him graduated, I thought, and let the book take care of itself. Whatever else, it will be good for him to find out just how hard it is to write a book.

The work began inauspiciously. The first drafts I saw were all that I had feared. Chip was too close to climbing: in one breath he would remember himself and describe what a piton was; in the next he would blithely talk about "taking all but two points of aid out of" a climb known at most to four hundred devotees of English gritstone crags.

And Chip was far too close to Henry. Virtually everything Henry said Chip took at face value. Not surprisingly, Henry's detractors and rivals tended to come off second-best. I would ask Chip, "How do you know this is true? "Chip would reply blandly, "Henry said so." "Did you think of asking X for his version of it?" I might urge. "Gosh, no," said Chip — or words to that effect.

We talked about biography. Boswell on Johnson, Richard Sewall on Emily Dickinson, Strachey on Queen Victoria. I felt frustrated; nothing was sinking in. And yet Chip was obsessed with Henry. He had spent uncountable hours tape-recording Henry's rambling self-appraisals and tales. He'd sat in his apartment and assiduously transcribed the tapes until, as one of his roommates confessed to me, "we're so sick of Henry's voice we could scream." I kept lobbying for *distance*. Distance on Henry, distance on climbing, with all its unspoken codes of toughness and internecine competitiveness.

I'd like to think that what happened next was my doing, but I suspect Chip too finally got sick of hearing Henry's anecdotes fill the apartment living room. He came to me one day in a fit of pique. Henry was spending the weekend at Hampshire. But Chip was fed up. Henry wanted *this*, he wanted *that*; listen to the incredible story he had told Chip *last* weekend. Chip was, I feared, on the verge of throwing in the towel. He had discovered "distance" with a vengeance.

The three of us got together that weekend for a drink. Drinking with Henry was always a formidable outing; pretty soon we were several pitchers into it. I had begun, I hoped, like a marriage counselor, trying to reconcile biographer and subject. But I began to lose what I thought of as my detachment. Pretty soon I was letting Henry have it, too, siding with Chip, implying that Henry ought to be grateful somebody wanted to write about him, rather than demanding. Henry, it seemed to me, regarded his life itself as what people in Hollywood refer to as a "property." I went to a few pains to inform him of this fact.

Dimly, in the midst of my woozy outburst, I recognized what Chip had sensed all along. Henry Barber, for all his faults, was a profoundly interesting person. Not simply because he was a true genius — he was different from anyone I had ever known. He was, like most intensely skilled practitioners of an art, self-centered, obsessive, alternately maudlin and cold, guarded about his personal "space," capable of great generosity, yet critical of others and self-conscious about his role in the world. Yet he had a lot of unique qualities: a distrust of machines, an unexplained Anglophilia, a deep hedonistic side, a strong streak of the self-destructive (revealed in his marathon drinking feats) side by side with the most precise calculation of his chances on dangerous rock. For the first time, in the midst of this absurd three-way quarrel in a tavern, I began really to believe Chip's book was worth writing.

The utter reversal was crucial for Chip. He found his perspective. His pendulum returned, during the succeeding months, to something like balance. There will no doubt be readers who feel that Chip's biography is still too close, too uncritical, to give an accurate view of Henry Barber's meteoric passage across the climbing scene. But I think he has ended up near where he should be.

Chip got his four chapters in and graduated. For a full year after Hampshire he plugged away at the book, determined to finish it. He climbed, made a furtive reconnaissance of medical school, and learned how to fly an airplane. Supporting himself by teaching flying, he burned the midnight oil in Boulder, Colorado, and finished the book.

The product, I think, justifies the labor. Chip's manuscript needed some editing, but not nearly so much as I feared when he first tackled his task in his last year of college. Henry Barber is, at this writing, still only twenty-eight years of age: very young to have a biography written about him. Chip, in fact, disclaims his effort as biography; but for all that, it remains, at the least, "a life in climbing." And Henry remains a fascinating character.

No biographer yet has captured the essence of the mystery that Wolfgang Amadeus Mozart embodied between 1756 and 1791. Prodigies and geniuses peculiarly defeat biography — their lives blend Foxe's *Book of Martyrs* with the most indulgent columns of sports magazines. It may be that Henry Barber was as good as he was mainly because he was so obsessive: he did climb on 320 days in a single year, and he built a "Foops machine" in his basement to practice the moves on a climb at the Shawangunks that no one else could make the second ascent of. But I doubt that there is a climber in the world who can read some of the episodes in Chip's book — especially those recounting Henry's boldest solo climbs, like the Steck-Salathé in Yosemite, or the made-for-television ascent of the Strand on a Cornish sea-cliff — without having to pause to wipe his sweating palms on his trousers. It may be a crude criterion, but it is a climber's ultimate one: only the most genuine tales can elicit it.

— David Roberts
Cambridge, Mass.
Winter, 1981

Prologue
Travels with Henli

W E CALL HIM HENLI because he hates "Hank" and clearly requires a nickname. It helps keep him from taking himself too seriously. When that happens, he gets agitated and anxious and rather fed-up. But when Henry is not worried, he is at his prime. At those times, we even call him Little Henli.

"This is where I'm at my best," he says simply. It is at the beginning of the trip, and we have been in the car only a few hours. Henry is driving; I am playing with the radio dial; Chip is in the back seat, knees to his chin, folded up like a deck chair among all our gear crammed into the modest Opel. This utilitarian order was not to last. We soon rearrange ourselves three abreast in the front seat.

By the time we crossed the border of Colorado into Utah, the sun was beginning to set, throwing bright, diagonal darts through the windshield. "On the road!" Henry screams above the static of the AM radio tunes.

> I feel like myself again. I got the steering wheel in one hand, a beer in the other. I know just where we're going and just which climbs we're going to do. Ho, boy! I'm ready to cruise!

He gives one of his high-pitched, crazed giggles and accelerates into the slanting sun.

Henry, happily, is enthusiastic to a fault when excited. He pays only casual attention to the task of piloting the car, so that he can direct his concern toward the well-being of his passengers. He half turns in his seat to assure Chip of the terror of climbs to come, narrowing his eyes with menacing promise. When he finishes his beer, he looks to us for a replacement, grinning like an idiot, happy in the assurance that we are as delighted with life as he.

Besides the fact that Little Henli is in a car — a moving vehicle being the next most appropriate surrounding for him after steep rock — he is in high spirits for other reasons. We have ventured into Colorado National Monument and, after winding through the red-bleached canyons where cliffs swell above and below the road like giant clay jugs, unfired and finger pressed, we get out of the car to hike down to "a beautiful finger crack that looks great from the road." We descend into a canyon and tiptoe along a narrow shelf. Up close it is a beautiful, thin cleft going straight up through smooth, red sandstone. Chip gazes at the delicate line of the crack, then looks down at his own large, rather thick fingers and shudders.

"What's the matter, Chippy?" Henry gives a diabolical laugh. "I've never seen you so quiet before a climb. If we make it up, I'll have to call it The Calm Before the Storm."

They both make it up. Henry names the climb Summerhill.

Henry doesn't look like a top climber, not the way the others do. The muscles don't show. But the forearms are like a blacksmith's — nearly as large as the biceps. And the incredibly small feet — size five or six, they look like. Taller than average, a bit stocky now, with arms far too long for the body and a reach like a spindly water bug. The long face and the moustache that droops, covering his facial expressions. Intense eyes that narrow to nothing. The inevitable white golfing hat. At twenty-eight, a noticeably receding hairline. A sense of total self-possession and absolute confidence. Inexhaustible energy flowing.

But mostly, it's in the head. He figures out moves faster than other climbers do. He commits himself totally: if he's going to go for it, he goes for it all the way. No compromise. None of the 'if's and 'but's that clutter the mind of the average climber. And he's figured out, as almost no one else has, how to rest on a climb. Complicated locks with hands, feet, and knees — not to mention the occasional elbow, even the head. He moves with a fraction of the effort that other climbers expend. It's weird.

* * * * * *

We drive and drive, finally pulling into the buzzing metropolis of Price, Utah. Main Street is filled with jacked-up trucks and lit-up store fronts; for dinner we choose a cafe with a pink neon sign in the window. Later, in the car, we tape for Chip's book. Henry talks about Australian animals for twenty minutes and then about the mysteries of soloing. When we turn on the light in the car, we find that a massive knot of tape fouled the cassette long ago. We curse and sigh, but maybe it is right that way.

That first night we sleep at a highway rest stop, the big trucks rolling nearby. Salt Lake City is just down the road, and the sky is fired orange by the Kennecott Copper factories. There are scores of foolish family restaurants serving breakfast in Salt Lake City, and a gray haze hangs over everything like a bad dream. In Cottonwood Canyon later, Henry browses through his climbing guide and leads the way to a whole mountainside of white rock — curving slabs, great shelf upon great shelf, a world of gigantic stone. I sit in the sun while Henry and Chip do a climb. I can't remember its name, but do remember its look, do remember that Henry free climbed an overhanging section that looked especially strenuous for the first time (throwing off the chains of the aid gear previously used).

* * * * * *

In the car again and back in town, Henry rolls down his window, leans out into the quiet evening, and shouts his greetings to the sidewalk strollers: "Hello, fat man!" he cries to a round gentleman taking an after-dinner walk. "You are a very fat man!" His crazed laughter dies away, and he falls into a reverie, swooning for his true love back east. After a period of reflection, he leans out into the wind and wails his desire, nearly falling out the window.

I awake in Idaho, in the City of the Rocks. Dr. Seuss could have invented it, the remnants of an arts and crafts session of mammoth children. A truck comes speeding down the road. Out hops a short man with an Ultra-Brite smile and an eager manner. His name is Dave, and he is our guide for the day. There is something about his rally-round-the- flag attitude that gives one the impression that, underneath his innocent tee shirt, he is concealing a coach's whistle that might be called into play at any moment.

With Dave in the lead we bushwhack single file through bramble jungles and swampy valleys to an island of a boulder and climb on a pockmarked rock. Throughout the day we wander in the desert heat, Dave always in front, ever pointing to something new.

On the road out of the City of Rocks, Henry spots a finger crack and forces the car to stop. When he and Chip get up to it, they give us an "It-sure-looks-different-from-here" look and smile shyly. Chip follows Henry's preparations for the attempt with one of his patented "Are-you-high-or-something-Henry?" gazes, but to no avail. After a few tries on the overhanging crack, Henry calls to us: "What'll you give me if I do this? I need a reward! How 'bout a kiss? Or a case of beer? I need some incentive." We promise a variety of things; luckily he doesn't make it.

*   *   *   *   *   *

As the Opel nears the town of Jackson, Wyoming and the Tetons, the frequency of Winnebago sightings increases. "I hate Winnies!" Henry screams. "Look at them all. I hate you, Winnies!" The streets are crowded with tourists, milling in and out of tacky souvenir shops selling ceramic jackrabbits with antlers and saddles and the like. We nearly hit a moose on the way back to our camp. It lumbers out of the underbrush, its knees seemingly level with the top of the tiny car. They are wrinkled and dirty.

In the morning, Henry bids us farewell and, with only a

chalk bag at his waist and EB climbing shoes on his feet (well, he might have had some shorts on), sets off to solo a long route. His casual goodbye is like that of a businessman heading off to catch the 8:13 into the city, but I think then, as I do many times, that any number of flukes — a loose rock, a wayward thought breaking his concentration, an awkward move with his bad shoulders — could make this a decisive farewell. Watching him stride away toward the mountain, I am impressed with his casual confidence and matter-of-fact conviction. I stopped worrying. You can't begin to worry about Henry.

* * * * * *

Henry drives. We sleep and regain consciousness in the heart of Yellowstone Park. Hot springs smoke by the side of the road and smell like hell.

Sometime in the late afternoon, eagle-eyed Henli spots some steep cliffs looming in the gray sky like Gothic fortresses. Henry and Chip do an intricate face climb completely without protection. On a nearby hill, up and across from us, there is a car flipped onto its roof. The accident must have just occurred. A family group, which I take to be the occupants of the car, is sitting a short distance away having a picnic. I look at them through my binoculars; no one seems to be hurt. They are munching potato chips and pouring cupfuls of something dark from a pink thermos. The car lies behind them like a dead, disfigured horse.

* * * * * *

Morning finds us at Devil's Tower, at the far end of Wyoming. Henry has driven through a rainy night. He has his own well-tested tricks for staying awake at the wheel. Sometimes he brushes his teeth — not just a quick brush, mind you, but a marathon hour-long session, toothpaste and all. Or, he will change his clothes completely, undressing himself at the wheel, only to put back on those same items just removed. Simpler tricks include raising one leg off the floor and leaving it suspended until he can no longer stand the pain; TURNING THE RADIO UP REAL LOUD, regardless of sleeping passengers; and, if it's raining, turning the wipers on only occasionally, demanding a great deal of concentration to stay on the road. You may still crash, but not from falling asleep.

Devil's Tower is a cubist rendition of a bunch of asparagus. Henry and Chip spend most of the day on a finger crack five rope lengths long, much to the delight and unrest of the tourists below.

That afternoon, Chip and I sit on the car at the border of Prairie Dog Village, next to a mobile home that unloads a family that feeds Doritos and Devil Dogs to the fat little critters scurrying about their mounds. Through binoculars, we watch Henry solo an intimidating climb called Hollywood and Vine up on the Tower. Henry usually keeps up a continual movement when he's climbing, especially when he's soloing, and we become a little concerned when he doesn't appear to be moving from a spot just below the top. Later, he tells us that he was trying to devise a way to make the necessary move without dislocating his weak shoulder. The move required an extension he knew would be too much for him. Needless to say, he made it. He then hitched a rappel down to the ground with some neighboring climbers. I like to picture that scene: "Excuse me, chaps, would you mind if I descend on your rope? I didn't bother to bring one up here myself." Once grounded, he is coaxed into some picture posing by incredulous tourists.

*   *   *   *   *   *

Next stop: the Needles, South Dakota. Here, nature makes her monumental tribute to the phallus. To enter is to drive into a Freudian dream. Great pinnacles rise solitary against the sky, or huddle together like embarrassed pubescent boys. We climb a bit, but it is the following day, with the promise of Henry scaling the infamous Super Pin, that we are waiting for.

We have dinner that night in, Heaven forbid, a family restaurant in Custer. Henry eats a huge plate of spaghetti, explaining that he needed his strength for the impending climb. Henry and food have a love/hate relationship. Although forever asserting a neutral attitude toward food — "I don't care if we have dinner or not," said with a sly and hungry glance at a well-laden table — only will power and not lack of appetite keeps him from eating constantly. He awakes the following morning in a chilly field, dew-drenched, and screams into the still morning: "Ahhhhhhh, Super Pin!"

After a cold bowl of cereal in a cold car, Chip and Henry do a warm-up climb. Super Pin deserves as much, in that it hasn't had a second ascent in ten years, perhaps due to its awesome reputation and the fact that the route totally lacks protection.

Henry prefaces his ascent of Super Pin by vowing,

As soon as I get this done, I'm heading straight east for Jane. This is the only thing standing between me and her.

His eyes flash and he giggles, "But not for long!" He is right enough about that. Henry does the climb. Chip and a fellow named Dennis follow.

Dennis is a typical Needles climber; has thighs as big as Ponderosa pine trunks and no fear, which some people might interpret as an absence of brains. Dennis takes us through some nearby woods in search of an out-of-the-way climb. He never falters in his composed and Zen-like acceptance of the rocks, some quite terrifying, all around him. At one point, he takes Henry up on a formation that looks like the ear of an enormous elephant. I am atop another rock and think that Henry looks like a recently swatted, flattened mosquito there, caught sucking blood.

When the light starts to fade, we pull out. Super Pin has been done. Henry is satisfied enough to return to the east to his lady love. Tipping our nonexistent hats to the huge grimaces on Mount Rushmore as we drive by, we settle into the front seat, resigning ourselves to the two-day drive ahead.

Where I-80 runs by Chicago, we hit the four o'clock traffic. Chip and I, in the front seat, look at the profusion of sweating, dirty collars in the cars around us and reaffirm to one another our commitment to elude the rat race. I turn to have Henry confirm our pact. He is in the back seat, covered by a beer-stained sleeping bag, stray books, and climbing gear. Although he claims that "I've never been able to sleep in a car in my life," he is, for at least this slight moment, sound asleep.

— Susan Minot

1

Collecting Cards

*H*ENRY BARBER EXHIBITED at an early age the qualities that would later distinguish him as a world-class rock climber — his dogged stubbornness, his desire to be the center of attention, his feistiness, his shrewd business sense. His first love was baseball.

In Little League, outside of Boston, he played on two different teams in adjacent towns, often playing two games on a single Saturday. Eventually he became good enough to play first base, where he earned the nickname "Stretch."

As his passion for baseball increased, he amassed a definitive collection of trading cards — nearly 10,000 of them. He memorized the statistics on the cards even before putting the gum in his mouth, and even today he can still quote an obscure datum. He later recalled,

> The main trait I developed during my baseball card days was the push to beat everybody out. You had to be good at wheeling and dealing, convincing some kid that he wanted to trade his valuable card for your worthless one.

From grade school on, Henry knew that he wanted to be in the big time, to be a person others noticed. He soothed that ambition not only with baseball, but by provoking fights. He was a "scrapper," he says, often picking on boys who were bigger or tougher than he. "It's the German blood," his mother says. "It runs in the family. His father is the same way, so stubborn you can't believe it." Fights were an everyday occurrence for Henry. He lost every one of them, because of his small size and weakness, but he never gave up; the victor would have to be dragged free from his victim.

What retrospection reveals as the turning point of Henry's early life occurred one day in ninth grade. A gang from the baseball team had thrown some school equipment from a moving bus as a prank. Apprehended, the culprits were cut from the team. They assumed that the solitary Henry had squealed, and decided to beat him up one day on his way to a game. Among Henry's wounds was a sizeable cut on his mouth where one of the attackers had kicked him. Henry tried to conceal the bleeding, but his coach asked him what was wrong. Impetuously the boy seized the moment to deliver not only a tirade against the thugs who had beaten him up, but against the coach and the baseball program as well. Jabbing the coach hard in the breastbone, he announced that he was quitting.

The summer before, Henry had attended the Aschcrofters (later Telluride) School of Mountaineering in southwestern Colorado. The day he gave up baseball, he came home, dropped his glove on the kitchen floor, and told his mother that he was going to become a great climber.

He worked as a janitor in the school gym to save enough money to return to Telluride the following summer, and started climbing around Boston with the Appalachian Mountain Club, the oldest group of its kind in the country. He met Ajax Greene, four years younger, who had started climbing at the age of eleven. In his trademark, a floppy orange-and-green hat, Ajax's father, an outgoing optimist and modest climber well-known to the AMC group, would drive the two boys to the local crags around Boston after school. On weekends he chauffeured them to the main climbing centers in New England. The year was 1970 — for Henry it was the beginning of a five-year obsession with climbing.

Returning from his second summer at Telluride, Henry looked at his school peers and decided they were

> wasting their time. None of them were leading a real life, according to the way I thought it should be led. They were all involved in parties and hanging out, so I just missed out on the entire social scene at school. The more I

AMC weekend group at the Franconia Hotel in 1970: (left to right) Glenn Sprowl, Ross Bronson, Harold Taylor, Bill Atkinson, Ginny Seymour, and Henry Barber/Henry Barber Collection

heard about the whole scene, the less I liked it and the more proud of myself I became. I was moving into the extreme sort of sincerity that I had been learning about at Dave Farny's school in Telluride, through the mountaineering guides, who were like bronzed lifeguards. I identified with them. They were my heros — mountain men who were complete individuals. To me, they were cool. They were all on their little trips where nobody else mattered. It all got a bit cornball at times, though. I remember one of the guides saying around a campfire one night that 'if you've ever loved a woman, you'll love the mountains.' At that point, I thought that kind of rhetoric was pretty moving, just because it was so removed from my experiences at school. I was having discussions with these people that seemed to mean something.

Henry was seventeen. He was climbing every day after school, and sometimes even between classes. Most of his time was spent with AMCers, virtually all of whom were older professionals of one sort or another; they had cars and could get Henry to the important cliffs on weekends. Around Boston he and his cronies climbed everywhere they could: at Quincy Quarries, long mined for granite and now full of wrecked cars and spray paint; on the mortared granite of the aqueduct known as the Waban Arches, where as a boy Henry had played "capture the flag;" on obscure boulders found behind shopping malls; and on the sides of college dormitories. There was an inconspicuous rock in the woods behind the Barber home on which Henry would practice traverses until well after dark, when his mother would call him to dinner. "We heard our fill of climbing talk at the dinner table every night," she remembers. "Every birthday and Christmas, it was piton-this and carabiner-that."

First photo of Henry to appear in a magazine. Yosemite early on. 1972–73/ Ken Wilson

The Barber family had been based in Rhode Island for several generations. After they moved to Boston, they returned for summers and holidays to the family place along the sea coast there, to relax and sail and explore. It gave Henry his strong taste for the ocean and sea-cliff climbing and water

Bouldering on Fort Independence in Boston/Bob Anderson

sports. His father, a vice president of one of New England's leading banks, was a major influence on his son, inculcating a Protestant work ethic, conservatism, and traditional family values. The Barbers had traveled quite a bit, and passed on that love to Henry, who freely shared most of his own adventures with them. As a result, in later years they ventured abroad to visit places where Henry had climbed, even following his itinerary; there they met people with whom he had become close. There is a great deal of mutual respect between parents and son.

Climbing soon took the place of beating up his brothers and picking fights at school for Henry. He was also interested

Bouldering at the Quincy Quarries/Henry Barber Collection

in Beverly Peale, a quiet girl with whom he felt comfortable talking. "I don't think many girls would have put up with him," his mother remembers.

> And he wouldn't take any foolishness from them, either. A few girls tried to pretend they liked climbing so that they could be with him. That didn't go over very well with Henry.

Already, at age seventeen, Henry was teaching rock climbing for the AMC beginner's program at the Quincy Quarries. As someone who learns by doing rather than reading, Henry gained considerable insight into movement on rock from hours of watching the mistakes and form of others. He also taught during the summers at Dave Farny's Telluride school, giving back to his students there some of the attention and advice he had received from the AMC crew.

The AMCers were fairly conservative professionals, physicists and professors who certainly were not doing wild things like the English climbers he was soon to meet. Though only average climbers, they were dedicated, energetic, well-rounded people, not the braggarts and competitors Henry would encounter on the climbing circuit.

Free climbing was often too difficult for the young climber, so Henry began to practice aid climbing, feeling that he would be more likely to excel at it. The repetitiveness and slow pace of aid work, though, with all that equipment dangling all over, was less appealing. So, he persevered with his efforts to learn free technique, spending innumerable weekends with the AMC at the Shawangunks near Poughkeepsie, New York, the most popular cliff in the east. Like baseball cards, he began to collect climbs.

I'd take my Shawangunks guidebook and make minus signs next to all the routes that I wanted to do; then I'd put a cross through it when I'd done the route. I'd put all the information about the climb by the cross as well. Before I'd go away for the weekend, I'd make a list of all the climbs I was going to get done during the two days. That saved time. We never stood around and looked at the guidebook. We just went from one climb to the next.

Even now I can't have a good day unless one of two things happens. Either I try the first of a number of hard climbs that I want to do in a day and fail. Then the whole day's blown as far as the plan's concerned. I'll just do a few easy climbs, then sunbathe, drink, and boulder — whatever's relaxing. The other day consists of having a sports plan — nine climbs or whatever — and I do all of them. I've accomplished what I set out to do.

By his own analysis, Henry is far from a natural climber.

The Life and Climbs of Henry Barber

When I started I couldn't do anything. I was so weak that
I was trying to get up to normal ability. When I first went
to Telluride, I couldn't even do a pullup. But I didn't get
good by doing exercises. I got good by climbing more
than anyone else around. Climbing that much had to be
planned, in order to achieve the goals that I had in mind:
to do the most difficult climbs, and the greatest number
of them, in as concentrated a period of time as possible.
There were only a certain number of hours in a day.

After about two years of effort Henry had reached the 5.7
level of difficulty (on a rating system running from 5.0 to
5.10). Ajax Greene remembers that at about this point his
friend started "galloping away from his peers." At the Shawangunks Henry and Ajax would begin climbing at 7 A.M., after
Henry had already soloed two or three routes. The last climb
of the day would invariably finish after dark.

Henry graduated from high school and entered the Babson School of Business. He was still living at home, and never
did spend time in a college dormitory. He was climbing on the
Waban Arches and the walls of buildings before school, during
breaks between classes, and after school. In 1972, he estimates,
he climbed on approximately 270 days. In 1973 the number
went up to 325. Ajax, then a perceptive ninth grader, observed
that

> Henry was pretty disappointed with school. He felt that
> the whole place was working against him, that no one
> really was involved with the students when he was there.
> Consequently, he never studied. He didn't work at all; he
> just got more and more into climbing.

Henry developed very few close friendships during these
years. Two of his regular partners were Ric Hatch and Bob
Anderson. Hatch was less ambitious than Henry, although
almost as talented, and was content to second numerous
climbs that he would have been scared out of his wits to lead.
Henry found in Ric a friend who "kept a lot of secrets for me."
These included routes at the Shawangunks which Henry

Early partners in the Boston area: (left to right) Greg Burns, Ajax Greene, Henry Barber, and Ric Hatch/Henry Barber Collection

never bothered to claim credit for, and numerous episodes involving soloing difficult climbs.

The pair met while each was soloing at Quincy Quarries. Henry was two years older and had a car; the two began to go bouldering together regularly after school, once Ric was free from Framingham High and Henry from Babson. During the summer, when Ric worked at a climbing shop in Cambridge, they were able to arrange frequent four-day climbing weekends.

Ric's unassuming good nature can be judged from a 'Gunks story he tells on himself.

We were doing a climb called Stirrup Trouble. Henry had it down pat. I don't really like to climb in front of a crowd, but it didn't bother Henry that much. We were doing it at the end of a day, just before driving back to Boston. He had only one runner in, and would have hit

9

the ground if he'd come off. All these people began gathering around, 'oohing' and 'aahing.' They all moved closer and closer to me, whispering all the time. Finally they got the courage to ask me what the route was and who that guy was up there. I just turned to them and said, "That's Ric Hatch." They all moved away, totally in awe of this climber Ric Hatch.

Another climber Barber met at this time was Mike Martinek, a graduate student who worked as a short-order cook and tied flies in his spare time; he was prominent in a group of a dozen or so youths who called themselves the CCC, or the Columbo (after the brand of yogurt) Climbing Club. They met frequently to climb but almost solely on small, obscure crags; they then gave slide shows of their exploits amidst a room full of controlled substances and trash cans of iced beer. Mike, always wild and loose, was in the habit of cruising around suburban neighborhoods offering twenty dollars to kids playing street hockey "if you can find me a nice rock face or a big boulder in the woods." For Ric and Henry — who was so straight then that he seemed "almost 1930ish, like from Officer's Candidate School," according to Martinek — the CCC provided a glimpse of another sort of lifestyle that they both decided to avoid, despite the great times they had with the group.

In his first year at Babson Henry had also met Bob Anderson, a young Tufts professor who shared his dedication and competitiveness. Anderson was immensely talented, intense, and heavily involved in a countercultural lifestyle at the time. Stories of freakish, drug-related behavior told by Anderson and Martinek had convinced Henry and Ric alike that their own path, however traditional, was the proper one. Henry remains adamant to this day in his aversion to alternative lifestyles.

In 1972 Barber and Anderson climbed most of the more difficult routes in the east, and opened up numerous previously unsuspected possibilities. During a single weekend at Cathedral Ledge, near North Conway, New Hampshire, Henry and Bob free-climbed five aid routes for the first time, all 5.9 or 5.10 efforts. In the summer of 1972, they added eleven aid eliminations in a burst of zealous free climbing, requiring a supplement to the new guidebook that was penned and published the following year by Henry. He noted the

> obviously egotistical reasons for writing this supplement, as my name appeared in it quite frequently. My major concern, though, was the ecology of the cliffs. Without this in mind, I probably would not have climbed many of the aid routes free and would not have repeated other climbs using only nuts.

At the time, first free ascents were more prestigious than new routes in the east (though the reverse was true out west). Although Henry had come up through the aid ranks himself, he had arrived on the scene late enough so that he was never inculcated with the dominant aid and big wall psychology of the 1960's, when the multiday routes on El Capitan in Yosemite were considered to be the highest forms of expression in climbing. He was the first of a generation that grew up not accepting pins and aid as given, right on the cusp between the very different worlds of aid and clean free climbing. There was an exciting sense, in fact, that climbers were now progressing beyond the achievements of the previous generation. So, aid eliminations became Henry's specialty and the focus of his attention. "They were easy pickings, but great for the ego," summarizes John Bragg, an active innovator and regular partner of Henry's.

Henry took a year off from Babson in early 1973 and, with Bob Anderson as his partner, climbed "like a madman" through the winter, "running around New England as fast as we could drive." The two were getting ready for a spring trip to Yosemite. Henry recalls,

> We were doing the hardest routes around. Anderson was outwardly competitive, and I just felt that I was pretty good. We climbed very well together, and so we started trying to do the hard stuff that had not as yet been climbed.

11

First free ascent of Recluse at Cathedral Ledge, NH (left). Bob Anderson toproping at Crow Hill (right)/Henry Barber Collection

We were stoked because we knew that we had our climbing pretty wired. We had just done the first ascent of Jane, a 5.11 at Crow Hill near Boston that took eight days to do, and we were chuffed as hell. We knew that there was no climb in the United States that was that hard. We worked on that one for a long time, trying to toprope it or lead it, finally leading it.

Collecting Cards

We weren't wasting any time, once getting up around seven at the Shawangunks and doing Matinee and Try Again, both 5.10 climbs, by ten in the morning. That was in April, one morning while it was snowing. Sometimes we were mismatched, with Anderson feeling his position as mentor somewhat and grilling me intellectually for long periods of time. I think that we both learned from each other.

While climbing with Anderson, Barber still felt the fresh, fervent intensity of someone on the rise in a sport or any other field of endeavor. He had not quite made it to the established forefront, although he knew that his name was being whispered. His level of energy and his capacity for large doses of severe climbing rose in proportion to the degree to which he was being recognized for his achievements.

At last the Yosemite visit took place. The eastern pair amazed Camp 4 locals with their nonstop activity on the hardest routes, and their very fast times on modern classics and routes climbed only once before. Henry had begun to make a name for himself.

An integral part of becoming a good climber was an adulation of men who served as role models, heroes, half-mythical exemplars. Says Henry,

There were people at the Shawangunks, like Jim McCarthy, Rich Goldstone, and John Stannard. I'd walk down the Carriage Road, wondering each time some guy passed by if he was Stannard.

At the time, John Stannard was the leading 'Gunks climber. An intense, dedicated, almost neurotically organized perfectionist, he had pushed the limits of free climbing far beyond the top achievements of climbers like McCarthy, who a decade earlier had represented the 'Gunks ultimate. Stannard was hard to miss on the Carriage Road. He walked with a slightly bowlegged sway, had long and slender but obviously strong arms that dangled awkwardly at his sides, and wore dark-rimmed glasses kept in place with a piece of parachute cord. The Stannard mystique had as one of its chief pillars an awesome climb called Foops. The crux section of Foops was a three-meter ceiling — a horizontal overhang so large that it extended farther than a leader could reach.

Done years before as an aid climb, Foops had seemed to earlier climbers intrinsically impossible to free. But in 1968 Stannard had performed the feat. He had patiently worked on a succession of extremely strenuous moves, accumulating knowledge from each failure, allowing himself to take repeated short, safe leader falls as he discovered the holds. Only extraordinary arm strength permitted Stannard to suspend all of his body weight from downward-pointing flakes of rock which he grasped between thumb and fingers — chinning bars over which he could not curl his fingers.

Normally at the 'Gunks, when a new route is freed the second ascent comes within weeks or even days. The extremely competitive scene guarantees as much. But Foops was so bold, so difficult, that *four years* after Stannard's success it awaited a second ascent. It was this climb that now became Henry's obsession.

After trying repeatedly to reach the lip of the overhang, he returned to Boston, where he built in his basement what was to be called the Foops Machine. He nailed various thicknesses of paintsticks onto the joists holding up the living room floor. Hanging upside down on the basement ceiling, his feet pressing on one joist, his right hand underclinging another, he practiced the reach needed to bring himself to the lip of the roof.

Anderson would often take part in the training sessions, as would others like Greene and Hatch. An average session included at least three six-packs of beer and an ample quantity of chalk for the hands. Gradually, the training partners halved the number of sticks until they represented small holds less than a centimeter wide but that would still support full body weight. Henry recalls,

> We all wanted to climb it pretty badly. It was almost turning into a kind of race, with this guy Dennis Meritt and his partner Sam Streibert going for it the same year

John Stannard on Open Cockpit, Shawangunks, NY/Heather Hurlbut

that Anderson and I were. Bob would come over to my house and say that some guy from Washington had done it. I'd get all hot and bothered but actually Bob was even more worried about it than I was. We were trying it at very weird times, though. The first time, it was snowing on and off. The second time, it was wet. I finally did it in the middle of January — a big scene. I just woke up one morning and said to my parents, "I have a feeling that I can do Foops today. Can I borrow the car?" It was like any other American kid asking his parents if he could borrow the car to go to the drive-in. I got in the car with Skip King, drove the four hours down there, got out, tried it, fell off, came down and had a beer, went up again, fell off, had another beer, went up and cruised over it, got in the car, and drove all the way back to Boston.

As the two became friendly, John Stannard was a considerable influence on Henry, though Stannard was not very talkative and was difficult to get to know. He typically took highly promising young rock athletes under his wing as partners. Henry never really served an apprenticeship with a master, however, the way Pat Ament learned from Layton Kor in Colorado, or Galen Rowell climbed with Fred Becky and Warren Harding in Yosemite and the Sierra.

Still, John Stannard greatly respected Henry for his climbing ability and served as a mentor of sorts. He was very concerned about Henry's penchant for soloing hard routes, but realized his exceptional ability outweighed his boldness and the obvious danger. The examples of Pete Ramins, author of many first free ascents with Stannard, who drove from Cleveland to the 'Gunks on weekends, and of Stannard himself, a Navy physicist who habitually drove eight hours up and back from Maryland every weekend, were sources of inspiration that fed Henry's innate drive to be good. John had a vision, one of clean climbing where pitons were eliminated and the cliffs saved from destruction, and he preached it with messianic fervor, winning over as converts the best of the young generation of 'Gunks climbers: Henry, Steve Wunsch, John Bragg, and others.

Barber on the second ascent of Foops in Shawangunks, NY, five years after John Stannard's first free ascent/Skip King

A later ascent of Foops; hanging at the lip/Henry Barber Collection

Like Stannard, Henry came to represent "an image of discipline and single-mindedness, the image of organization, with lists of routes he wanted to do, a clear plan," Bragg notes. "But he wasn't a real pioneer at anything, more a real good climber who followed in others' footsteps and improved on their performances." There was some jockeying within the group to do the hard leads but largely these climbers felt like members of the same team. There was, though, friction with Henry over his self-centeredness; he appeared at the time to be interested only in his own climbing, and not in that of others.

At last, after Foops, Henry was gaining some recognition, and even with friends like Ajax and Bob the competition could be sharp. At this point Henry began to indulge in a practice that threatened to alienate other climbers, whether or not they were friends. Ajax recalls a 1973 incident:

> I had gone to Ragged Mountain in Connecticut with a friend and done a short climb on a toprope. It was hard,

5.10, and I named it Defecation Delight. I was the only one who liked the name. Henry went and led it the next weekend. I followed him on it, and at the top, when we were talking, it came up that he wanted to rename it. I was pissed off and asked him, as a friend, not to change it. He still did. Traditionally, whoever first leads a route is free to name it, though if already named, that title is usually kept. Another climber, John Shelton, had the same thing done to him. He'd toproped a climb called Foobah. Henry came and did the first free ascent, changing the name of the climb to Suspense. Shelton was bummed out to no end by that. It got so that if he did a new route, he wouldn't tell anyone about it just because of his experience with Henry. The only aspect of Henry's personality that can cause friction is that he's about as inflexible as one can be. He's set in his ways, and this part of him, I think, was coming out more and more as he began to hit the big time.

After a blitzkrieg spring marked by an insatiable drive to climb all over the east, Henry made a second trip west to Yosemite. "We walked in there," Henry remembers, "and they were expecting us." While the previous year's trip had been little more than an impressive visit by an outsider, on this stay he made his first creative contributions to the local scene. He did a very fast ascent of the Nose, mastered all the highest caliber lines, and with his first ascent of Butterballs, a 5.11 finger crack drew his first real recognition from the locals.

But it was Henry's solos that revealed the truly innovative stamp of the brilliant climber he had become. With his two-and-a-half-hour solo of the Steck-Salathé route on Sentinel Rock, Henry took his first internationally recognized step in the world of climbing.

With the recognition came the fulfillment of the fantasy that had haunted Henry since grade school, that had made him long for the respectability of playing the infield during his baseball days: he was now the center of attention. On Friday and Saturday evenings at the 'Gunks the climbers would gather at a bar called "Emil's." From being a hanger-on, on the

fringe of the beer-pitcher conversations, Henry had graduated to a place at the focus of those nocturnal gossip sessions.
Aspirants sat in rapt silence on the edge of his circle, making
sure the beer never ran out, fueling Henry's long soliloquies
about the state of the art.

In Henry's view, though, the repetitious questions and the
constant attention from up-and-coming climbers became tedious. He developed an aloof detachment to counter it. Hatch
was bothered by the new turn in Henry's character; he wondered whether the two of them would have ever become
friends had Henry been like this from the beginning. By 1974
Ric found himself alienated by the intensely competitive
climbing scene and began edging out of the sport. He saw
climbing as something personal, to be shared between two
people. Ajax Greene, on the other hand, saw his old climbing
partner in the role of the western gunslinger. Having knocked
off the best rivals in 1973, Henry had become the man to
beat.Greene recalled an incident in Yosemite to illustrate his
point:

> In the California Sierra in 1974, Henry dislocated his
> shoulder. He wasn't climbing that hard the following
> year, so John Bachar, one of the best young climbers,
> started calling him 'Cold Turkey,' taking off on the name
> 'Hot Henry' that he'd gotten in '73. Henry went and did a
> very hard climb that hadn't been done, but that had
> already been named Fish Crack. Henry renamed it Cold
> Turkey when he did the first ascent, just to get back at all
> of them. It still appears, though, in the guidebook as Fish
> Crack.

In looking back at his former high school classmates,
Henry decided that he was

> leading a better life. What I was doing was better than all
> the other kids driving around in their parents' cars every
> weekend and partying. My direction in life was impor-
> tant, and theirs was mundane.

Likewise, he had become

disillusioned with the way a lot of climbers expected so much from other people. So many of them have slovenly behavior, no scruples, bad manners — little things that add up to an individual going nowhere.

In the winter of 1975 he returned to Babson from his year off. Shortly afterwards he came home and announced to his parents that his career as a student had come to an end. In a recent talk with the dean, Henry had told him, much as he had straightened out his baseball coach, about the twenty-eight different ways Babson lacked educational credibility. He asked the dean rhetorically, "Under the circumstances, Dean Staake, would you stay at Babson?" The dean told him what he wanted to hear.

For better or for worse, Henry Barber had become a full-time climber.

2

Western Adventures

DESPITE HIS EXPERIENCES in the Shawangunks and elsewhere in the east, it is in the west that Barber really learned to climb — first as a student at Telluride, later as an instructor, and finally as a practitioner, neither learner nor teacher, moving from one climbing area to the next. It is not surprising, then, that in the west Henry feels at his best. Far from the admirers and critics, from an identity in print and in pubs, hidden in eddies like the Needles of South Dakota or Devil's Tower nearby in Wyoming, or on the remote limestone crags in the Bighorns to the west, his energy peaks. There are no crowds to influence decision-making, no one is there to perform for, and no one will give you a hard time. While in earlier days he did strive to see his name in lights, that need has metamorphosed into a desire for quality, to be just plain good at the sport. At the small crags it is possible to climb freely for yourself and to study the shadow you cast on the rock, with nothing to lose. In the freedom of the west, Henry is at home.

One of Barber's very first western climbing efforts was nearly thwarted by the law in Colorado. At the age of fifteen, with two peers named John McDermott and Jim Dixon, he had traveled from Telluride to Boulder for a week of climbing. On arrival the three were promptly arrested as suspected runaways.

Phone calls to their parents managed to spring them, and the police dropped them off at a grocery with instructions to buy food and then head home. Instead they went to Castle Rock in Boulder Canyon, where they spent the next six days doing "desperate" routes. As Henry remembers it,

Virgin River, Zion National Park/Reudi Homberger

Every climb was a major effort at that point. There's an easy roof there that people nail for aid practice. Most of them do it in an hour. It took me almost a day. We were always so knackered. There was a lot of swearing, grunting, and moaning.

Everything was awesome to us. One day we did the famous Country Club Crack. Took me hours to nail the first pitch, but we finally made it to the first ledge, really beat. Meanwhile, some guy had soloed a flake next to the crack. We thought he was crackers for solo climbing. He did the whole thing in the time it took us to go ten meters. And we thought we were really good and fast.

Somewhere on the second pitch I was exhausted and having some real difficulty. I'd tied my stirrups such that it was almost impossible to get my feet into them. Well, I passed out with one elbow through one of the loops and went swinging out into space. Hung there for I don't know how long. I had just overexerted myself so badly that I went unconscious. I was dutifully following what it said in the books: You've got to really space out your pitons. It didn't matter how fast you went, as long as you made it absolutely desperate to clip into your next piece. Dixon said to hell with that and rappelled off, and Mc-Dermott came up, swearing the thing up and down. He was always really good at swearing.

The three eventually made it home to the east, planning adventures for the following seasons. As he became more proficient, Barber returned each summer to Colorado and to Telluride to work and to teach. Potential new routes around Telluride began to appear feasible. A friend named Tom Stimson elected to take part in some of these endeavors. For instance they climbed on a two-pitch stone pinnacle they named The Mummy which resembled vertical dust. The climbing was difficult and unprotected, with no spot that resembled a belay ledge. After placing a bolt that was at best questionable, the two climbed together without belaying; Henry held numerous short falls by Stimson on his waist as he led the final pitch.

Having managed a climb of this caliber, the two moved to the Ophir Wall down the road. Stimson had never used Jumars, the ascending devices used to climb a fixed rope tied into an anchor above by the leader. As a result, the first of the five or six pitches on the climb took Stimson well over an hour-and-a-half to ascend.

I'd figured that we'd be off by four in the afternoon. Stimson had to get in early because his parents were at the camp, worrying about him like crazy.

Late in the afternoon, after four, a storm moved in. We hadn't brought any rain gear because we knew we'd be off before the weather. It took us most of the day to get up two pitches. I thought that I was a great aid climber, but it would take me a couple of hours to lead a pitch. Definitely not a star. Tom was jumaring the third pitch, and while he was on rope, the lightning began. I was trying to be optimistic, but then it was just too damn close. I turned down to him and yelled something like, "Get rid of the hardware! It's right on us!" He threw all the hardware off, including his really nice camera.

I couldn't believe it. We didn't have a thing left. I thought he was going to cry. He didn't have his hammer anymore, and I suggested that he might have been hasty in winging all of the gear. Somehow the equipment had gotten stuck in a bush about fifteen meters down. For him to go down, get it, and jumar back up only took about two hours. It was a comedy of errors like a bad Walter Bonatti story of an epic climb. We did get up, though, and somehow we did find a way down the back by a horrible gully. Stimson's parents were apoplectic when we made it back to camp.

The adventures were by no means confined to climbing. One time Henry was hitching from Yosemite to Telluride, where he was due to start working as a guide for Dave Farny's mountaineering school in two days.

My second ride couldn't speak very well, since he was

shaking a great deal from all the speed he'd eaten. He dropped me in Sparks, Nevada where there were a mere ten or fifteen other people attempting to hitch as well. Most of them scared me — Hell's Angels types. Regardless, everyone on that road got picked up before me. A scruffy guy came up to me just as a cop pulled up the ramp; he turned to me frantically, and said, "Hey, you want some reds? Want some ups? Here, I'll . . . ."

"Nope, that's ok! I don't need any today," I answered, and started walking away backwards, just as he started to throw bags of illicit pills into the dirt. But the policeman wasn't looking. A few minutes later the freak was on his hands and knees, picking red and white pills out of the dust. I ditched him quick, and started trying to flag down drivers with an orange poncho. After six hours there, I did indeed get picked up. Unfortunately, the guy was a do-gooder who thought it necessary to stop and help another car broken down by the side of the road. I waited for him about an hour-and-a-half — because I knew that he'd be taking me a long way. He let me off five minutes down the road.

At midnight, Henry was in the middle of the Nevada desert. Not a headlight was in sight. Down the road he could see a gas station: Savin' Sam's. No change in his luck came with the morning or, for that matter, the afternoon. Desperate, in the early afternoon Henry attempted to obtain water from the gas station. Even for a dollar a pint, it was not for sale. He continued,

I wanted to kill myself. One of the drivers that passed would have done fine, too. I saw some graffiti on the guard rail near my pack. It said, "Been here for two days and two nights; want to die." Engraved next to this was, "Stick around, buddy, and we'll burn down Savin' Sam's tonight." Another said, "Been here for forty-eight hours. Humans stink!"

A woman stopped in the late afternoon. As she did, a couple with a dog hurriedly advanced.

> I leaned in the door, yelling that the girl down the road, running towards us now, had a guy and a dog in the bushes. I took my rucksack, which weighed as much as I did, and threw it in the back seat, right on top of her two little daughters, jumped in, and said how it was lucky we got away from them, all running for the car. The woman gave me a frightened look, as if to say that she wasn't so sure my arrival was a big break.

With his usual mixture of mild hyperbole and an eye for the outlandish, Henry looks back on another early trip west. He recalls the story of the Eldorado Canyon epic with obvious delight, even though he has told it in virtually the exact same phrases dozens of times. They drove straight up to the steep, rough walls of Eldorado Canyon.

> In '72 when Bob Anderson and I headed west for our first road trip together, we thought that we were the hottest thing to touch down on God's earth since the Martians. We were just about in flames by the time we got to Boulder.
>
> We'd had one can of juice since we left the east thirty-five hours or so earlier, and, of course, hadn't had any sleep because we'd been talking about all the great routes we were going to do.
>
> We went straight to the Bastille to do the touted Northwest Corner. Bob went up and didn't like it, so I took over the lead. As he came up the pitch, we couldn't hear each other that well, so on the next pitch we decided to use tugging signals: three tugs meant off-belay. Well, Bob went too far left, into a route called X-M, a really hard little section, got in a shaky pin about halfway and tied it off, then fell. I figured that he was off-belay because of the tug. I let out the rope and unintentionally

lowered him. He bounced due to sudden rope stretch. "There's the second tug," I thought, and just started letting out all the rope, as I thought he was pulling it all in. Actually, I was lowering him into the middle of an over-hanging wall.

There were two guys across the canyon, looking up at me with what I could see as horrified expressions, yelling at me. I couldn't hear them, and couldn't see Anderson. I yelled back, "Yeah, it's a great route!" Anderson was screaming at the top of his lungs, but I couldn't hear him, so I started climbing, lowering him even further. It was hard to figure out when the damn pitch was going to end. I just wasn't aware of what was happening until I moved around a corner and looked up at the pin, then down where the rope was going. Then I did a very fast double-take. The pin was bad for sure. It was a long way to the ground at this point. I saw Anderson way down there, just as I was saying, "Where the hell are you?"

"I'm where you put me!"

Somehow he managed to pendulum about fifteen meters across the face until he could grab part of the Bastille Crack. He was completely undone, wheezing and panting. Our first climb in Boulder.

After they had their bearings, which came quickly after the epic on the Bastille and then their impressive and touted fourth ascent of the Naked Edge back in Boulder, Anderson and Barber traveled to Yosemite Valley in northern California. Every spring that fabled chasm, with its immense and unflawed granite walls, serves as a kind of international rodeo and Boy Scout jamboree for devoted climbers from all over the planet. They hone their skills, engage in intense competition, and work on their tans. The thundering waterfalls and perfect weather draw hard-core climbers to thousands of beautiful routes of extreme difficulty, tracks across a vertical desert. At Yosemite the two young men "knocked off" routes in very systematic fashion. Their lists were meticulous. Such calculation precluded all but the occasional epic. The Valley

George Meyers belaying Barber on the first ascent of Butterballs, at the Cookie/Jib Knight

regulars were impressed by the versatility of a young eastern climber such as Barber, who felt at home on the hardest routes up steep cracks or on the friction slabs of the Apron. The positive reinforcement Barber received spurred him on through the trials of learning the Valley techniques and the rules of the local game.

During their fifteen days in Yosemite, Barber and Anderson were able to climb some of the more difficult routes. They even managed a few very fine free ascents: the Sacherer-Fredericks, a long route on Middle Cathedral Rock that served to bolster their egos, since theirs was the second ascent, coming a full ten years after the first; and the first pitch of La Esquela, a short lie-back problem at the base of El Capitan. They stayed primarily with the shorter routes, since they both found multi-pitch climbs to be "boring in their repetition."

To conserve the little strength that he maintains he had, Henry was forced to learn rapidly to climb the unusual flaring chimneys and off-width cracks of the area proficiently. He and Jim Bridwell, one of the permanent Camp 4 residents who has long been in the climbing vanguard, did the second ascent of New Dimensions, a four-pitch climb rated 5.11 on two leads. Barber used his "almost ineffectual nuts," strung with light cord, while Bridwell used pitons.

> In the Shawangunks, we were playing a sort of game with nuts. We'd try and ignore all of the fixed pegs on a route and do climbs 'all nuts;' they were just coming into vogue at the time. At the Gunks, there was a whole rating system that corresponded with doing climbs without any pegs. The Valley people thought that this was absurd, that pitons were the only way. Their outlook infuriated me. But I was leading things then with nuts that were simply foolish, as my smallest nuts were doubtful at best. On the last pitch of New Dimensions, while Bridwell was leading I was getting fairly gripped because I knew that he was a good climber. I was wondering how I was ever going to get all of the pegs out while I was trying to do such hard climbing. I got up there, and it looked like a lot of pitons. Somehow, I took them all out, but was totally exhausted from hanging around so long.

The early years out west were crazed delight, running wild with the heady successes racked up in each area visited, eating superhot cheap Mexican chili and burning gas by the tankful. By the time of Barber's second visit to Yosemite in 1973, he was beginning to feel like a top gun, although he had still put up relatively few first ascents and none in the Valley, specializing instead in very clean ascents of former aid or high-quality routes. The promise and challenge of a proposed trip to Britain that coming fall encouraged Henry to climb all of the hardest routes he could, often by lining up a succession of partners for each part of the day so that he could work in at least three 5.10 or 5.11 climbs.

The breakthrough came on a thin finger crack called Butterballs. It was a route that Steve Wunsch had been up on about eight times and gotten pretty far on, but had not completed. So I heard about it and went up there and did it. Just barely, but at least without any frigging around. I didn't think Wunsch, whom I knew from the 'Gunks, would mind.

This was about the time the whole "flash" business started. The second ascent of Butterballs was done the following season on the second day of attempts, with a rope hanging down through all of the protection that had been left there overnight. That was a "flash." People were yo-yoing climbs for days on end, hauling hand-over-hand up the rope to their high point rather than climbing the bottom section over again. Then, if they made it, they'd have "flashed" the route. Not in your wildest dreams.

It was during this Yosemite stay that Barber really 'arrived' in climbing terms. He was only nineteen, but he already had six years of rock experience behind him — the last three of which he had pursued the sport with single-minded intensity. In this year, 1973, he began to make a name for himself by climbing a famous and difficult route, 500 meters long, called the Steck Salathé. His achievement was not in the climb itself; many had ascended the popular route before him. It was in his style — he did it alone, without ropes or protective gear of any kind. He also completed the climb in two-and-a-half hours; it normally takes a long day. This was by far the fastest time in which the route had ever been climbed. Royal Robbins, the man who a decade earlier had been the single outstanding Yosemite climber, hailed Barber's achievement as a landmark in American mountaineering.

The west is huge, open, and free. When the quality of climbing or company is exhausted in one area, there are always highways that lead elsewhere. From his vacations spent in

Aspen and then Telluride mountain schools (following a string of childhood camps in New England), Henry had learned the beauty and freedom of the mountains. Climbing and traveling out west came naturally after the years of long hikes and river trips in the canyonlands. It was inexpensive to travel then, too.

In 1972 he and Anderson drove to Boulder, then on to Yosemite, spent two weeks there, hitched back to Salt Lake City, and took a bus to a job in Colorado for around $100 — just under a month's trip. The money covered the incessant peanut butter and jelly sandwiches, all the beer they could drink, and gas. The trip to England in 1973 cost a grand total of $600 for two-and-a-half months, including an airline ticket whose cost was diminished by price wars.

It was all money Henry had saved while working during the summers at Dave Farny's in Telluride, or had borrowed from his college bank account during his year off from Babson in 1973 and 1974, when he financed trips to Australia and Britain. Through hard work, hustling climbing gear as a salesman for several different small manufacturers, and lecturing and giving slide shows, Henry eventually repaid the loans and began to achieve the personal solvency that allowed his international climbing career to continue. He's always resented those who assumed he had the means to climb as he wished, and ardently projects the accurate image of a hard-working and self-made man; he is quick to criticize climbing bums or the lazy in any endeavor.

The people Henry did choose to emulate were ones he felt had a lot more in their lives than an intense devotion to climbing. Ironically, he had to go through a stage of single-mindedness of purpose, climbing to the exclusion of virtually everything else, to even be able to meet and come to know luminaries like Joe Brown, Royal Robbins, and Yvon Chouinard. The former two were heroes of sorts from the very first to Barber; they were doing the hard, frightening, and impressive free climbing that Henry aspired to master. After years of travel, though, the more integrated lives of Brown and Chouinard drew him more.

In the fall of 1974, Henry flew to Las Vegas and on to Los Angeles for lectures. After staying with long-time 'Gunks reg-

Mount Johnson in Alaska. The route attempted follows along behind the ridge/Reudi Homberger

ular and close friend Bob Johnson, a soft-spoken high-technology engineer, Henry was driven up to the Great Pacific Iron Works shop that housed Chouinard's rapidly growing climbing hardware and softgoods concern. Arriving just before the lecture was due to begin, Henry was shocked to find a penciled note on the door: "Lecture canceled — same time next week."

Chouinard, a diminutive, low-key mainstay of the Yosemite big wall years and probably the foremost equipment designer in the country, was wintering in the basement of the Iron Works then and living at the beach during the summer. The pair got along well, trotted off to the Valley for a week of climbing, and then returned to ease Henry into the delicate art of surfing.

The following summer, under the wise leadership of lawyer and 'Gunks elder hard man Jim McCarthy, Henry, Tom Fisher, Joe Bridge, and Yvon journeyed together to attempt the 1,700-meter-high east ridge and face of Mount Johnson in Alaska. In one of the most successful big wall ascents in Alaska the previous summer (1974), a lightly equipped party of three had found a way up Mount Dickey's 1,600-meter face, just to the north of Johnson in the Great Gorge of the Ruth Glacier, south of Mount McKinley. McCarthy, no innocent on big arctic walls, felt Mount Johnson would go. Glacier travel by snowshoe to the foot of the unbroken granite wall followed a dramatic flight in, but the climbing attempt was thwarted by very dangerous conditions — climbing above scanty protection in wet Alaskan weather.

Back at the sunny Iron Works, Yvon and Henry played and then taught an ice climbing class together in the High Sierra. Later in the fall, when asked who he could recommend

Barber leads while Chouinard belays in dismal conditions on Mount Johnson/Reudi Homberger

Barber starting the long traverse on the dike on Mount Johnson/Henry Barber Collection

as a climbing equipment representative in the east, McCarthy (who was also part-owner of a climbing shop in the Shawangunks) recommended Henry. The job involved extensive travel around a territory, which covered virtually all of the northeast; it was a natural step for Henry, and helped spur a major shift to a more settled and stable lifestyle. He was giving up the comet's-tail existence he had known prior to that time.

The Life and Climbs of Henry Barber

Work, climbs, films, and vacations in the wilds of Baja and northern Mexico would bring Henry into contact with Chouinard repeatedly, and he came to respect Yvon's drive, personal style and ethics, as well as his expanding business. The hard climbing was blended into a multiplicity of other interests with Chouinard, something Barber was coming to admire.

The interpersonal politics surrounding first ascents and high-level climbing were often a source of tension and harsh judgment for Barber in his early years. Climbers new to the forefront of activity, especially younger ones like himself, had to gain gradually confidence and distance from their own involvement in the sport before they could artfully handle the pressures of the limelight. With exposure to the graciousness of the Australian scene, and later the non-reporting ethic of the Norwegians, Henry began to evolve away from the need for publicity and ownership of routes.

When they were climbing in the east in the early 1970's, Henry and Bob Anderson would dash up routes like Matinee and Try Again (both strenuous 5.10 climbs) at the Shawangunks by 7 A.M. on a snowy April morning. Then they would relax for the rest of the day and do five or six more routes. Barber recalls,

> People would ask me how it was, and I'd say: "a piece of cake." I didn't have the grace then to say that it was hard. I was intense, and, I think, fairly obnoxious. But it's very difficult to say anything to another hyper climber without offending him. So, in '70 and '71, I didn't say much about any route.

The second season in Yosemite was not all proud banter. With the right partner, Henry occasionally recovered the zaniness and healthy challenge that drew him to the sport's practitioners in the first place. Diana Hunter and Bev Johnson provided some of the summer's best times. Diana, an equally brilliant climber, took a fatal fall on easy terrain during the descent from a peak in Rocky Mountain National Park not long after. As Barber remembers her,

I was always getting in bizarre situations with the women with whom I was climbing. Diana Hunter used to make you feel like you were high — loose and free. We'd go dancing, and she'd start doing these improvisations on the floor, writhing around. I'd have to be loaded, but she'd do it straight. One day, she completely painted herself with climbing chalk, walked into a bar in Yosemite, and acted as if nothing was wrong.

She once led me up a 5.11 route in Eldorado called Wide Country. I'd tried my hardest but didn't feel good enough about the moves to commit myself to an unprotected section. She was very good, creative to the point where sometimes it seemed that she wasn't concentrating on events that were going on around her. Whatever felt good, she did. I think that's why she was killed. Her ability certainly wasn't the cause for her death, because she was a brilliant climber.

Henry seems outwardly untouched by the deaths of peers and friends in climbing. He analyzes this reaction as a certain callousness. It may be, however, that his incessant traveling and his tendency to be a loner mean that each of the people he knows adds up only to a handful of memories, a particular trip, images of a series of climbing days sometime in the past. Some protection from the realities of death comes in the form of a distancing defense mechanism that operates to allow him to continue climbing. When a friend takes risks at something he likes doing, Henry remains detached, but when a real freak accident — apart from climbing or driving fast — occurs, it hurts Henry deeply.

Bev Johnson was well known around Camp 4 as an immensely attractive and well-endowed campground ranger who climbed hard. As Barber describes her,

Bev is an incredible athlete. She managed to follow some routes that I thought were desperate — in her cross-country ski boots or sneakers. We always had our laughs.

At one point that spring, we rode the bus up to Mirror Lake to see some friends climbing on Half Dome.

We were the only people on the bus, and at one of the stops, about forty Hell's Angels got on. We were sitting, minding our own business, licking yogurt off our fingers. All of a sudden, there's this head between us, from the seat behind. He looks like your classic motorcycle outlaw: bald with a profusion of scars covering his face. He says in the lowest voice I'd ever heard, "Can I have a lick?"

Bev turns to him, giggles, and says, "Do you have a spoon?" All I could think of doing was jumping out one of the windows. They were all screwing around in back of us, and after a few minutes, Bev notices that her bag is gone. She starts yelling about how someone stole her bag. I was muttering to her how it was cool, that she might not want to make a scene. The same guy leans between us again and says, "Somebody stole your what?"

"Oh, nothing. Everything's cool," I was saying. I thought that we were going to die. Some girls beside this guy had sneaked it back to their seat and were going through it. They didn't care; they gave it back, and we got off after what seemed like a year.

Beverly would go on to be a part of the first all-women's ascent of El Capitan and, years later, make the first and only solo woman's ascent of the 900-meter cliff.

In the summer of 1974 Barber made a long western trip with Ric Hatch, Ajax Greene, and a girl friend named Heather Hurlbut. For once Henry was less hyperactive than usual. The four spent some time on Heather's farm in Kansas, wandering around the sprawling fields or simply sitting on the porch. "I was realizing," says Henry, "that between one climb and the next there were some sights to see, rather than just time to be filled." In the aftermath of his journey to England, Henry's friends noticed a marked change in outlook. While still taking climbing very seriously, Henry was also equally dedicated to having a good time with the people involved, drinking and carousing a lot, and being more well rounded. Suddenly there were other pursuits in life besides climbing, and one learned about them through the folks that practiced them.

He had met Heather at the Shawangunks, where she climbed on occasion, but her feelings about climbing were to cause Henry some difficulties during the two years they kept constant company together. As he puts it now,

Women have been a major problem in my climbing career. Some didn't mind it, and they enjoyed the time for themselves. With Heather, it was more of a problem, as she didn't want me gone all the time — a perfectly normal reaction. The main friction was that she couldn't accept my soloing, which put real doubt into my actions. It became more and more apparent during the trip that summer with her.

In Boulder in the summer of 1974, Barber encountered another kind of problem. The climbing crew there was ambitious and began on the most severe routes. Barber tried Kloeberdanz, a climb he would not complete until three years later, with his second on Jumars to get by the large roof. He soloed T-2, an eight-pitch climb considered one of the 5.9 classics in Eldorado.

With Ric Hatch as a second, Henry at one point led a six-pitch climb called the Diving Board, an overhanging 5.10 off-width crack, extremely intimidating, which at the time was getting few ascents. Henry had just finished the crux moves of the whole route up around a chockstone and was only six or seven meters below the top. The leader had to do an easy but strenuous 5.6 move emerging from the side crack to finish on easy ground. As he moved back into the crack, he pulled outwards, extending his shoulder too far and dislocating it.

I didn't fall off, but I couldn't get it back in. It was very hot. We hadn't had anything to eat or drink, and were quite tired. I went into shock almost immediately. I did manage to get down below the chockstone before passing out for about fifteen or twenty minutes. Ric couldn't see me and didn't know what was going on. When I yelled down to him to talk to me so I wouldn't stay in shock, he

Barber on Kloeberdanz/Dudley Chelton

was speechless. I'm not sure he knew what to do at that point.

Hatch recalls that he, indeed, could not see Henry.

All I remember was him yelling, "Talk to me, talk to me!" He didn't fall. He didn't have much strength, so I think that he pretty much just jammed his hand into the crack and dropped off his stance onto the jam to relocate the shoulder, passed out almost immediately, and then kept coming to and going out.

Between fainting spells, Henry was able to clip a sling onto a nut in the crack and slide a leg through it for support.

I'd sit there and try to get my mind off the predicament. This was probably the worst place in Eldorado that you could get stuck. I'd think about sex, but then I'd think about climbing and where I was. I'd look across at the Bastille, getting hot flashes, seeing the Bastille turn colors, shimmering in a sort of mercurial silver. I'd never been out of control like this. I was feeling really desperate.

Recalls Hatch,

I belayed myself up to him. The anchors were pretty uncertain as he'd fixed a hanging belay. We talked for awhile, making sure that he was still there. Even though I wasn't that good, I took Henry's rack, about an eighth as big as mine, and led through. I was at the crux of a 5.10 off-width crack, trying to protect it with tiny #1 wired stoppers. It took me a long time because I had to aid quite a bit of it. He dragged himself up the last pitch of the thing — I'm not sure how.

Henry continues,

Whereas it had taken us an hour-and-a-half to get to the point where I was hurt, it took us three hours from there.

I used small wire nuts wrapped around the rope as prusik knots, and aided a lot of the finish.

Hatch recalls no trip to the doctor, though, since "Henry was too much a purist. He was in a lot of pain, though." Barber didn't sleep, and was very shaken by the experience.

Despite his shoulder, Henry went on to Devil's Tower and the Needles, where he did some very hard and very gratifying climbing. Yet the diversity and scale of Yosemite continued to call him back, even though he found the scene itself more repugnant with each visit.

Henry after having completed second ascent of the Super Pin in ten years/Sue Minot

Chip Lee seconding on the second pitch of the Super Pin in the Needles, South Dakota/Henry Barber Collection

When I came back from Australia in '75 and went to the Valley, I'd have to say that was the grimmest scene I've ever been part of. I went up to try a route called Oreo. Ron Kauk in particular was working on it, but he'd been away for a few days. I didn't feel like I was stealing his route or anything, so I just went up on it. He happened to drive up to the area just as we finished the first pitch. He jumped out, forgetting to set the hand brake, and sprinted up there and made quite a stink about the whole thing claiming we were on his route while the borrowed car rolled off into some rocks and bushes. After Australia this kind of thing was almost a culture shock for me. He calmed down, though, and joined us for the first ascent. It was just his initial reaction that blew us away, him yelling at us to get down from 'his' route. But that was the way everything was being done in Yosemite at that time, so it was hard not to think like that. People were just spending too much time in that one place. They didn't know anything else. The times I've been there, however, I have not been one of the more popular people in Camp 4. Around me, everyone's mouth has been sealed.

With three six-packs of beer in him, he recalls, Henry went up to try Axis on Arch Rock — like Fish Crack, a route that had been named before it had been ascended. "I fell off a boulder while we were putting on our shoes and went into a pile of rubble below. It was the three sixes, I think."

Nevertheless he climbed the route without too much trouble. It was wet in spots. No one had been climbing much in a period of stormy weather, even though the routes had dried in some areas. To an outsider, the lack of activity typified the inbred, lackadaisical air of the local climbing scene.

The night after we did the climb, I was sitting in a restaurant at the Yosemite Lodge, packed with two-hundred tourists at dinnertime, when one of the guys who'd been trying the route comes up to me and says, "You stole my route!

"What are you talking about?

"You know what route. You know what I'm talking about. You stole my route!

"For God's sake, man, don't cause a scene. Get a grip on yourself. Maybe you'd better leave."

It was Kevin Worral, completely outraged. He was getting pumped up over the thing right there in the restaurant. His fists were clenched and he was snarling. I just told him that I'd explain it all to him later. It was out of hand. One of the guys working on another route that I wanted to do said that if I went up on it, he'd blow me off with a ten-millimeter cannon. Everyone was juiced up at this point, to the extent that people were loathing me. I left the restaurant on that particular evening, bought the guy a beer, and tried to explain the whole Australian scene and how noncompetitive it was. I don't think that anyone really got the point. It was like saying that a certain explorer couldn't go and discover a set of ruins because they're mine to discover. Well, let's wait about twenty years and they'll crumble; then nobody will discover them. It was all fairly juvenile.

Ron Kauk attempting a first ascent of the Fish Crack in Yosemite. Barber achieved the first ascent the following day/Henry Barber Collection

The Life and Climbs of Henry Barber

Henry saw the problem as one involving the evolution of the sport as a whole. Technicality was becoming paramount in any climb worth being considered a classic. Climbing in areas such as Yosemite had reached a gymnastic level in which competition appeared to be a primary motivating force. Barber saw that people around him were training as gymnasts; they devoted themselves to a single-minded purpose, to be excellent, and sought recognition for their abilities. Henry had never trained athletically since he was always practicing on the more severe routes. He feels that

> If you have the strength, the body, not the mind, begins to dictate the possibilities in a situation. You stop being creative. For me, climbing has always been a contest to achieve harmony between brain and brawn.

The antithesis of Yosemite at its worst, for Henry, is a major cliff called Granite Mountain near Prescott, Arizona. Many of the routes there were put up by a number of excellent climbers based at Prescott College in the early 1970's. Yet the area remains isolated and little-known.

> When I was there, I couldn't believe how high the quality of the climbing was. Everything was desperate. It was so much healthier than Yosemite. People climb at Granite Mountain because they want to climb, not to knock off a few new routes this season. It appeared to me that a healthier viewpoint exists in Arizona, as it does elsewhere in locations that aren't overrun with climbers trying to make the papers.

In the summer of 1977, with Chip Lee and Susan Minot, Henry spent ten days of nonstop driving among eight different areas, and led ten first ascents or first free ascents and a plethora of others. The reserved, often snobbish, attitude that he saves for the times when he climbs at the major areas, frequently in front of a gallery, was nowhere to be found. There was no need for it. At an isolated crag just off the road on the way to Devil's Tower, with no sign of even a stray cow,

*Barber leads the second pitch of Outer Limits in Yosemite while Jeff White
belays/Reudi Homberger*

The Life and Climbs of Henry Barber

Barber uncoiled his rope and mentioned to his companions that he felt at home. He committed himself to a twenty-five-meter run-out above protection; a belay was useless on the 5.10 limestone, which kept shelving off as he moved away from his holds. Susan, not wanting to watch, read in the car.

Barber on a girdle traverse in Pembrokeshire/Pat Littlejohn

3

England and Emergence

WHEN HENRY BARBER stepped off the plane at London's Heathrow Airport in the fall of 1973, he expected to be greeted by Richard McHardy, a wide-ranging British climber he had met climbing and carousing in Yosemite Valley. The two had spent time together there briefly only months before. McHardy's nonchalance in the face of imminent danger was an obligatory ingredient in the character of the traditional front-rank British climber — the "hard man." He had woven a wealth of animated tales of valor on inspiring routes done in the rain with minimal equipment, projecting an air of daring and discovery that primed the interest of the eager young American, some ten years his junior.

McHardy had treated Henry to a story of a typical adventure on a severe solo climb in Wales, his home turf. It was hard to fathom it all, sitting in sunny, idyllic Yosemite drinking Dos Equis Mexican beer among the parched, perfect climbing boulders protected by fifty-meter Ponderosa pines. But McHardy, the product of artful storytelling in a hundred English pubs, recreated the wet moss and blowing fog and the forbidding rock buttresses fading in and out of view. It was a solo climb, performed alone and without the protection offered by a rope and a partner to hold it in case of a fall, an extremely committing and bold style indulged in by only the best climbers. McHardy thought he might have wandered off-route onto harder and unknown terrain, and was aware that the crux — the most demanding move on the climb — was supposed to be yet above, near the top. Finally Richard said to himself in his thick Lancashire accent,

"Richard, where are ya?" I said, "'I doon't know.'" I wanted to take a loook at me guidebook, but I couldn't le' go to fetch it from me pocket. So I just kept going.

Although he managed to finish that climb and so tell the tale, McHardy has not always been so fortunate. A metal plate completes the contour of his skull in one spot, the aftermath of a thirty-meter ground fall onto broken talus blocks beneath a route at Llanberis Pass in Wales. Henry, himself an avid and accomplished solo climber, heard the story and absorbed the air of color and commitment it exuded, and soon made tentative plans to visit Britain in the fall.

Henry also knew another Englishman, Pete Minks, casually from the Valley; Minks was noted for his recent involvement in a filmed ascent of the notorious north face of the Eiger in Switzerland, among other accomplishments.

Henry had asked Paul Ross to write a few letters of introduction and give him tips on where to climb and drink. Ross is a compact and tight-lipped climber, fortyish, who operates a climbing school in New Hampshire and is a dedicated new route pioneer. He learned to climb in his native Lake District in England and in the Alps with all the young hard men involved in the surge of modern interest in rock climbing in England in the early 1950's and onward, most of them later to become famous: Don Whillans, Chris Bonington, Joe Brown.

It had been the British who had invented mountaineering in the nineteenth century, and ever since they had enjoyed the reputation — sometimes deserved, sometimes not — of being the best in the world. The motive for Barber's English tour that fall, as much as anything, was to test his skills against the legendary and dangerous routes to be found on small rock outcroppings from Cornwall to Scotland.

His early years as a boy from a small town in eastern Massachusetts, a boy who gave up other sports to become a climber, were punctuated by reading about the great heroes of this strange new enterprise. They were largely British and French climbers, since few Americans were well known in the sport in the early 1960's, and, the tales were of wild times and places: riding huge stones at terrifying speeds down the cog railway at

Snowdon in Wales, hitchhiking up to Scotland in winter to climb the notorious gullies on Ben Nevis, trekking into the Nepalese Himalaya to ascend Annapurna. Henry wanted to go to Britain to see the places and famous personalities once he had become an accomplished climber himself. He wanted to hear the stories firsthand, to do sea-level girdle traverses along rugged sea cliffs with the waves at his feet, and to drink in the pubs and cavort with heroes like Joe Brown and the others, now that he was one of their kind.

British climbing itself also had several appealing aspects for him. First there was the apparent seriousness of it all: long run-outs above pieces of protection, stones carried up on the climbs as natural chocks, the climbing in continual rain and wind. The British had a strong sense of properness — or ethics — about the way they climbed long before similar concerns surfaced in America in the late 1960's and early 1970's. The history of very difficult technical rock climbing on small crags in the early 1950's, and of routes at home in New Hampshire like Repentence — put in by Englishman John Turner in 1958 and not repeated for twelve years — was very appealing to him. Henry felt he could do the famous climbs and do them in good style. Also, the English climbing scene had more tangible stars who showed character and zaniness; such figures were absent from the low-key and nascent domestic stage.

In addition to all this, the people spoke English. The audacious Barber had conjured up the image of what's known as "flash" in the climbing world — accomplished by climbing a hard route on-sight on the first or second try in good style, a form of one-upmanship. Henry was only nineteen though, and traveling alone; he was used to being seen as a brash newcomer on the make, but he had a phobia about encountering a non-English-speaking society. It would be easier to make a splash in a place where he could communicate well with the locals and get around. Despite innumerable travels worldwide since that first trip abroad, Henry still does not speak any other language fluently (though he knows enough of several to get around), and he retains an uncertainty mixed with obvious fascination about other cultures, as well as a hint of parochialism.

Following his bold performances during the 1972 and 1973 seasons in the Valley, he was under much pressure from peers in Yosemite and elsewhere. The September 1973 issue of *Summit* magazine contained a letter criticizing an earlier article lauding Henry's amazing speed ascent of the classic Nose route on El Capitan and his first free solo of the Steck-Salathé. Its author commented that, given the rash of recent deaths in Yosemite, why was the magazine giving attention to such ill-considered acts as solo climbing big walls? Henry was stunned by the letter, his first taste of the power of the press.

Royal Robbins replied in the following issue that the solo was an act of vision. When the two met briefly in a pub, Barber expressed his appreciation and eagerly said he hoped to climb with his hero Robbins. Personality differences and the circumstances prevented the partnership from occuring, though, and Barber was left to fend for himself among the local climbers, who were not ready for the aggressive, eye-catching performances of an outsider. So Henry withdrew to seek a more favorable environment. He felt he could handle the English. "As it turned out, I couldn't deal with the English — I couldn't deal with them at all," he reminisced later.

Unfortunately, when Henry touched down at Heathrow, he learned that Richard McHardy was off to Dhaulagiri in the Himalaya, the fifth-highest peak in the world. He was met by Barbara McHardy and introduced to some of the local climbers at a pub called "The Moon" near Stoney Middleton, a popular climbing area. Off the plane only a few hours, he was already in the thick of it. He said of his first evening,

> We were throwing darts and drinking a lot of beer. They wanted to see if I was up to par, and I wanted to be sure I was.

Henry approached this situation as he does all others — he owned it. Well above average in height and barrel-chested, he has arms that appear far too long. It is these arms that one notices, and the grin matching the intensity of his eyes. It's

Henry on the Dangler at Stanage Edge/Tony Riley

hard to say if the look on his face is angry or not. Strangers can't tell. He moves directly at things, without preambles or peeking ahead.

The British climbers were waiting for him. In the second week of his visit, *Mountain,* the British climbing magazine that is more widely read and credited than any other in the world, published an article on Barber's Yosemite exploits. The somewhat cool account by its editor, Ken Wilson, nevertheless vaulted Henry into worldwide prominence within climbing circles; the article concentrated on his Steck-Salathé solo, his Nose blitz in a day-and-three-quarters (normally taking two to five days), and ascents of the most desperate free climbs. It gave currency to a nickname until then used half-ironically by his friends: "Hot Henry" Barber.

Whether or not he wanted to, Henry thus stepped into the middle of one of the most competitive scenes in sport. Many of the British hard men, jealous guardians of their demanding but not ethically pure standards, would have liked nothing better than to see Henry fail. He was in top form, however, and had some inkling of the kind of situation he was entering. Beyond the merely personal levels of pride involved and the play of personalities, a minor chapter in the climbing rivalry between the United States and Great Britain was about to be written.

To add to the tensions that his trip was bound to produce, Henry came armed with an extremely austere notion of climbing purity, a style composed of what climbers call "ethical" choices as to what kinds of aid and safety protection ought to be used. Henry's style was in some respects quite at odds with British practices. Finally, Henry's personality — intense, demanding of himself and of others, verging on arrogant — was bound to rub some of the studiedly casual English climbers the wrong way. In a *Mountain* interview published after his trip, Henry summed up the potential for conflict in this way:

> People tend to frown on ego, but I think ego is good, so long as it isn't obnoxious to others. This is my problem: I can't conceal my ego.

For the next few days Henry climbed with alpinist Rab Carrington at Froggatt and Curbar edges, two gritstone cliffs in Derbyshire. He found himself more interested in "the history and color behind the routes" than in the technical moves involved. Ideally he had hoped to penetrate the inner sanctums of British mountaineering by meeting and getting to know some of the legends of the generation before, men like Joe Brown and Don Whillans, known to American climbers from celebrated stories told the world around.

But a far different assortment of cronies awaited him. English photographer and climber Tony Riley remembers that

> the thing that seemed to strike him first, and in which we all took great delight, was that the groups and friends I introduced him to were brought together totally without reference to climbing ability.

Henry instinctively classified climbers by their ability and performance and sought to be with the best, though he had learned to climb with a club of only average climbers who were nonetheless intriguing otherwise. This difference in approach created a gulf between the visitor and the hosts.

After climbing on the gritstone edges around Derbyshire for several days, Henry went with Tony Riley, Malcolm Cundy, and two others to Scotland. The five of them drove to Ahcasheen, where Henry had his first glimpse of the Scottish hard men. He recalls sitting and staring fixedly at them as they would repeatedly "wuf down a wee dram" (a shot of scotch) followed by a pint of bitters.

The first night in Scotland proved to be a long one. The following morning passed unnoticed.

> At two o'clock we went off to do this climb, the Three Buttresses of Ben Eighe. Usually, people start at six in the morning for this thing. It's a 650-meter climb. We were still drunk from the night before, and we were pretty much stumbling through these horrible bogs, just about

crawling on our hands and knees to get up to this place. It was a pretty good day, but I don't think I've ever done a worse climb in my life. The rock was nice — very hard sandstone with scoops and pockets, but very mossy and dripping with water and mud. Everything was loose.

One of Henry's most noticeable traits as a young stylist on rock back home in New England had been his omnipresent outfit: white painter's pants, loose and baggy and immaculately clean, with never a touch of dirt around the knees from some indiscretion such as getting up onto a ledge in desperation; a white golfer's hat, a trademark directly borrowed from Robbins and kept to this day; and a clean oxford dress shirt or tee shirt. Never the torn, filthy clothes repatched and sewn with mismatching thread, that others climbed in. The crisp whiteness made a statement of calculation and control, almost a dare. It was a dare that the rain and mud of English climbing took.

Tony Riley remembers the first day in Scotland differently.

We set off towards some unclimbed gully after a debauched night. Just below the entrance to the gully we ended up slithering about on some loose mud and scree in quite an exposed position, all soloing. I remember Henry was last across. We all thought this was hilarious, because for us it was part of the enjoyment. Later on in the day, he unroped from us, preferring to solo up a nearby, cleaner rib while we hauled ourselves up some horrible loose rock, mud, wet ice, and clumps of grass. It was as though he couldn't enjoy what we were enjoying because it didn't present him with 'The Situation' — making the hard move on hard rock, something totally personal with rules and ethics. That was definitely a group day out.

For Henry, this was all part of

my first epic day in Britain. The whole trip to Scotland

Nick Escourt on tyrolean traverse during sea level girdling. Note the foot dragging in the water/Henry Barber Collection

was a marathon — like driving from Boston to Cleveland, Ohio to climb for the weekend. The climbing on Ben Eighe was about as good as the climbing in industrial Cleveland, too.

They continued to Glencoe to climb on the Etive slabs. Here Henry had his first shock of the trip. The character of the smoothly angled slabs demanded friction climbing, a technique requiring maximum contact with the rock from the soles of one's feet and the flattened palms of one's hands. Friction climbing is frightening at best — and on the Etive slabs Henry found a complete absence of cracks into which the climber might hammer reassuring pitons or insert nuts. Unlike many similar American cliffs without protection, there was not a single bolt — an aluminum rivet driven into a hole drilled into blank rock and used like a piton, though considered ethically more questionable — on any route. Glacier Point Apron in

Brian Griffith on the etive slabs in Scotland/Henry Barber Collection

Yosemite looks like a veritable pincushion of pins and bolts by comparison.

"I'd never heard of Scottish climbing before," says Henry.

> I'd never even known much about Scotland itself, and all of a sudden I was presented with these horror climbs. I was starting to become a little awed at the state of things on this trip.

He was to learn that the Scottish pride themselves on their intimidating rock and ice lines, and have an ongoing rivalry with the lowlander "Sassenachs" coming up from England to the south.

Henry found himself on a long climb with Malcolm Cundy, nicknamed Piken and fabled among the group for his extremely poor vision. Essentially refuting the fact that he was legally blind, Piken habitually drove straight through radar traps at high speed without stopping, whereupon his eyes would crazily wiggle back and forth in their sockets in excitement. Close to two hundred meters off the ground, Henry tried to anchor himself to the rock after leading a pitch (or rope length), in order to belay Piken up by passing the rope around his waist and pulling it in as Piken ascended below. The only protection he could place to tie in to was a stack of several thin pitons called knifeblades, piled back to back to make a mass thick enough to wedge into the crack. It was the kind of anchor a climber is reluctant to pull or place his own weight on, much less to expect to hold a fall by his second. Not a single piece of protection secured the rope to the rock between the two, separated by a full forty-meter rope length. Henry recalls,

> So here's Piken coming up, and his eyes are darting all over the place. I'm up there yelling at the top of my voice, "Piken, don't fall!" And he's saying, "Where do you go?" I would reply, "See that piton over there?" Then I thought to myself, *Of course he can't see that piton over there. He can't see anything! We're gonna die!*

By this point in his tour, the word was out that the "hot" young American was living up to advance notices. The *Mountain* article had thrown the spotlight on him more than ever. English superiority was being threatened. Henry's purism had managed to offend, as well. In Britain during the 1950's and 1960's, the reliance of climbers on artificial aids like pitons and bolts had remained much less thorough than in America, where it had become common practice to nail one's way up otherwise unclimbable walls, placing pitons wherever necessary. The British "odd peg" ethic, first developed by masters like Joe Brown, lingered into the 1970's. This generally accepted belief dictated that a leader ought not to place more than two or three pitons per rope length, but that he could hang from those to rest or use them to aid his progress past a nasty spot.

Henry brought to Britain an extremely "clean" notion of climbing, one that had just coalesced in America within the past two years or so. He felt, in common with many other leading American climbers, that a climb ought to go all free or not at all. Thus, he eschewed the use of pitons for anything more than protection in the event of a fall, and often chose to ignore fixed pins already in place and instead to insert his own "clean" nut protection. He refused to use pitons for rest or aid, finding any means possible, however difficult, to bypass them. A route relying upon even one or two points of aid was simply not a free climb.

The growing commitment to free climbing evolving in Yosemite and all over the country, and the rise of popular concern for the American environment, had by about 1970 spawned the concept of "clean climbing." This movement espoused climbing on easy and difficult routes alike without the traditional reliance on pitons hammered into cracks for protection, and with a minimal use of equipment in general. The emphasis was now on individual technique on the rock and the style and spirit of the ascent, rather than on a dependency on technology, epitomized by big wall climbing. Repetitive use of the hard-alloy pins in the same spots on a climb led to the deterioration of the cracks. Lightweight, soft aluminum nuts jammed into cracks without the use of tools or force were slowly becoming the accepted replacement, especially among the most skilled practitioners of the sport, and heavy hammers and pins were left at home. It was scary business.

Prominent climbers like equipment manufacturers Yvon Chouinard and Tom Frost of Yosemite fame, and John Stannard on the east coast, led the crusade with eloquent arguments in the pages of climbing magazines and catalogs and by personal example on the cliffs. The clean climbing movement was spiritual revitalization for a sport beginning to stagger under the complexity of vast quantities of gear and the concomitant near-certainty of success.

By the early 1970's, routes on short cliffs had taken on a far more serious nature. The leader was forced to rely on carefully honed physical and psychological skills in confronting the increased dangers inherent in demanding free climbing. Even the famous big walls of the Valley, ranging from three hundred to a thousand meters and requiring two to six days to complete, began to be subjected to an increased amount of free climbing, reducing the times but raising the necessary level of talent and commitment.

The short crag became an entity in itself, not simply a training ground for trips to the great ranges or big walls. An increasing number of climbers saw the whole of the sport embodied in seemingly obscure gymnastic problems from a few to a hundred meters long. As the focus of attention and innovation came down from the heights, the pressures to perform correctly intensified, illustrating the continually evolving code of unwritten ethics that each locale generated. Everyone was watching.

Henry Barber grew up and into climbing precisely at the point at which the sport made this sudden alteration of its trajectory. He came to epitomize this new age of purity and ethics, having made a name for himself in America by virtue of his boldness and style. The move to clean climbing had not as yet reached England. Henry brought it with him.

To many of his British ropemates, this austerity practiced by an upstart newcomer looked like as a kind of one-upmanship. And it violated a time-honored code of climbing: when in Britain, climb as the British do. In addition, Henry was climbing with his usual fanatic intensity, exhausting one partner after another. Back in Sheffield with Brian Griffiths, he had marathon days during which the pair would negotiate a dozen routes at each of five crags. On other days assorted partners would take turns climbing with Henry. At night he would be involved in the serious drinking at the pubs, and sometimes in lunatic caving expeditions. As the days went by, Henry met more and more climbers, and his reputation preceded him. He perceived his notoriety as an obstacle. When he finally was introduced to climbers like Joe Brown and Mo Anthoine, pivotal figures in the development of British rock climbing, he found that they wanted little to do with him. This rejection was an unanticipated blow.

Brown in particular was one of only a handful of heroes Henry openly emulated, along with several other British notables, Lionel Terray and Gaston Rebuffat of France, and Americans Royal Robbins, Chuck Pratt, and Yvon Chouinard. Brown and Chouinard came to represent for him the climber

Joe Brown before the start of sea-level girdling/Henry Barber Collection

as Renaissance man — superb, innovative performers bristling with charisma and creative energy, deeply intrigued by a broad range of subjects like fly fishing, surfing, design, business, media. They were the first glimpses he had of ways he might want to be, of where the art of climbing hard and well might lead.

In part, the reaction to him was impersonal — a generic dislike for "Yosemite hard-cores," those who lived and breathed the indigent Valley lifestyle. He reasons,

> All these British fellows were very defensive because they had heard all of these 'hot' comments. It was so hard to get into their inner circle. The only way to break in, in fact, was to drink and play like a madman.

62

Ignoring the sometimes strained atmosphere, Henry kept climbing with those who would join him. The desire to break into the core of British climbing persisted but went unfulfilled. His response to what he saw as "the British reaction to me" was to become all the more intense in his climbing. By nature of personality and reputation, he was highly visible, forcing the locals to consider American free climbing achievements, as he freed many existing aid routes — always his specialty.

Cenotaph Corner, sometimes an aid and sometimes a free climb, depending on the ability of the leader attempting it, has long been considered a landmark in British climbing. The steep crack at the back of a forbidding corner was first mastered in 1952 by Joe Brown, in a major psychological breakthrough. The extreme technical difficulty of moves far above protection did much to elevate him to the status of first-rank hard man, and to raise the standard of British rock climbing in a rebirth of interest in hard, short, free climbs that brought the British up to the level of attainment then prevalent on the Continent. The climb helped usher in an era characterized by boldness, gymnastic difficulty, and ethics, not dissimilar from the clean climbing revolution underway in America twenty years later.

While at the pub as usual one evening, Henry was asked if he would like to go to a wake for a climber who had just been killed in a motorbike crash. He reluctantly agreed, imagining the rather morbid scene, and accompanied a crew of the regulars over to Al Harris's house. The rain was heavy that evening, and the night dark. When they arrived, however, they found most of the guests outside despite the weather. Al had rigged up a jukebox in a field adjoining his backyard, and it was blaring full tilt. Cars were driven in and out of the party at random, and a staggering amount of liquor was consumed. The party continued until dawn, when Al insisted that Henry remain as a guest and climbing partner for at least a fortnight.

Little climbing took place in those two weeks. After long nights of drinking at the "Padarn," Henry would be up at seven, ready to head out to the crags. The stereo would grow louder as the morning progressed. Al, a man of leisure "on the

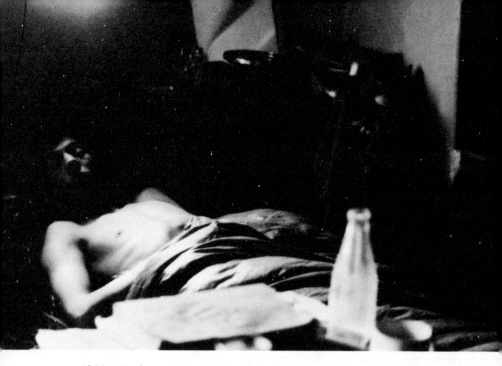

Al Harris after one more tough night/Henry Barber Collection

dole," would have the TV on as well as the black lights, the reason for which escaped Henry. Inevitably, the frustrated American would go off soloing.

After two weeks of indifference, Harris and Cliff Phillips agreed to accompany Henry climbing. Al had turned out to be one of the wildest and craziest people Barber had ever met, with a total disregard for personal well-being constantly demonstrated by drinking and driving to excess. Once Harris bet his then-regular partner Pete Crew, one of the leading lights of the early 1960's, that anything Crew could lead in his best rock shoes Harris could follow in his finest dress winklepickers — pointed black leather Beatle boots popular at the time. Crew took up the challenge and lost to Harris, who drove home his point by climbing in an oversize mackintosh as well. Any sport with a rough, desperate element, like dirt bike racing, appealed to Al. Henry, on the other hand, was an ex-Little League baseball player from a nice town in the suburbs of Boston, son of a conservative New England banker; he despised the very idea of people on the dole, not out working hard for an honest living.

Phillips had been the best solo climber in Britain some years before, had made the Eiger film with Pete Minks and Leo

Pete Crew on Mousetrap in North Wales/Malcolm Cundy

Dickinson a year or so earlier, and had recently fallen seventy meters to the ground off a climb called Blackfoot while soloing. He had reportedly fractured his pelvis, broken an arm, jostled his organs a bit, and suffered lacerations on his head that later required something like sixty stitches to close — but he had nonetheless crawled out to his car and driven to the Padarn pub as usual.

The two locals chose a line called Surplomb for the disparate trio, a classic Brown-Whillans route in the Llanberis Pass. It still had one point of aid, which the leader uses to move right at six or seven meters off the ground. Henry explains, his brow knitting:

It was my first limestone climb. Right away I could tell
from the look and feel of the rock that limestone was
going to be my nemesis. It was just beginning to get dark.
I had been up since six in the morning, trying to get
somebody to go climbing. I was angry and frustrated.
They all think I'm hyper; I think they're full of it. Surplomb was pretty hard. It took me a long time to figure
out, going straight up instead of right, to eliminate the
aid. It was just about dark when I got to the top. Phillips
came racing up behind while Harris soloed up another
route on the side. Al got to the top and said, "He did all
right, didn't he?" I said yes, that this guy was all right.
They were both up there congratulating each other, and
all of a sudden they both started laughing. It turned out
that Harris had given him a shoulder stand to get him
over the hard part. They wouldn't tell me at the time.
Harris was saying things like, "Well, I guess you Americans aren't so good anyway, are you?" I was pretty bummed out.

Tony Riley feels that Henry's seriousness, intensity, and
his imposition of American ideas about ethics were simply
anathematic to the British.

The least enjoyable times I had with Henry were when I
took him to some locality to find a hard route he had read
about, just the two of us. It all seemed a bit boring. He was
into his own thing — seeking out and killing. We didn't
relate much on that level.

There was much more to climbing than moving on rock
or ice, maintained people like Al Harris and Cliff Phillips.
There was salmon poaching up in the lakelands, heroic drinking in the pubs, and car racing on the narrow roads. Henry
learned about the car races between Al and Cliff down Fach
Wen, a tortuous road taken by the average driver at twenty-
five or thirty miles per hour. The road is a lane-and-a-half
wide, framed by stone walls and houses on one side and steep

Barber on Surplomb, his first lead on limestone/Tony Riley

drops on the other. Al and Cliff used to race at around ninety miles an hour.

They devised rules to the game that held that it was only a one-car race, with the driver on the first run becoming the passenger on the second. The passenger wore an American-style football helmet, was tied into the seat with climbing webbing, and was covered with a bed mattress, for safety's sake. The rider, as it was told to Henry, inevitably screamed uncontrollably throughout the whole three- or four-minute run. The course ended with a double right-angle corner which ought to have been taken at about twenty miles per hour, but which was regularly negotiated by the pair at forty. At 2 A.M., after a good day of salmon poaching, this was considered excellent fun.

The Life and Climbs of Henry Barber

Henry began to feel that it was more than his seriousness that got the British dander up; he even felt that his very style of climbing was being criticized. The contrast can be gleaned from Henry's description of the style of the old master, Joe Brown.

> He's fluid, but he's immaculate at the same time. He's one of the finest climbers I've ever seen. You go sea-level girdling with him, six meters above the sea, boulders everywhere. If you ever fell, you'd knock yourself out and drown for sure. There's green slime hanging off the walls, and he just pads across it like it was nothing. He makes hard 5.8 moves on this terrain look as if they were easy 5.2. It doesn't matter what the conditions are like for that guy.

Henry climbs in a much different fashion than Brown; one rarely sees Henry pad across anything. Instead he exhibits a highly polished and carefully calculated process in which each move appears to be made mentally before it is acted out. It is a glimpse of his vision of the world, his sense of being on stage, as if someone were always watching and judging, the cameras always rolling.

> It seemed that in their eyes there was absolutely nothing that I could do right. I didn't climb correctly. I didn't drink enough and didn't enjoy myself enough, i.e., I didn't get into these insane car races. I was too keen, too young, and not mature enough. But you could never get any of these guys to open themselves up and talk to you about it. So I thought that they were all jerks. That's all changed now. The whole scene's changed, in fact, and I feel a lot different about it now. Britain's still the most competitive situation in climbing, though.

It became increasingly difficult for Henry to find climbing partners.

> I was continually frustrated because I wasn't getting to do

the climbing that I had hoped for. Finally one day I went climbing with Pete Crew, who I'd been playing darts with. We did five routes at Tremadoc, a very popular cliff. I said to him afterwards, "Pete, you know, that's the best day I've had in Wales. I've done more climbs today and more climbs with you than anybody else." And he was miserable. That blew it for him. It just wasn't good to go out and be that keen. If I'd done seven routes with some-body else and five with him, then that would have been just fine. But to do all of these routes with me completely blew people's image of him. What he should have been doing was drinking tea until eleven, doing a route, drink-ing until three, doing a route, and then heading for the pub. It was all a front. This was what the entire trip was like. Whether we were having a good time or not, basi-cally I was too keen. Everyone was paranoid about climb-ing with me.

After the initial two weeks at Al Harris's house, during which Henry had trouble budging Al out of his armchair, Harris suddenly was seized with zeal. Paul Trower and Henry ran into him in Llanberis Pass. Al excitedly insisted that the trio had to go off climbing for the rest of the day. He'd just come from an appointment at the bank, and he was dressed appropriately in a white shirt, red tie, black pants, brown leather jacket, and climbing shoes.

They went to Tremadoc and began soloing what Harris and Trower said were the classics. Recalls Barber,

They're trying to get me to do all these routes that they're doing. There was this incredible psychology working. I made a point of asking them how hard the climb was that they were on, and I'd do a climb one grade easier. I didn't want to make them think that I was trying to beat them at their own game. Instead, I was trying to have a good laugh. But slowly, I started upping the ante by soloing some harder climbs. It went this way for a few routes until we got down to a thing called Fang. We were all up on it, and just as I did the crux moves, they decided to traverse off instead, still soloing, to a different finish. They obviously realized that the jig was up. I just didn't want to climb below them.

I had just done this one discomforting move when suddenly I heard this tremendous crash. Looking down, I saw that Trower had fallen off. He'd grabbed this vine and pulled the whole thing away. Al looked up at me. Mind you, Paul has just fallen thirty-odd meters unroped. Perfectly calm, Al said, "Henry, can you come down? I think Paul's gone a long way."

The two of them raced down to where Trower lay upside down in a bramble bush, unconscious, with head wounds and a dislocated shoulder. Harris pulled him out and said, "Paul, are you all right? We have to get you to the pub. We've got to get you a drink."

Upon reaching the car, blood covered Harris's once-white shirt and his bright red tie was askew. He kept reassuring Trower, "Don't worry, Paul, everything will be all right. The pub's not far."

"I jus' wan' t' go home, lad. Jus' ta' me home," Trower replied.

Henry convinced Harris to take Trower to the hospital instead of the pub. Harris's sense of urgency was directly translated into the speed of his vehicle. Coming into Bangor he passed a car on a blind corner at just under eighty miles per hour. As they came around the corner they discovered a car headed straight for them.

Henry screamed. Harris squirmed a little in his seat, saying "Oh maan, thi' is great! I wish I had a siren! Thi' is great! Paul, di' ya see tha' pass?"

"I jus' wan' t' go hom', lad. Ta' me home."

"Oh maan, thi' is great!"

Harris's car, still in the middle of the road and traveling at about seventy miles per hour, had squeezed through with cars on his left and right. Just as he was finishing the pass, a Triumph Spitfire began passing him. Nine cars were headed their way. Harris was in the middle of the road, still, with a car on either side of him.

Al turned to Henry after watching the Spitfire pass and said, "Oh, maan, di' ya see tha'?"

The Spitfire completed the pass, pulling in front of Harris onto the center line, still passing another car they'd come up on. At this point, there were two cars in the correct lane with Harris and the Spitfire on the center line beside them. Harris pulled out around the Spitfire, producing a three abreast situation, with Harris now in the left lane and oncoming cars only a hundred meters away.

"Oh maan, thi' is great! Loo' a' this."

At almost ninety miles per hour, Harris completed another pass, getting around the Spitfire and by the first of the oncoming cars on the center line before he pushed his way into the right lane. The Spitfire, not to be outdone, passed Harris again. Harris answered the challenge. Henry kept watching the floor. Mercifully, the hospital was at last in sight.

Trower remained in bed for a week, nursing his shoulder and concussion with the aid of the beer that Al and Cliff Phillips brought him, along with the requisite pile of pornographic reading material. He was in good hands except that his blanket, bedpan, and other hospital items would often disappear at the end of his friends' visits. Years later, in the fall of 1981, Al Harris was to disappear too. He met his demise in a similarly wild drive, after one drink too many and one corner too sharp.

Henry left Wales, went to the Midlands, and then to Yorkshire. Here he climbed with John Syrett, who did not seem concerned with the reports that were circulating around Wales.

> Whatever reputation I had when I went to Great Britain had been lost in the time I spent in Wales. All of the reports of the American were that he was too keen. He wasn't "doing as the Romans do." He was just being an ass.

Syrett, however, did not display the competitive attitude that Henry found prevalent among climbers he encountered in Wales. For half a week the pair climbed on numerous outcrops without donning a rope. Days on the rock with Syrett were a relief, since he was the first person in Britain who could climb at Henry's level who was not trying to intimidate or sandbag him. John was taking time off from university. His soft, boyish face belied his age — some five years older than Henry — as did his quiet manner. Since he worked all night stocking shelves at a supermarket, he regularly overate free food (with typical British frugality) to such an extent that he would spend the mornings feeling nauseous and vomiting; then he would drink with Henry or another in a pub in Leeds called the "Fenton" from noon to three, solo respectable routes all afternoon with Henry, and finally head back to food and pricing at the supermarket. Everyone has his own routine; that was John Syrett's.

Near the end of his two-and-a-half-month stay, Henry visited Ken Wilson at his flat in London. Wilson is a pivotal figure in the reportage of British climbing, the locus of news and opinion about the practice of the sport there and abroad. His highly organized, aggressive, businesslike nature had made him a magazine publisher, editor, author of several books on climbing, and well-published photographer. In part because of his big bones and stocky build, he is not an especially good climber, though he pursues the avocation religiously and very seriously. Wilson loves the great routes, the limelight, drinking and debating politics and ethics with the stars, and reporting about all three.

He had heard about Henry's exploits while on a climbing trip to the States at the end of the 1972 season, when Henry had blitzed most of the hardest short free climbs in Yosemite; the two had met briefly in Camp 4 in the Valley and Wilson had taken a photograph of him. But he had been reserved throughout Henry's visit. The significance of the visitor's achievements and the psychology of his presence promised good copy, though, so Wilson eventually sought an interview just two days before Barber's departure for home.

The timeliness of the report on the Yosemite happenings, just at the beginning of Henry's tour of Britain, was characteristic of Wilson's strong sense of the force of the moment and the power of print. Henry, for his part, began to perceive the politics of exposure, though he claims that at the time "it never entered my mind to keep up a rapport with magazine editors to get good press," the way he saw Pete Livesey and Ron Fawcett calling in news of their latest performances. He feels that Wilson was not particularly interested in helping him out, and never made an effort to "save my neck" from critics. On the other hand, the editorial voice of *Mountain* could have made much of his controversial use of chalk, the powdered magnesium carbonate favored by gymnasts to dry and protect their hands and improve their grip. And Wilson had indirectly planted in him the notion of climber as media star, unknown in America, where there were far less public and media involvement in climbing and virtually no professional climbers (beyond a handful of mountain guides). *Mountain,* through Ken Wilson, had introduced Henry to another world, but it was not a wholehearted endorsement.

While at Wilson's one day, Henry ran into Pete Livesey, reputed to be one of the top British rock climbers. Livesey had just returned from Yosemite, one of only a few climbers in the country to seek out the secrets and rigors of short and big wall routes there at the time, an early model of the modern English rock specialist. At home he was heavily mining the Lake District and Yorkshire for new routes and pushing standards on limestone, largely ignored until that time. Notwithstanding his job as a school teacher in Yorkshire, Livesey was a wild-looking, egocentric combatant, some ten years senior to Henry.

They talked awhile and immediately there was an abrasiveness, but they arranged to meet in Bristol. From there the pair headed to Avon Gorge and did a few routes. On the second day they traveled over to Cheddar Gorge, another limestone area, to go up on a famous climb called Coronation Street. It was raining hard. The day was cold and very miserable. Pete insisted that they do the climb they had planned anyway. He led the first pitch; Henry followed and then tried to lead the second. "I didn't like it and came down and proposed rappeling off, figuring it was not worth the discomfort. Pete had led the climb before, and went up to do it anyway, out of pure competitiveness. Thick mud was running down the pitch when I came up." Barber continues,

After that we went back to Avon Gorge and did the third ascent of Yellow Edge, a very rotten, overhanging limestone climb. You move on these scoops in the rock-like fossils, very sharp-edged. They break off when you pull on them. It's really grim.

I led the first pitch — a very devious lead, but interesting. He led the second. Like a lot of others, he'd downgrade things to make himself look better. On that pitch, in the middle of some moderate moves, he grabbed a sling to lean out and look above him, though clearly not using it for aid. At the top I said to him, half-joking, "I won't tell Wilson if you don't," trading bribes.

"About what?" he casually replied, coiling the rope.

"About that sling you grabbed down there."

He was being incredibly competitive. I was on his home ground — crumbling limestone — and was just trying to be as mellow as I could. But at the same time I didn't want him to get away with anything. So he turned to me and said, "I didn't grab any sling."

Steve Wunsch, an outstanding American climber and longtime friend of Henry's, says,

A lot of British climbers were really upset when Henry came in and did things like Vector all on nuts, ignoring the fixed belay pins. I love doing things like that. I do things the way I've always done them, and it doesn't matter if it accords with some local tradition or other.

Henry had beaten them at their own game once or twice, and had shown contempt for their hallowed odd peg ethic; the British climbers had closed ranks and retaliated with pranks or indifference. When Wunsch did the first free ascent of the Left Wall of Cenotaph, it had, of course, "been done before." No one ever knew who had done it, but someone always knew someone over there who knew someone who had. "I must have heard it a hundred times. You can't tell them that something's good unless you convince them that they invented it," Wunsch says.

Henry on Quietus at Stanage Edge/Tony Riley

But ultimately British climbers had to acknowledge the extraordinary 1973 tour that represented Henry's first stab at international climbing. In just over two-and-a-half months he had managed to climb 160 routes. Ken Wilson swallowed his habitual aloofness to underline the significance of Henry's visit in the pages of *Mountain*:

> Hot Henry Barber arrived here in September with a shopping list of routes culled from our magazines, and despite poor autumn weather his results were impressive. His best climbs included Quietus, Rasp..., Tensor..., Fang (solo), and Sickle (solo). All of these routes were climbed without aid, but his run came to an end on Zukator where fatigue and technical difficulty caused him to seek sanctuary on a piton. These visits underline the fact that the British have little justification for being complacent either about technical or ethical aspects of their climbing. However, they still appear to excel in the *joie de vivre* that is such an essential element in climbing.

4

"Hot Henry's Here!"

CLIMBING HISTORY is normally fashioned in small increments. Rivals in a local area press new routes, and cliques form and evaporate fluidly and spur each other on. They contribute to the gradual improvement of standards through inspired leads of new lines, through a purer style of ascent than previously thought necessary, or through technical innovations like devising unusual means of protecting an ominous-looking lead. Change comes about from this sporting competition within the loose collective of regulars, and from the occasional infusion of energy and new ideas unaffected by preconceptions or local taboos that a visiting outsider brings. In rare instances a great leap forward is made by a single individual who finds himself in the right place at the right time — with the right stuff.

The great Austrian mountaineer Hermann Buhl well exemplifies the personal act of genius. On a summit attempt on the virgin 8,000-meter Himalayan giant Nanga Parbat in 1953, Buhl's partner fell behind from fatigue after leaving the highest camp, still close to 1,200 meters below the summit. Rather than accept defeat, in an incredibly bold overnight push involving a standing bivouac at over 7,700 meters (25,000 feet), Buhl struggled onward to make the first ascent of the mountain — solo.

Likewise, two fine California climbers, Dave Rearick and Bob Kamps, found themselves in the vicinity of Colorado's Longs Peak in 1960, just when Rocky Mountain National Park rangers decided the time had come to issue permits for attempts on the unclimbed, unrelentingly steep face of the Diamond — the highest-altitude big wall in the continental United States. Colorado climbers had coveted the chance for years, but the Californians persuaded the rangers that their credentials were the best around. In three days of skillful aid climbing they forced a direct line up the awesome wall. As with Buhl's epic solo, their audacious and spontaneous ascent of an intimidating major route was a significant and highly acclaimed breakthrough.

Almost never, however, has a lone outsider arrived at a local crag and at once had a major impact on the route possibilities it offers. Local climbing areas are like home stadiums in sports — the regulars tend to perform better there than the visitors. They have had months or years to get used to the idiosyncrasies of the rock; they can work repeatedly on a climb until they get it "wired;" and indigenous rivalries serve to push standards higher than they might otherwise reach.

Henry went to Australia in March of 1975 because he wanted to see what the climbing was like there. Possibly no other well-known American had climbed on that remote continent. In a whirlwind tour lasting forty-four days, he accomplished a feat that may be unique in mountaineering history. Not only did he climb the hardest routes at every crag he visited, but he also added dozens of new "desperates." Most important of all, he raised standards so consistently that two new ratings of difficulty had to be adopted to accommodate his climbs.

"The first that I ever heard of him was in one of the issues of *Mountain* magazine," recalls John Smart, an active Australian climber living in Canberra. Smart is a well-kept, quiet, and conservative high school teacher. Somewhat surprisingly, given his large-boned physique, he is concerned with the ethics and style of movement on rock.

> The general feeling was that, "here's this little Yankee upstart — this young kid who thinks he's crash hot." We didn't have much of an idea about him.

Shortly before Barber was due to arrive, Smart was climbing with another Australian, Ray Lassman, when the latter suggested that he would be all for climbing with Barber, if given the chance. Smart replied,

> It might improve your climbing, but how can you climb with a bloke who's so much better and is obviously egotistical about his climbing? He does it for perhaps very different reasons than we do.

It was a touch audacious to go jetting off to Australia. Henry had managed a 65% free ascent (ignoring the aid normally relied upon) of the legendary Nose route on El Capitan in Yosemite Valley with an Australian named Keith Bell; they had done the route in the record time of a day and three-quarters. A number of other hard free ascents of routes like Outer Limits, a short but severe crack climb, had been accomplished with Rick White, another member of the strong Australian contingent normally found in the Valley.

The idea of a trip Down Under originated, then, in the summer of 1973 in Camp 4, the traditional mixing place of international rock climbers. Pictures of Ball's Pyramid (a 570-meter sea stack off the Australian coast) started cropping up in the magazines, followed by an article about Frenchman's Cap in Tasmania in *Mountain*. Although he denies having any articulated sense of designing a career as a climber, Henry felt that the next logical step after England was to go to another English-speaking country. (Henry does not speak any foreign languages fluently, in spite of all his travels, and remains a devoted Anglophile.)

> I chose Australia because it was far enough away and would be adventuring out, like going to the Alps (where it would be difficult to do something significant, because of the standards). Few Americans had climbed there. I've always had a desire in my climbing to go places where others aren't journeying. If they spoke French or Russian or Chinese there, I never would have gone.

By now Henry was living partly off of the honoraria he

commanded for giving slide shows. At the tender age of 21 he was a member of the Board of Directors of the American Alpine Club, a nonpaying but very prestigious position allowing maximum access to the sources of influence in the climbing world.

The AAC needed new, young blood at the time. One of the older directors had volunteered to resign if he could be replaced with an active climber, and Henry was recommended for the position. It involved considerable expense, flying to meetings all over the country three or four times a year, but once over his initial awkwardness, Henry felt he had something to say and drew upon his able salesmanship to present his positions boldly. He "learned a lot and grew up" from the experience. One director has indicated that he was especially welcome because of the fact that he was beginning to work for a living, and was not simply a climbing bum on the dole, something that bothers Henry as much as it did the staid directors.

Just prior to his departure for Australia Henry had attended to lectures and business obligations in the east, flown to Oregon for an AAC meeting, and lectured in Las Vegas (followed by a caving trip lasting till 4 A.M.) and Los Angeles. The plan was to finance the Australian trip by giving talks around the continent (trading on his reputation in *Mountain* magazine and the success of his recent trip to England), and then, afterwards, at home in the States he would lecture on Australian climbing, which few climbers in America knew anything about. For these and other reasons, he wanted to see as much of the country and its ways as possible and to sample as many varieties of climbing as the Aussies could throw at him. In theory it was simple: total immersion in all that was Australian climbing. But when he loaded himself onto the plane to fly to Sydney, he was exhausted. He had had, by his count, six hours' sleep in the previous four days.

From Sydney, a city of about four million but with only 300 to 400 climbers, Henry flew north to Brisbane, along the continent's relatively urban east coast, to meet Rick White, owner of a major climbing shop there and one of the state's most active climbers. White is swarthy, ardently competitive, and secretive about new crags he has ferreted out of the bush. As Barber recalls it, his first local conversation with the climber went as follows:

> I called him up and said, "I'm here." He said, "Gidday." I didn't know what he was talking about. He meant, "Good day." The accent's incredible. They say things like "eineen" and "nineen" for eighteen and nineteen. "Goodonya" means "good for you." When they make a toast to something, they say "giddeyhinya," and "fair dinkum" is a rhetorical question, meaning "really?" The whole thing takes a little getting used to.

Within minutes after Henry dropped his luggage at White's house the pair were out bouldering on some lava-like blocks outside of Brisbane. It was a typically humid day, with the temperature above ninety degrees Fahrenheit even though the Southern Hemisphere summer was over. While walking through the woods to the boulders, Barber began to recall stories he'd heard of the Australian wildlife. The exotic koalas and kangaroos and other creatures were certainly one of the major attractions of the trip, for Henry has a deep-seated fascination with animals and all that is animated and irrational, beyond his proven powers of persuasion and comprehension.

> This Tasmanian businessman on the plane had been telling me stories about the snakes. There are approximately a hundred and twenty species of snake in Australia, and about eight-five percent of them are poisonous. He was saying really nice things like, "If you ever get bit in Tassie [Tasmania] — don't worry, because we only have three snakes there. They're all poisonous."
>
> While we were bouldering, I was thinking, "What have I come to?" These blocks are grimy and dirty, and I'm thinking about the snakes. And it's not like New York City's nearby. It's not like I can go to the theater or the symphony. There aren't even any drive-in movies around. I was pretty down.

Koala in Grampian Mountains in Victoria, Australia/Henry Barber Collection

Barber had a meager $200 in his pocket and no sure source of income. He was depending on lectures to be set up by White and Bell to pay for the trip. The money he had borrowed from his college fund upon leaving Babson College for the last time a few months earlier was already exhausted.

Immediately, while working on several short boulder problems, Henry recognized the growing local competitiveness in the group, especially from Rick White. By the end of the session Henry had located one or two new moves that gave the others trouble. At the end of the afternoon, while downclimbing a trivial corner on the razor-edged lava rock, he slid off in exhaustion and gashed his leg badly. A huge scar still shows. When telling the story, he always lifts his pant leg to show it and slowly runs a finger or two up the rough texture of the incision.

From the pace that first day, Barber guessed that he would be getting no more sleep over the next six days than he had during the last. White had told all of his climbing friends that "Hot" Henry was coming to Australia. They began calling from cities all along the coast, eagerly waiting for his arrival at the local crag and ready to guide him to all the newest unsolved problems.

The following day White and Barber drove out to Frog Buttress, a remote crag featuring short cracks that attracts climbers from all over Queensland. On the hike in, White regaled Henry with stories about the local fauna. Carpet snakes, he recalls,

> are the fourth biggest snake in the world, and they live at Frog Buttress. They just laze around in the trees. Taipans are the second biggest poisonous snake in the world, next to the king cobra. They also live in Queensland. I was thinking about this a lot. Just so you don't get bored, there are spiders half as big as your hand crawling all over the place.
>
> We did one route called Blood, Sweat and Tears, a route that Rick had put up. On the way to do the next one, Corner of Eden, Rick started yelling about a snake that was on the climb. I went running over to get my camera, right through a wasp nest, and got stung twelve times on the neck. This is within an hour of my first day at the crags.
>
> Rick was telling me not to worry, that he'd only seen a handful of snakes at Frog Buttress. Well, we were walking around after doing Corner of Eden. I was following Rick through dense forsythia-like bushes full of flowers, bending down to duck under floral arches. Before I knew it we were both flat on the ground. He'd jumped backward about two meters. A snake had come out of the bushes right in front of him, passing through the bushes at eyeball height.
>
> We hadn't walked twenty meters beyond that spot when I looked down by my foot, and maybe twenty centimeters away is this death adder lying in the grass. They're only twenty-five centimeters long, but they cause more deaths than any other reptile in Australia. Tiger snakes are more poisonous, drop for drop, but they're not as dangerous as the adders because they have grooved fangs. If they bite you through a sock or clothing, a lot of venom gets absorbed by the material. Adders have hypodermic fangs. They're sluggish, though, so I started taking pic-

tures of this snake. I came real close to it with my macro lens and looked up at my depth of field adjustment. Just when I looked back at the snake, I saw *another* one about ten centimeters from my foot. I think that I now hold the world's record for the longest backward standing broad jump.

After two days at Frog Buttress, the climbers took the third day off. Barber used his respite to dash off twenty-seven letters in order to set up a lecture tour on his return to the States. Then the team was off again.

Most of the areas Barber visited in his first days of climbing in Queensland had numerous possibilities that had not been tried, and he began to put up new routes almost immediately. At any given time, several climbers were lined up and ready to work on the hardest or classic climbs with him. Often, he was climbing five or six routes a day with various partners, then soloing if the pace slackened. One of his most difficult solos occurred early in the tour when he went up onto the Womb, a 5.10 off-width crack (too wide for solid jams with hands and feet) at Wyberba, in the south.

After a week in Queensland, Barber and White drove south to the Warrumbungles, a range of steep igneous plugs and dikes in northwestern New South Wales. American highways had spoiled Henry. Somehow he always expected to find the same cultural standards and material comforts wherever he traveled; in fact, he almost demanded them, despite his avowed desire to explore and to experience the altered sense of place that strange lands offer. By American standards, the Australian equivalent of our interstate system would compare with back roads in West Virginia; White frequently had to pull his car onto the shoulder if a truck approached from the opposite direction.

The twelve hour drive to New South Wales was routine stuff for Aussies on a climbing outing. Rick's Citroen body could be raised or lowered over the axles, which helped them negotiate several kilometers of highway flooded by a meter of water. Henry found the driving quite different from the breakneck races in which he had taken an unwilling part in England.

They're obsessed with trying to take Fiats and Austin Minis, which have a clearance of several centimeters, over rough dirt roads with troughs and boulders in them. A Citroen's just no challenge. Once you get one of those cars in there, it doesn't matter what climb you do because you've already made it.

White kept promising his passenger that he would see some kangaroos and, soon enough, Henry spotted one from the car.

I jumped out and started shooting some film, wandering around in the grass, trying to be sneaky, getting closer and closer. I took about twelve pictures that were absolutely worthless, but finally I was getting closer. I looked to one side and saw a dozen of them feeding. I think that I was a little excited and yelled, "Bloody hell, there's a whole pack of them!" They all looked up, but luckily they have very poor eyesight. You just get in the shape of one of them, and they think that you're a kangaroo. They're pretty stupid.

Besides snakes, spiders, and kangaroos, I began to be very interested in koalas. I was told that there are about two hundred and thirty kinds of eucalyptus trees, and about ten or fifteen of them have tannic acid running in them. Koalas crave tannic acid. They eat it all day long and get stoned on it. The government is constantly trying to manipulate the wildlife. They tried to bring a lot of koalas up from Victoria to live in the Warrumbungle National Park. They built a wire pen around a few eucalyptus trees which they'd transplanted. Of course, it's a lot hotter in the Warrumbungles than it is in Victoria to the south, so the tannic acid isn't running in the trees. All the koalas are escaping out of this pen that's only a meter high. The gamekeepers spend all their time catching the koalas and putting them back in the pen. They all died off, eventually, the ten or fifteen they had up there. It was the details of fiascos like this that interested me.

Dogface in the Blue Mountains of New South Wales. The cliff line in the background goes on for miles and as yet has not seen much climbing/Henry Barber Collection

The first route that Barber and White did in the intricate Warrumbungles was a famous one called Lieben.

"It's eideen, up on Croiter Bloof," Rick said to Henry.

"What?" Henry replied. Finally, the American figured it out: "It's eighteen, up on Crater Bluff."

Over the years Australian climbers have developed their own unique rating system. Grades 1 through 4 correspond to the same numbered grades in the American Yosemite Decimal System and pertain to trail walking. An Australian 5 is equivalent to the American YDS 5.0 to 5.1, for easy roped climbing. Above this there are two or three Australian grades for every single American decimal. An 18 was, Henry found, the equivalent of an American 5.8. He was quite impressed with Lieben, for the 5.8 section was unprotected and the route had first been led by Bryden Allen in 1953. An advantage of the Australian system, conceived early on by John Ewbank, is that it is open-ended: as new climbs become increasingly difficult, higher numbers can be applied. Faced with the same dilemma, the originally closed American system (which culminated at

5.10) has had to resort to awkward designations like 5.11 and 5.12, each subdivided with the letters *a* through *d* or with plus and minus signs.

At the time of Henry's Australian visit, the hardest climbs in the country were graded at 22, and virtually all included the use of some aid, in an extension of the British "odd peg" ethic. After a few climbs, Barber judged that an Australian 20 was equal to a hard 5.9 or 5.10 at home; 21 or 22 was 5.10 and above. As in the United States, there were variations from one area to another and fierce debates about grading particular climbs. Since Henry's itinerary would take him to many of the major areas, locals were especially interested in his opinions of the difficulty of various routes, and how they compared to classics and new lines in Britain and the U.S.

The 600,000-hectare Warrumbungle National Park — a labyrinth of soaring spires, bottomless gorges, and improbably steep forest lands — is also the location of Bluff Mountain, one of the highest cliffs in Australia, though only 200 to 300 meters high. While the Blue Mountains west of Sydney offer mostly delicate face climbs and crack and corner routes, the Warrumbungles demand more creative technique — bizarre pinch grips, wild stemming moves, and thorough knowledge of the undercling. Barber had heard tales of the 'Bungles from Keith Bell while in Yosemite, since it was Bell's home territory. Henry kept a low profile and was content to repeat established routes, quite typically taking a respectful interest in the kind of lines pioneered by Allen and Ewbank a generation earlier in the 1960's. They were an odd pair, a gentle academic and a younger, outspoken dropout, but their personal chemistry and visionary grasp of the potential of the cliffs and of future trends dominated the Australian scene for a decade.

The crew climbed illegally on the Breadknife, an incredibly thin wafer of deteriorating rock hanging over a popular hiking trail, and then they drove the many hours back to Queensland.

The pace was debilitating. It was something that became a Barber trait, almost a point of honor and certainly a matter of pride. The adrenaline flow of constant motion and perpetual play figure prominently in his self-image. He feels secure in his knowledge that few could do as much as he did (and does) in so short a time, and he recites the deeds and doers with a deep-sea fisherman's sense of improving on the truth and affirming one's manhood.

One evening Henry watched shark movies on television until one in the morning, only to be brusquely awakened at 4:30 A.M. by "Trevor the Revver," a friend of White's, who insisted they go climb for the day at Wyberba, only four-and-a-half hours by car from Brisbane. Henry recalls,

> We went out there, and I was completely wasted. This pace went on for the entire trip, it seemed. As soon as I got out of the car at Wyberba, I was stung by about ten wasps. One never stings you; they all get you. We did the first ascent of Late Afternoon Flake, then two first free ascents, and then I soloed the Womb. We drove back about one in the morning after drinking with Rick. Trevor was back at four A.M.

Trevor was a highly energized oddity in the world of Australian rock, cut from the classic British wild-hard-man pattern but from local fabric. He worked as an insurance salesman of one sort or another, and loved to drive at speeds better reckoned with in high-performance experimental aircraft. While timid as a rope leader, Trevor was aggressive as a sleuthhound in unearthing new routes and secret crags hidden in the bush. He was an obvious partner for Henry.

> It was hot enough so that I was drinking about a quart of milk, a quart of soda, a half-gallon of water, and, seriously, close to a gallon of beer a day. I was averaging about two to three hours of sleep a night.
>
> I began to meet some new people — a guy named John Fantini, who took me climbing, and another guy named Fred From. They all called him "Fred-from-the-Bush." He never wears shoes, just wanders around in the bush in bare feet with all these snakes and spiders and leaves with thorns in them all over the ground. He doesn't care.

The climbing and drinking continued unabated. On Henry's last day in the state, after three hours of sleep, a group of regulars drove an hour to Frog Buttress, knocked off three first free ascents and two first ascents and were back in the pub in Brisbane by noon. They downed a quick couple of pots of beer, then rushed over to Kangaroo Point and flew up a few routes, since Henry had not climbed there yet. He was supposed to fly to Canberra that night for a lecture, but he found that the airlines were on strike. Two more days of the same manic pace followed immediately.

That night the team partied until 2 A.M. Fantini rushed the visitor out to the crag first thing in the morning to do the first free ascents of old aid routes called Venom and Badfinger. According to Barber,

> These were difficult climbs. It was oppressively hot, grimy, and uncomfortable all the time. The pace and environment and fauna had about them an air of desperation so trying that the climbs became reasonable by comparison. Every climb was the same — just hard. Since I couldn't distinguish between the climbs, I may have been screwing up the rating system some. I couldn't tell. I'd just tell them that such a climb seemed harder than some other and then they'd rate the climbs for me, although I insisted that nothing I did — except for one called Manic Depressive — was harder than 23.

As John Smart remembers,

> On his one day climbing around Canberra Henry did a few climbs and made them all look easy. We'd never seen this sort of thing before. There was an aid climb that had been done only recently, called Soolaimon. It was a corner with a large roof at the top and only a hand crack running out of it. Henry freed the climb at grade 21. Since he was there it's had only one other ascent, by Rick McGregor, who took two days and eight falls and then regraded it at 22.

Barber on the first free ascent of Soolaimon/Henry Barber Collection

McGregor is an itinerant New Zealander who also frequents Yosemite and Eldorado Canyon in Colorado.

Smart continues,

> After that day Henry sat on our living room floor, looking exhausted. We told him that we were off to Mount Arapiles in Victoria. He said "All right," and off we went.

Mount Arapiles — from an Aboriginal word meaning "mystical mountain in a desert" — is just that: a three-kilometer-long band of hard sandstone cliffs about 300 kilometers northwest of Melbourne rising abruptly out of vast, rich wheat fields and sterile, scrubby desert. Close to 600 climbs are found on about a dozen crags. Arapiles has been one of the continent's premier climbing areas for just under twenty years. Smart says,

> It's a thirteen-hour drive. We got there at about five in the morning, napped for about two hours, and someone jokingly said to Henry, "Why don't you go and do Kama Sutra? That only has two points of aid left in it." He wanted to do a climb first to get used to the rock, so he and Ray Lassman did Eurydice. He wandered up the route, not putting in any nuts. This was surprising to us, as it is a grade 18.

Ray turned out to be an ideal partner in many ways for those frantic days. He is a scraggly, bearded computer nut with an unruly head of hair not unlike desert shrubbery, and a compulsive manner. Between bouts of effusive gregariousness, talking to everyone at once, Ray would make hell-bent attempts to follow Henry's leads and would regularly take wild, spiraling falls, the overhangs echoing with his screams and laughter. According to Smart,

> Henry then went up to Kama Sutra, a large, jagged roof, and again wandered up, putting very few nuts in the overhang. He graded it at 23. He traversed into the roof section from the side, and ran both pitches of the climb into one, so that when Ray tried to follow, he found no

*Henry's first free ascent of Taste of Honey at Mount Arapiles in Victoria/
Charles Massey*

way to aid through the difficult moves. He became completely spent and was left swinging in space. There was no way to lower him to the ground, so Henry untied from his belay and walked without any anchor to the edge of the rock, downclimbing several tricky moves, lowering Ray to John Smith's shoulders on a ledge below, all a good hundred meters off the deck with the full weight of a climber on his waist. We thought this an amazing effort in itself. This sort of mind-blasting all the time was giving us an insight into the character that he was. It just seemed unbelievable to us at that time in Australia.

It would be several years before there were full-time climbing bums in the country, most of them informally residing at Mount Arapiles and living on the dole; they forever changed the caliber and tone of life on the rocks in that ripe continent. At that moment, though, its innocence and promise suited the American's hyperactive personality, weaned on similar all-night drives to the west, with sunrises over parched plains, gloating on the expansiveness of it all.

Smart continues,

We came down that afternoon to the camp area at Arapiles. A few of us were bouldering on a rock that has twenty or so routes on it. Henry came down, and I pointed out a route called Garden Street. Only about three people had done this before. He shuffled back and forth for about five seconds, dipped his hands into his chalk bag, and then just walked up this problem. Some people saw him come up this side of the boulder and came over to watch. I told him to do it again so I could watch, but slowly this time. He said to wait a minute, that there was something else there. He moved about a meter right, dipped his hands again, and did this problem that no one even knew was there. He then moved about a meter to the left and did one there that had never been seen. I asked him to do the central one again, please, and, in fact, I think that he did them all about two or three times again for the spectators, just dusting his hands down in chalk each time, proving that he was a caliber of climber that we had never seen in Australia before. Subsequently, a few climbers have done these boulders, but never in the same style as Henry.

Luckily they arrived back at the climbers' camp in the pines at the base of the cliff in time for the traditional Easter egg hunts in the dark, groping around for eggs hidden in tree branches ten meters off the ground, and for the ever-popular sport of chasing ecidna, a cross between an anteater and a groundhog. The crux of the chase is a dramatic speed digging contest, since the ecidna tunnels straight down into the ground when cornered. There was little time for sleep.

The difficulty of the climbing continued to exceed the abilities of Barber's partners. Often, he rappelled routes after leading them, cleaning the protection, since no one could follow. Consequently he began to solo more frequently. He tells one story about a climb called Bard.

It was about 5.3 or 5.4 and about one hundred and fifty meters long. It took about nine minutes or something. Later I was sleeping in camp. A woman friend named Kim Blanch was in the tent with me. A guy comes in late at night to a camp right next to us. He says to his friend, not knowing that we were right there, "Hey, do you know what? Hot Henry's here! And you know what? He's free climbing everything in sight!" His friend says, "Really!"

"And you know what?"

"No, what?"

"He soloed Bard in nine minutes!"

"No, really?"

"Yep. He started at nine minutes to five and finished at five. He went right by me like a shot."

The next morning, another guy comes up to their camp. I'd just told Kim the story of the night before. The same guy from the night before was walking around. I woke up Kim again and told her to listen to this. Sure enough, the guy repeats the exact same conversation.

The Life and Climbs of Henry Barber

"Hey, you know what? Hot Henry's here. . . ."

I had to keep my hand over Kim's mouth to keep her quiet because she was laughing so hard. This is the sort of thing that I run up against all the time, and I just have to be quiet about it. I didn't want to get up and embarrass the guy, so we lay there for about an hour-and-a-half. Then this other guy comes over trying to give me some addresses so I can line up a South Australian lecture. He says to the camp right next to us, "Hey, you seen Henry Barber?" They say, "Nope, he's not around here." Then the guy who's looking for me catches sight of the picnic table and says, "Oh, there he is. He's right over here."

The guy who'd told the stories turned about eight shades of red when he saw me. It was a bummer. He said, "Well, sorry about that."

"Well, I wouldn't worry about it," I said, "I've made an ass of myself before, too." And, of course, I was making an ass of myself when I said that to him. It was funny, though.

While driving to the four-day meet at Arapiles with a cast of characters that included a "Hum Zoo," a "Mr. Boobs," and a dog named Sasha, Henry had ended up in the back seat with a pretty, blonde, and outgoing gym and sex education teacher that everybody liked from the onset. Kim Blanch, although not really a climber, was "zooey" enough to fit right in; she later hitchhiked over the Khyber Pass alone. "Kim took care of me after all those hard climbs," Henry says; she served as a source of emotional release and confidence in an otherwise cooly combative male enclave. His habitual lack of close friends and climbing partners, even when traveling, has caused Henry to seek solace from the pressures of performance in relationships with women struck up on the road. Kim was to return the visit by a trip to America the following year that lasted 342 days, much of it passed with Henry, who remembers with chagrin that "she was definitely the marrying type . . . ."

Outside of Melbourne in the Grampian Range the climbing continued: Henry would lead; his seconds would be unable to follow. With Matthew Taylor, Henry tried one of the few

Henry on his attempt of Manic Depressive, the hardest set of technical moves pieced together during the Australian trip/Matt Taylor

climbs he would not be able to finish, an overhanging wall called Manic Depressive, estimated to be a 26. Before backing off, though, Henry pushed himself to the limit.

> I'd say that it's the hardest set of technical moves that I've ever strung together. When I go back there, if I complete it, I'll undoubtedly grade it two grades harder than anything else. Nobody else has even been able to do the first move. I got damn close to finishing the route — about ten moves up.

The performance so impressed Chris Baxter, Henry's erstwhile guide, that Chris shied away from showing him any other routes that might go free. A few other efforts were unsuccessful, too, though some of them were years ahead of their time. At Arapiles Barber had gone up on a grossly overhanging aid line called Procul Harum, not climbed until three years later when Kim Carrigan beseiged the route over several days and graded it a 26.

The frenetic pace continued, with visits to the endless route possibilities of the far southern island of Tasmania, home of the three poisonous snakes, and on to Adelaide in South Australia. In Canberra a surprise dinner party greeted Henry, with guests arrayed in "formal" attire. Ray Lassman wore a black velvet suit "and was immaculate. But, then again, come to think of it, Ray never travels with shoes."

By the end of the trip, word about Henry's sensational performances was preceding him everywhere he went. In the Wolgen Valley of the Blue Mountains, west of Sydney, Henry found himself in the midst of what the Australians call a climbing "meet." First impressions left much to be desired. Henry found himself

> in this sandstone valley that has several hundred kilometers of cliff line, all sandstone. An incredible place, but these people were out of control. They were racing around in their cars, tearing up these beautiful fields.

They were *out of control,* way out beyond "fun" and into the murky and indistinct edges of unpredictable behavior. It was unsettling.

On a climb called Flashpoint there, Henry sensed a new kind of pressure.

> I had to be very careful how I rated each climb. They were all ready to jump on me. I'd done at least one first ascent or first free ascent in every place I'd been, and so I felt obligated to give Flashpoint — which hadn't gone free yet — a try.
>
> It was just like soloing. There were about fifteen people watching. It was raining. It was slimy and desperate. I had to rid my mind of all these extraneous thoughts, but it was hard. There was such pressure not to fail. Even though I climb mostly for myself, sometimes you have to dance to some different music. My reputation was at stake here.
>
> Kim Blanch was as bothered as I was by the pressure these people were putting on. Well, I happened to make

Henry on first free ascent of Kachong, Mount Arapiles/Charles Massey

the climb, and finally got my second up with no small amount of swearing and tugging.

In forty-four days in Australia, Henry had climbed in twenty-seven areas in six of the eight states — far more than any Australian. He had traveled over 9,600 kilometers. Of the hundred routes he had climbed, sixty were first ascents or first free ascents. He says,

> When I got to Australia, there wasn't one 22 that didn't have aid in it. So I was the person who was open-ending their system. A lot of 23's sprang up immediately after I left. I was just giving them a proper perspective.

The Australians weren't the only ones who were dazzled. In an article on Henry's climbs in *Mountain,* the typically restrained Ken Wilson described the tour: "Henry Barber went on a rampage during his first visit to Australia, freeing dozens of previously aided routes and establishing hard new climbs." The encomium continued, noting Henry's "hurricane pace," "spectacular freeing 'displays,' " and the "relatively stunning importance" of his achievements.

Henry, meanwhile, sees the overall effect of his visit as "helping the Australians out with their grading system by knocking off all these routes." There was, he reflects, only one negative aspect of his impact: the introduction of chalk.

John Smart agrees, explaining,

> I don't think that chalk was in use before Henry arrived in Australia. It's used fairly widely now. All the new limits, with only a few exceptions, are being pushed with chalk. I think that there is little doubt that it changes the nature of a given climb. Many of us blame this partly on Henry's visit but mostly on the States in general. American climbing has obviously gotten to the point where climbers there can't afford not to use chalk. And I think that it's a case of egos in the sport. For many of us here, climbing is still a wilderness activity, and we don't want to see all of the

really superb routes clogged up with chalk. It's a matter of conservation versus the frail egos of those who are doing very well with chalk. For doing well, though, you have to take your hat off to them.

Hats off or not, Henry modestly downplays his visit.

The scene was just in its infancy. Like a child — anything could influence it or push it in any direction. That's why the climbs that I did and the style I used had such an impact on the evolution of the sport there.

Greg Child, in a recent survey article on climbing at Arapiles in *Mountain 78*, wrote that "Most of his achievements were aid eliminations which further emphasized the philosophy of pure free climbing, which was only beginning to surface amid repression from reactionary rock factions. . .and opened the local eyes to the idea of hard climbing and pushing oneself."

In the wake of Henry's trip and the widespread favorable publicity that showered on both the visitor and on Australian climbing, a number of other talented Americans (and Englishmen) — including Ajax Greene, Tobin Sorenson, and Mike Graham — have visited the continent and made an impression, but none had the opportunities of Barber. The gap in standards had been largely closed.

By the end of his stay, Barber had convinced himself and all the others about a number of things. While John Smart and Ray Lassman had initially wondered what drove someone like Henry to climb with such a voracious appetite and under such intense pressure to excel, Smart realized "in the end that the reasons that Ray, Henry, and myself climb are all pretty much the same. It's just that we do it on different levels."

In Australia international professional climbing as a career arose as a real possibility for the first time for Barber. He had established a definite personal style. What a year earlier had been a tentative probing into the cherished mysteries of English climbing and forced participation in all of its attendant joys — salmon poaching, pub running, mad driving to the crags — by a young visitor who only wanted *to climb,* had been translated by Henry into a lifestyle all his own, with a pace in climbing and travel and misadventure that few could match. Henry had created demanding new lines and an entirely new standard, cleaned up the ethics of local areas with free ascents made in impeccable style, and arranged for slide show lectures both on the road and afterward at home to pay for the whole venture. It had been both a risk and another logical step outward in an ever widening spiral from New England and the west, and it had worked.

Business, unusual places and people, manic energy, and very pure climbing at the cutting edge now characterized the Barber style. His purpose was clear: to be bold and extremely alive, and to live to tell about it at great length. Henry was confident, more so than ever. He *knew* he could make an impact, could define himself by his professional presence almost anywhere. He aimed to perfect his tour-de-force method and use it elsewhere, in other countries possessing significant climbing potential that were relatively unknown to the west. He was looking for something different, uniquely personal — places where he could leave his mark, like a timber wolf circumnavigating its territory. Eastern Europe in particular held such promise.

Henry was an established international star, but what he would find in his next foreign campaign would be far different from what he encountered in Australia. On the soft sandstone pinnacles of East Germany, it was a scene decidedly not in its infancy.

5

At the Feet of the Master

CLIMBERS LIKE TO SPIN YARNS about climbing almost as much as they like doing it. Vast geographic distances, lifestyles, and generations separate climbers. Much of what they know about particular areas and about each other has been distilled by the grapevine into archetypal stories of grueling epics in the big, remote ranges by fascinating individualists sparkling with wit.

The kind of stories that emerge about a person or place in the climbing world, while often embellished by a hundred barroom retellings, embody the prevalent mythology that guides mountaineers in their choice of dreams and wanderings. Occasionally the tales are more real than anyone ever imagined.

What little word escaped through the Iron Curtain from Dresden pictured an established climbing tradition that was pure, simple, and utterly uncompromising. Virtually no western climbers visited Dresden. Its short, very technical routes were thought of only as practice for grander alpine routes by both local and foreign climbers. The long standing tradition of very clean and devilishly hard climbing was sustained by this neglect, and by a general continental lack of interest in pure free climbing that lasted until the mid-1970's. Even the British stayed away, perhaps because of their own temperaments or from intimidation based on the stories they had heard. After the 1930's, travel was restricted by political developments, and the isolation became entrenched.

Barber, anxious to explain the tradition, said this about it:

To give an idea of the Dresden style of climbing, one time Herbert Richter, the former Master of Sport who taught the top climber Bernd Arnold how to climb, was trying to make the first ascent of a beautiful but dirty handcrack. He was up there on a vertical face laboriously cleaning it out with a knife, trying to dig out all of the moss and dirt. He kept carefully climbing down to rest, and then back up very difficult moves to keep working on this thing.

After numerous trips up and down, he was beginning to tire and began slowly downclimbing delicate terrain. He suddenly slipped, plummeted about eight meters, and completely broke one of the double nine-millimeter ropes that was protecting him. Ignoring the bruises and adrenaline, he went back up on the remaining single strand, finished cleaning the crack, successfully downclimbed it, and came back the following week to do the first ascent of the route.

No one in this country or England would ever consider doing a climb in that style — having a rope break and going back up there to finish the job. It would just never happen anywhere else but Dresden.

The cathedral-like clusters of a thousand soft sandstone towers, in surrealistic forms that seem to be born of the same Teutonic imagination that produced Beowulf and Grimm's fairy tales, fill the wooded, rolling countryside around the River Elbe and its tributaries. Saxon climbing tradition in the two-hundred-square-kilometer area formally known as Elbsandsteingebirge, hidden in the southeast corner of socialist East Germany (GDR), is identified in the west by the name of the wet, worn, once-proud city hastily rebuilt in pragmatic style after its firebombing by the Allies in 1945: Dresden.

Fritz Wiessner is an 81-year-old American alpinist and retired chemical engineer who began during his youth in Dresden a sixty-year climbing career that spanned the globe. Hard new routes there and in the eastern Alps dominated his early years, before he left Germany in the late 1920's to seek refuge from the Third Reich in America; here he set up his own firm and went on to discover very difficult rock and alpine routes throughout the continent and in the Himalaya. For years he had been saying that the deadly serious rock routes of

The Pinnacles in the Dresden area/Henry Barber Collection

Dresden have produced specialists that are among the best free climbers in the world.

Steve Roper, a well-known Yosemite big wall climber and guidebook editor active in the 1960's, was the first American-born climber to travel to Dresden since Oliver Perry-Smith was a student and leading light there just after the turn of the century. Roper spent two weeks in Saxony in 1973 with Wiessner (and his daughter Polly), who annually returns to climb and visit friends. A clever article by Roper in the Sierra Club's esteemed journal *Ascent* (July 1974) was the first description of modern rock climbing in Dresden to appear in the United States.

Wiessner had shown a gripping film of Saxon climbing at the American Alpine Club (AAC) annual meeting in 1967, but

Fritz Wiesner at 77 leading steep rock in La Baou near Nice/Henry Barber Collection

that was the era of pushing big wall routes. The clean, austere style was too far removed from the focus of American efforts at the time to stimulate enthusiasm. The free climbing movement was to begin several years later, about the time the idea of conservation of the rock through "clean" climbing (the use of nuts instead of pitons) gained prominence through the efforts and writings of Robbins, Stannard, Chouinard, and Doug Robinson. Roper, however, was retiring from big wall climbs at the time and expressed his curiosity to Wiessner.

Wiessner, ever the alpine diplomat concerned with the flow of ideas between Europe and the U.S., invited Roper to visit Dresden in 1969, but the trip was cut short while the pair was warming up on the Calanque limestone in southern France, when Fritz had unexpected heart trouble high up on a wall. The account of the 1973 trip greatly impressed Henry, who thought it one of the best articles on climbing he had ever read. "Though the climbs nowhere exceed eighty meters in length," wrote Roper, "there is great continuity. Steep and continuous. Intimidating. Scary."

Three years after Roper went to Dresden, in the spring of 1976, a second American group followed. In his AAC activities Henry had come to know Fritz Wiessner, and had indicated his interest in Dresden. One day early in the year, the 76-year-old Wiessner called Henry (then aged 22) and asked if he were serious about wanting to visit the area. When Barber responded affirmatively, Fritz invited him along for a March expedition. If he liked, said Wiessner, he could invite a few others, too. The outcome was that Steve Wunsch, a superb 29-year-old free climber active in the Shawangunks and Colorado and also a climbing equipment representative who had nurtured Henry's interest in Dresden, and Ric Hatch, Henry's 21-year-old local climbing friend from Boston, joined the party.

The group understood that this trip would not bear much resemblance to what *Mountain* magazine had called "Barber's whirlwind tour of Australia," and that they would have little effect on the standards of East German climbing. By the time they arrived there were over five thousand routes in the area. After a century of extreme climbing, the very strict ethics regarding protection were fixed like laws. Pitons and metal nuts were not allowed; consequently, even the fiercest routes were poorly protected and very steep.

Henry thought beforehand that

> it was basically going to be terrifying. My way of getting psyched up for major events is deciding that they're really way beyond me. I build them up to be impossible; I don't study them.

He feels that as long as he is on guard and paying attention, as long as the situation is new and exciting and challenging, he has the internal resources to rise to the occasion and pull it off. This "blank slate" philosophy of approaching problems intuitively and without prior knowledge figures heavily in his soloing methodology, business, and pursuit of new interests. Act first with exuberance, experience directly, then gradually read the history and fill in the details after the fact.

After Fritz's standard warm-up tour with the group in the

French Calanque, near the Riviera, and other lesser-known areas, they arrived in Dresden. It was cloudy and drizzling, with huge banners of socialist propaganda flashing everywhere in the clean but grey and rundown city. Almost immediately it felt depressing.

Dresden is not an accessible scene for the outsider — the climbs are too intimidating, the people too pure. At first, Barber, Wunsch, and Hatch had difficulty in even comprehending the minimal, exotic protection on some of the climbs. On their first day of climbing they visited the Bielatal. Wunsch, in his continuing dedication to strict ethics and local practice, immediately took off his shoes like the Germans, who routinely climb barefoot. Later on, when they were doing their hardest climbing, this turned out to be a mistake, since his feet were still tender from earlier efforts. Henry started out wearing shoes on the harder routes, while toughening his feet on easier ones.

The first day was sobering. Barber remembers,

> We got to the Herkulessaulen Towers. Wunsch was climbing in his bare feet, and after two routes with Fritz, goes up on the south face of the Hollenstein. Fritz is saying, "Oh, it gets many ascents. It's done all the time. It's no longer a Master route," — one of the hardest. Well, it *was* a Master route — one of the easier ones but unbelievably desperate. I finally managed it at the very end of our trip. We were immediately blown away. Neither Steve nor I could figure it out.

Meanwhile, Fritz was busy leading those hard 5.8 routes well known to him, at age 76.

The climbing that had so impressed Roper takes place on near-vertical pinnacles offering routes on all sides in cracks, on corners, or on faces pocked everywhere with solution holes, like the aftermath of a plague. Climbers go barefoot to allow more adroit use of the big toe in pockets, and to promote friction when the holds disappear on rock seventy degrees and steeper. Also, climbing shoes are difficult to come by in East Germany, even for those who have the money. Often leather

*Barber on the south face of the Kanzelturm in the Bielatal area/Henry
Barber Collection*

anklets are worn to protect the upper part of the foot in cracks.

But it is the system of protection that sets Dresden (and Czechoslovakia just to the south) apart from the rest of the world. Rudolf Fehrmann (1886–1947), a regular partner of Perry-Smith's on new routes, was the prime mover in the establishment and observance of a strict ethical code; he was also author of the first guidebook to the area in 1908. The prevalent belief in the area is that chocks, as well as pitons, scar the dense but friable sandstone cracks. Indeed, the tops of many towers have meter-long sets of grooves where the rope has been repeatedly pulled down after a rappel off a ring on the summit. So instead of the metal protection universal elsewhere, Dresden climbers employ knots that they tie in slings of various diameters and cunningly jam in cracks or pockets while balancing on small holds until they reach *Ringen*. These rings are large iron bolts about twenty centimeters long, featuring a ring about half that size in diameter and so thick that it barely allows a carabiner to be attached. The rings are placed only by the first ascent party; subsequent leaders must not add protection. The rock is so soft that holes can sometimes be drilled by hand without a hammer, although at times it takes several hours on successive days.

The result of this system of protection is that most routes have one to four rings; Fehrmann's vision limited their use to three or four at most. While American climbers run out a full rope length (fifty meters) on a given pitch, East Germans belay at each ring. As a result, most pitches are only twelve to twenty meters in length. Most leader falls are especially serious unless held by a jammed knot, since they are held directly on the belay ring and the displaced leader often hits the hapless belayer on the way by. The death rate for climbers has always been high in Dresden.

After their humbling experience on the Herkulessaulen Towers, the trio returned to the Bielatal for the next few days, doing easier climbs and learning the intriguing history of the surprisingly high standards. Many of the climbs they did there were conceived by Oliver Perry-Smith (1884–1969), an American from Philadelphia who spent his student and early years in Dresden. He did most of his climbing between 1904 and 1913, building his reputation as a legendary climber and audacious skier. He drove a flashy Bugatti far too fast and lived his life at the same pace. Stories about him are reminiscent of those told about Layton Kor, the tall, tough, and insatiable Colorado climber active in the 1960's until he abruptly joined the Jehovah's Witnesses. In an article on Perry-Smith by Monroe Thorington in the 1964 *American Alpine Journal*, Rudolph Fehrmann recalled an incident involving Perry-Smith leading a loud-mouthed beginner up a tower.

Left, the ingenious art of knot placement — a Bernd Arnold specialty. It can actually hold a short drop. Right, a typical steep hanging belay. Note the old equipment/Henry Barber Collection

All went well in the beginning, but then hand and foot-holds gave out. "Goddamn, I can't hold you," sounded from above, "I must cut the rope. I have no desire to fall on your account." A cry of anguish from the depths at last brought Oliver to call to me: "You, Petrus, have him on the rope, you must pull him over to you." And so it worked; the poor fellow swung through the air. . . .As the victim hung free in the air and flailed with arms and legs, Oliver slowly spoke memorable words to me, which I can never forget: "See, Petrus, the lovely picture, how he hovers, like an eagle!"

Perry-Smith put in some thirty-two ultra-hard first ascents. Near the end of his climbing career, just before he returned to the U.S., he was found in a bar one afternoon by some aspiring climbers. They badgered him for his drinking, saying that he was going downhill. Perry-Smith, after a few more drinks, went out that afternoon and soloed the first ascent of a route now known as the Perry Riss, roped, but completely without protection. One can still make out where he later returned and carved his name, "Perry S," in the rock halfway up the 5.8 to 5.9 crack to quell doubt about his impressive ascent.

The Perry Riss (or crack) was done first in 1907 and remains a classic, despite its utter lack of protection. Henry feels that even today the

brutal simplicity of the rules ensures that all leads are serious undertakings. But because of the route's popularity, the Federation placed a ring by Perry-Smith's initials, in contravention to the ethic of placement only by first ascensionists. The decision to add a ring was a long and arduous one, and required a meeting of and vote by all the Masters in Dresden. On only a very few routes has the Federation added rings; it normally upholds the original style of ascent. A tree used to protect a dangerous 5.8 layback crack was cut down several years ago by the Federation. Since that time, several people have been fatally injured on the climb.

When the three Americans went to do the Perry Riss, Barber soloed the route, since that was the original style. On a later ascent he stopped at the ring, untied from the rope and passed it through, retied, and continued since this was the practice before carabiners were invented. Wunsch, right behind Barber, led the climb, but without using the Federation's ring. All three found the route difficult, a tribute in itself since the climb had first been done seventy years before. The Perry Riss, however, is not an exception in the history of climbing in Dresden. Perry-Smith and others in 1905 were putting up routes of a severity not equalled in the U.S. until the 1950's. In 1907, Perry-Smith contributed to the rising standards with a route on the Monchstein that would be a respectable 5.9 in the U.S. today, all without pitons or nuts.

Barber notes that,

> Fritz was excited that I'd soloed the Perry Riss, and told everyone about it. None of the climbers could grasp any of this because they consider all of their climbs to be really safe. They don't indulge in solo climbing and find it frightening. Plus, their political culture teaches that the GDR needs the workers for the working. They are not supposed to be risking their lives. The Federation simply forbids solo climbing, although a lot of their routes are just soloing anyway.

Henry's personal philosophy about style had evolved considerably since his first trip abroad to England three years earlier. Initially at home in the east and while on the road, Henry had flaunted his own clean and highly controlled style, refraining from pulling on slings or resting on protection or even getting his omnipresent white golfer's hat and white painter's pants dirty. It was a self-imposed ethic and was applied universally, wherever he might be. In England it met with considerable resistance from the locals, who felt their indigenous odd peg ethic and casual free climbing style directly challenged by a brash outsider. The same was true to a lesser extent in Australia.

But by the time Henry arrived in Dresden, he had not

Barber in the midst of a very difficult stemming problem and one of the second ascents done during the first trip to Dresden/Ric Hatch

only further refined his own sense of what was proper and sporting, but had grafted on a newer ethic of stylistic relativity: when in Rome, do as the Romans do, unless it severely contrasts with your own beliefs. The experience of conflict in Britain, and gradual exposure to the many different ways that people in different places respond to similar problems, had generated an undercurrent of understanding that countered the arrogance of his early years.

This nascent ethic combined with two other major personal prejudices — his longstanding fascination with the history of climbing in an area and his resulting respect for the minimal protection and equipment and correspondingly severe risks of the pioneering climbers, and his continuing mistrust of technology and complexity in any forms. As a result, Henry was openly receptive to the obviously pure state of the sport in Dresden. It was the first glimpse of where his incipient ideas might eventually lead, and it proved both terrifying and addictive. The harsh simplicity of the rules led to a place out near the edge of control and survival where no rules made any difference.

One of the more difficult routes, and one that adequately reflects the sophisticated nature and elevated standard of Dresden climbing, is the Rost Riss, a Master route. Prior to 1976, the hundred most demanding routes in Dresden were elected to the category of Master routes by members of the Mountaineering Federation, once they have had second ascents to confirm their quality. When a new route deemed more challenging than others already on the list is created, number one hundred is deleted and the new line added in the appropriate spot on the list. At present about five of the hundred climbs were put up as early as the 1920's and still retain Master status.

Masters of Sport, as they are known, are state-sanctioned climbers who have led twenty-five Master routes each year for five years to gain the title, and then an additional twenty-five each year to maintain it. While the Rost Riss is a product of such standards and competition, it is by no means representative of the hardest climbing being done in Dresden.

The Rost (or Schwager) Riss, a crack climb put up by Harry Rost in 1954, lies in the Schramstein, a group of pinnacles relatively close to the city. The route begins with a finger crack that Henry likens to Butterballs (5.11) in Yosemite Valley, except it is more overhanging. The climber considering such a route must take into account that he will have to tie knots in sling rope of various sizes along the way in order to protect himself.

The crack moves over a one-meter overhang that would draw a 5.10b rating in Yosemite, to a ring twenty meters above large, broken boulders. On the equally serious second pitch, the crack becomes fist size (like Yosemite's Goldrush, 5.11) and has its crux a few meters above the belay, then ascends for another sixteen meters of difficult climbing with no protection. Another ring materializes shortly thereafter. On the third pitch the crack becomes off-width and unprotectable with knots thirteen meters above the second ring. The climbing here is similar to Cream in Yosemite (5.11).

The Rost Riss is a relatively popular route. Henry, despite several attempts, could not do the climb, one of the few failures he is unabashed about. In the U.S. climbs of comparable difficulty were not made until 1972. Barber feels that

> no crack climb as serious as this one, with little protection and sustained difficulties, has ever been done in the United States and probably never will be, due to the use of nuts and "Friends," mechanical camming devices.
>
> One reason that the Rost Riss is done with some frequency is not because it's easy for them, but because people are used to the style of the climbing. The climbers in Dresden aren't contrived and calculated in their movement like I am. They're much more natural. The tougher the climbing gets, the more contrived people get in the U.S. — that's the way they learn here. They clean the routes, or use pitons, or rest on protection to do the climb. The style always varies here. But in Dresden there is only one style to rely on.

Gradually, after three or four days of climbing, the Americans began to feel more comfortable. Wiessner, in his formal and gentle fatherly way, had waited until then to introduce them to Bernd Arnold, a handsome, modest man who would never let on that he might well be the finest rock climber in the world.

Bernd is a solidly built, shaggy-haired, and casual 34-year-old who lives with his wife Christina in the village of Hohnstein, about thirty kilometers outside of Dresden. He runs an inconspicuous print shop there that he has managed to keep a private business (he has a half-dozen employees; shops with more than seven become government concerns). Unlike the government print shops, Arnold's does not print propaganda. He specializes in custom work for the private sector, and as the sole manager of the business, he is able to climb whenever he wants.

> For me and my friends, rock climbing is a passion. It is a search after the very moment of happiness that you are able to experience, that most people who stay down below never feel. I prepare for the sport with a lot of training. My life rotates totally around climbing, even my professional life.

When Bernd arrives at the foot of a compact, complex,

Bernd Arnold high on Black and White on the Devil's Tower in Dresden/ Henry Barber Collection

and dead-vertical sandstone face, its moods and intricacies not fully discernible from below, the commitment is evident. The shoes, the shirt, virtually everything he's wearing comes off. Only light running shorts, a chest harness tie-in, and a few rope slings for protection hamper his fluid, intense search for the subtlest topographic irregularities that might be of use. A neat solution hole, as clean-walled as those one might hammer dowels into to join the pieces of a wooden bench, appears and Bernd studies it, smoothly raises his right foot to a point from which he can tentatively ease his big toe onto its rim and twist it back and forth until he has discovered all the texture that will just barely allow him to transfer weight onto the foot. Higher he encounters a similar pocket, almost a mate. He stops and ties a knot in one of the rope slings, such that one strand is tight and the other rises over the backs of both loops, forcing the knot to bulge out at the sides. When it is inserted into the hole — like the finger grips in a bowling ball — it is torqued into a camming action against the walls and holds body weight while he begins the laborious process of drilling a hole for a ring. "Who knows how he does it," muses Henry, "it's all magic to me."

Arnold is not a member of the Communist Party and not a Master of Sport. He has no interest in becoming either one. There are numerous Master routes to his credit, yet many of his most difficult climbs are not rated, since they have yet to see a second ascent. Over forty of Bernd's routes have not been repeated. Says Barber, who is often reserved with praise,

> He's probably the most natural climber I've ever run across. He flows and doesn't hesitate, and knows all the tricks in the world for placing knots. He's thirty-four years old and has been climbing for twenty-one years. Here's someone who's been putting up the highest quality climbs of virtually anyone in the world for about thirteen years and just now feels he's doing his best climbs.
>
> Bernd's routes are incredibly mature. You have to be very mature to climb them, with an overall balance between one's climbing and one's inner self.

Arnold leading " . . .one of his more desperate leads." Note the tied-off drill bit for protection in the foreground/Henry Barber Collection

Henry was struck by Bernd's highly evolved approach to movement on rock. His lines are largely calculated-risk death routes, where it is mandatory to assess one's limitations precisely in order to manage the emotional pressure of gaming for ultimate stakes. The existential isolation of a slow journey through an austere psychological and physical landscape with-

117

out landmarks or certainty of success weighs heavily in his finest routes. Henry maintains that Bernd would never be alive today if he employed a typical American or British attitude of "we'll just launch out there and see what happens."

> After twenty-one years, Bernd thinks he's finally got it all together. Look at these guys in Yosemite or England who have been climbing for a few years and are putting up 5.11 crack climbs. They think they're doing the hardest climbs in the world. And they don't know what they're talking about.

Simply understanding the commitment and complication of Bernd's climbs was difficult for the three Americans. Their concept of risk, vital to performance at this level, was very much at odds with that of the Germans. The new routes of Bernd are artful calculated risks, and because of that, Bernd feels that they are safe. His sense of control over his movements is so complete and so finely tuned that no element of risk is allowed to enter as long as he is rationally making decisions. Henry did not think that "what Bernd was doing was safe, as to me it was totally incomprehensible that the soft rock and knot protection would hold a fall." The Americans could not, in three weeks' time, evolve to the point where they could either trust or ignore the safeguards and feel confident about the outcome based on calm analysis of their own powers — and the laws of probability.

Both Herbert Richter and Bernd Arnold felt that Henry and the other two were capricious and unsafe in their style; especially so was Henry's reliance on an inflammable mixture of adrenaline, confidence, and fear to surmount difficult, unprotected leads. Henry, however, felt that his climbing had progressed into a very different realm of assuredness by that time. Early on in his career he fell frequently. He took probably a hundred leader falls in 1973–74 while he was forcing Foops and other extreme moves in the 'Gunks and elsewhere, but only some fifteen times has he come off unexpectedly. In the course of climbing innumerable first free ascents of old aid routes in the period before Dresden, Henry had worked on a stylistic innovation by insisting on downclimbing from hard moves instead of routinely falling. Doing the first ascent of Yellow Crack in the Shawangunks was a breakthrough for him; here, climbing with John Stannard and John Bragg in late 1974, Henry had reversed the difficult moves three or four times from seven meters above the protection. By the time he finally forced the moves, he was confident that he could back down from any point. It had become "safe." He had crossed over to another notion of control, of reversibility, and could climb his way out of fear.

In Australia the following spring, this innovation became integrated into his style. If he was thwarted on a route, if he had to be lowered to a stance or belay, he would downclimb and pull the rope through the protection, and then he would relead the pitch to the previous high point without the benefit of a toprope. This was a way of giving the climb the best chance, and, while not nearly so severe as Jim Erickson's ethic of never returning to a climb he had taken a fall on, it was nonetheless progress toward a purer vision of the sport and a bold personal statement.

> What you learn by climbing all over the world are the natural, logical responses to a particular place — seeing, without being told, that there's a rational way to do things dictated by the local conditions and ethics.

Observers speculate that Henry takes great risks, but they are not able to see back beyond the moment of danger to the wealth of crises and confrontations with self in extreme situations that have been resolved successfully in the galaxy of moves he has made in his past.

A few days after their climb with Bernd Arnold, Wiessner introduced his guests to Herbert Richter, a forty-six-year-old physicist working in Dresden. Herbert, who is a bit of a clown, has fluid jowls that appear too soft for a rock climber and hair that stands on end like some frightened hairy mammal's. Like Arnold, Richter is no longer a Master of Sport, following

Herbert Richter/Henry Barber Collection

trouble with the Federation. Herbert was attracted by the myriad long cliff walls around Saxony. However, all of the climbing there takes place on pinnacles, since the Federation has adopted the ideology of the eastern bloc that one must reach a summit — and a cliff does not have a summit. Herbert ignored this reasoning and put up beautiful climbs, both with aid and free, of which the latter has been strictly prohibited since Fehrmann's time. The Federation began to issue warnings about Herbert's status as Master of Sport. He persisted in his personal explorations and was eventually removed from the list. Now he is not allowed to climb outside of the country on official trips to Poland or the Soviet Union.

Arnold's case is different. A few years ago, he began to put up routes that were of a more difficult standard than any in Dresden. They unfortunately lacked any sort of protection, so he installed as many as five to seven rings on his routes, when the unwritten law limits rings to three or four. Once, on one of his more difficult routes, the drilling position was so tenuous that he placed a peg in order to avoid a ground fall, and did not attempt to cover up that fact. Official sentiment mounted against him until he was asked to join the Communist Party, an offer he had already refused numerous times; this caused him to lose his Master status.

Herbert states neither Bernd nor Herbert regret exclusion from the Federation.

> What interests me most in climbing, especially while our American friends were here, is the human contact that's involved. In my youth, naturally, I was capable and fit, rather ambitious, but what was most important to me was to be climbing with good friends; the common push with reliable and cheerful comrades. In short: the blue flowers of romanticism. Even today, I experience them more than ever.

Barber found the situation of the masterful two non-Masters a paradox. Bernd is by far the best climber around, so of course the Federation wants him to represent the system and the party.

But he's only concerned with his own little place, like a doctor who only works on ligaments or fingers. He's not interested in playing anybody else's game. Bernd epitomizes truly creative drive. He's not in Yosemite Valley with the best Australian, the best Polish and American climbers coming from all over the world to engage in a friendly competition. In Yosemite that has had a negative effect, as people have rappelled down and cleaned routes and chipped holds to fashion new routes under pressure. In a place like Boulder, Colorado, guys like me came in and made just enough impact to keep the locals like Wunsch, Erickson, Roger Briggs, and Dave Breashears spurred on in one of the most creative atmospheres ever developed in climbing.

But Bernd has never had that. It is unbelievable that his striving continues, that he is happy with what he has and what he does. His freedom to create and express is his inspiration.

Both Bernd and Herbert took it upon themselves to show the Americans all of the classic climbs and many of their new routes, inaccessible to all but the best climbers. Bernd recalled that it was raining on the day they all met.

We drove to the Shrammensteinen, and after some brief thought, I decided on the Direct Wall of the front Tohrstein. You wouldn't be surprised by rain on this route as it is protected by overhangs. We climbed in two groups: Henry and Ric, and Steve and I. As I was leading, I laid too many slings, out of my concern for my partners. I hoped that Henry would do the same. We all laughed about it on top.

For many Saxonians, mostly conservatives, it was a sad sensation that strangers could climb this difficult route immediately. For me, it was satisfying. I suspected all along that it was possible.

Arnold had good cause for concern on the route, since it had been rated 7c, the hardest rating given in the guidebook.

The book, however, has little relevance in terms of the more difficult climbing in Dresden. Over the past years, Arnold has extended the rating system to include 8a-c and 9a-b. The most difficult climb that existed in Dresden at the time of the Americans' visit was 9a, the b rating presumably being left for future installment by Arnold. The best climb they managed was an 8c.

Richter immediately took a liking to Henry, calling him "Pumper Billy." On one occasion, he showed Henry a climb at the Pfaffenstein, just off the river, one of the easier Master routes. It was the most overhanging off-width crack Henry had seen anywhere. He stared up with widening eyes as Herbert said (as he did so many times during the three weeks),

> "This . . .is a . . .pumper. You like . . .my English? My English . . .is . . .perfect. Yes? Yes. Herbert's English . . . is . . .perfect. This . . .is a . . .pumper. OK, Pumper Billy, . . .this is . . .yours.

Herbert met Henry as he came down from what had been a marginal success on the route.

> "You like that . . .Pumper Billy? It was a . . .pumper, yes? Say . . .'Yes, Herbert, it was a . . .pumper.'
> "Yes, Herbert, it was a pumper," Henry replied obediently, amused and exhausted.
> "I . . .thought so."

With Bernd and Herbert as guides, the American found that almost every climb they did was a "pumper."

Henry particularly remembers doing the third ascent of a route called the Herrenparti, or "Gentleman's Day Out," with Bernd.

> We're on the last pitch of the route, and he shows me this little trick. He takes a four-millimeter sling and places it around a *senture,* meaning "sandwatch" or "hourglass" in German. This *senture* in the rock he uses is about the size of a pencil. From there you make a thirteen-meter run-

out on 5.10 face climbing. Fortunately, he lets me lead every pitch so that I can truly enjoy the route. Every minute I was with him I was terrified.

Then he takes me over to the Nordpfeiler on the Ganzfelsen, another one of his Master routes. It's had six ascents: one with me and three others with him. Every time his new Master routes get a second ascent, it's usually with him on the lead. The Nordpfeiler is this perfect arete, laid back at about eighty-five degrees. You're just swimming up this thing, like a native climbing a palm tree. We all did it in bare feet, except for Ric who had his shoes, and every one of us nearly fell off. My turn came, of course, when I was almost twenty meters out from the ring, facing a forty-meter fall. Every hard climb was like that. That was our little day out in Rathen with Bernd.

As the days unfolded, the Americans led and followed increasingly difficult routes. Early in the trip Steve Wunsch managed to lead the first pitch of the Feuerwand after a ten-meter fall off the crux on his first attempt. This was perhaps the most sustained pitch they succeeded on while in Dresden. Wunsch brought a revelation in style to Dresden when he completed the entire first half of the climb in one continuous pitch, clipping slings into the four rings along the way as protection instead of using belay points. This was the most important contribution of the Americans and was emulated by the top German climbers.

The second pitch of the climb was not much easier. It is normally begun with a shoulder stand by the leader on top of this belayer, since the Germans consider the team as the attacking unit. After eliminating the shoulder stand (which the Americans considered aid), Henry fell six meters, yanking Wunsch up against the rock through his belay anchors and knocking him senseless. He almost dropped Henry the rest of the thirty meters to the ground. "At that point, we had just about negative progress," Barber says, taking their long falls into account; they did not finish the climb.

They somehow got up many of Arnold's climbs, but the

trio began comprehending Steve Roper's sense of paranoia as the trip wore on. They found it more difficult to keep up the momentum in the constant mist and rain, among the massive prefabricated housing projects, and at the same climbing area day in and day out. The rock was superb, but the motivation meager. "Imagine climbing with the same person every day at the same place," Henry muses, grimacing. As an outsider it was very hard to create and perform well in that atmosphere. Ric and Steve especially felt this way, and, except for Steve's brilliant lead on the Feuerwand, neither successfully led any Master routes.

While Barber, Wunsch, and Hatch were well-traveled — all three having managed a comfortable life in the new business of climbing — their East German counterparts could only fantasize about trips to other climbing areas.

> My biggest dream is of Yosemite. I have a very clear
> picture in my mind of what it must be like. The rock looks
> unique, making me wonder about the free climbing

Arnold on a typically steep friction climb on the Gansfelsen/Henry Barber Collection

there. But there are always borders, making it necessary for a great deal of planning and organization in order to go to other mountains. Probably the major reason why I became interested in rock climbing, and never spent too much time in the high mountains, is that during my youth when I was learning, all of the borders were closed until way after the war. While in the early sixties I was a member of the national alpine team, allowing me to climb in the high mountains, in the U.S.S.R. and Czechoslovakia, my fondest memories are of the Sandsteinfelsen cliffs here along the Elbe.

Beginning about 1974, Herbert has worked on land near his house, digging out a filled-in quarry by hand so he can have a climbing area without rules or restrictions. Each year he excavates more of this personal temple, like a gentleman archeologist at the turn of the century — Heinrich Schliemann discovering the ruins of Troy — and climbs here as he wishes. He has put in short aid climbs and filled the buttress with a maze of lines otherwise illegal, since it has no summit. Five years ago, during Henry's first trip, it was roughly ten meters high and sixteen wide; by 1979, when Henry returned for a second stay, it had doubled in height and was perhaps sixty meters long. Herbert still climbs and digs there today, like a miner who believes he has found the mother lode.

The restrictive nature of the Dresden scene, a far cry from the delightful anarchy of the rock world in England or Australia or the U.S., contributed to tensions building between the young climbers and Wiessner, who mainly wanted to climb the old classics. Fritz had been a powerful original in his day, with a list of Dolomite firsts and the first ascents of Mount Waddington in British Columbia and of Devil's Tower in Wyoming (1937) to his credit; he also made a solo trip to within 250 meters of the summit of the then-unclimbed Himalayan giant K2 during a controversial expedition in 1939. The younger trio was naturally drawn to the innovative routes of their friends Bernd and Herbert. Fritz, while full of the greatest admiration for both, felt that "Bernd's routes are almost psychopathic in conception, and Henry almost psychopathic

Bernd and friends on a new route on the Welturn near Rathen/Henry Barber Collection

in his style and movement." Life together brought out differences between Wiessner, a formal chaperone and gracious host of the old school, and the three fun-loving rock jocks in their twenties.

127

Succumbing to the pressure, Henry opted out of climbing one day and spent the time wandering around the zoo instead, oddly drawn to and frightened by the animals of another land. The next day, when he felt like climbing, it was raining.

I was pissed off, and so I hopped a train out to Schmilka alone, took a ferry across the river, and walked up to the Meurerturm tower. I decided to solo this arete that Bernd had showed us but not indicated how hard it was, only noting that it was a Master route. So I went up on it, and it turned out to be probably the most committing thing I've ever soloed. The climbing just kept getting harder and harder. Finally, I ended on this arete, pulling on these tiny edges that are about to break off. There were only these pockmarks, no holds at all, and strictly friction for the feet.

Bernd came to dinner that night. We sat down, and I started drinking like fury. I was the most strung out I've ever been as a result of all the fearsome climbing. I'd had it. All I wanted to do was to get out of there alive, to be able to leave and say that I had a good trip. We had about three or four days left.

I drank about eight beers, almost a bottle of wine, and some apricot brandy, and was so dazed already that I was just bringing myself to normality. Bernd was amazed at how little training and how much drinking I was doing.

Bernd leaned across to Ric and queried cautiously, in his slow English, "Does he do this every night?"

"Yes, every night," said Ric.

"Why doesn't he train?"

"I don't think he needs to. You know that corner on the Meurerturm? The richt kunte?"

"Ya, ya. Ya, ya."

"Well, he soloed that."

"Without rope?"

"Yeah."

"Balls of steel. He has . . .balls of steel."

The climb had been rated 8b on the East German scale.

The climbing was equivalent to 5.10d face climbing in Yosemite Valley.

One day Henry decided to go to Czechoslovakia and he
needed a visa. He was introduced to a man named Hans,

> an important fellow in charge of all the Interhotel, who
> drove me up to Berlin, as I had to bribe the Czech officials
> to get one. Once in East Berlin, we were hurriedly dodg-
> ing in and out of all these huge hotel kitchens and mazes
> of back alleyways to meet our contact, when Hans looks
> both ways to see if it's clear and says to me, "Don't say
> anything to anybody. Your're my assistant, my friend, ok?"
> and then rushes into another hotel lobby. His employees
> and friends would come up and talk to us and I'd just
> smile and say "ja, ja . . ." and nod my head in agreement,
> as they'd know straightaway that I didn't speak German.
> This was in East Berlin, and a little like a Tyrone Power
> cold war spy film.

On the way back to Dresden after obtaining the visa, Hans
nonchalantly asked Henry if he wanted to get his swimsuit and
go for a swim? They would meet Renatta, the rather comely
wife of one of the members of Bernd's climbing team. When
they pulled up to a fancy club outside Dresden, Hans casually
added, "You don't mind if we don't wear our swimsuits, do
you?" and began pulling in. Henry wondered for a moment
just what kind of scene this fellow was proposing, but replied
that he did not mind at all, especially if Renatta was coming.

The pair drove down a driveway surrounded by orna-
mental hedges and fruit trees, and out of nowhere six naked
people came walking around the corner. Henry thought, *well,
okay, it looks like a great place* — except for one thing: there were
hundreds of cars there. They parked and wheeled around a
huge hedge, to confront about five hundred stark naked people milling around, engaged in conversation and swimming.

> We started talking to this real skinny guy and this real fat
> one, who must have weighed over a hundred kilos, and
> I'm freaking out as we're both in all our clothes. I was

casually observing the array of appendages all around, and whispering to my companion, "Hey, c'mon — let's take our clothes off!" in a real low voice. I was feeling really uncomfortable walking all around this place looking for Renatta. It was the first time I've ever felt awkward because I had my clothes *on* . . . .

We never did find Renatta. Finally Hans relented and drove me back to the relative safety of Bernd's mind-bending routes on the towers.

His eye still on one or two more major routes, Henry decided to attempt Bernd's two-pitch 1972 center route on the Meurerturm, next to the one he'd soloed. The full extent of the protection on the climb is a ring halfway up the steep face. The last moves on the climb are the most difficult; here the climber must ease into a narrow, holdless groove. Bernd's strategy for the climb had been to station a third climber — a member of his "team" of five that pass him hammers and follow him — on a separate ring higher than the belay. His job would be to pay out the rope from the belayer, since Bernd felt that the rope drag might be a deciding factor in the completion of the final moves.

On his first attempt, Bernd fell from the last move, going thirteen meters onto the ring supporting the third man. Since he badly bruised his ribs in the fall, he was forced to wait a week before he could make his second, successful effort.

Henry, fearful of the rope drag after hearing the story, decided to climb on a nine-millimeter rope, normally considered too weak for leading. "I figured that you're out there anyway. You might as well go for it all the way . . . ." When he got fourteen meters off the ground, he noticed that his rope was just blowing in the breeze. No one was belaying. He glanced down to see Hatch and Wunsch intently flipping a coin. Wunsch lost the toss, cursed softly, and soon followed up the first pitch to belay off the ring. Neither climber had taken the pitch lightly, since it involved 5.9 climbing with the possibility of dropping twenty meters into the boulders.

The crux moves in the second pitch occurred directly above the ring and belayer. Henry clipped numerous carabiners into the ring, since he found himself grimly contemplating their breakage.

> I wasn't fooling around. I was gripped.
>
> I launched off this ring, carrying no hardware — there was nothing up there. It was 5.8 or 5.9 for about seven meters on really sharp holds. All of a sudden eight meters up, there are no holds. Everything is rounded. It had been raining all week, and there was a slight film of dampness on the thin lichen covering the rock. I was just pissing myself. Wunsch was down there cowering at the belay, terrified, because if I fell off, I was going to land right on his head on the way by. I was so excited that I was leading and not belaying.
>
> I was climbing very quickly and suddenly began to feel very calm. I moved into this little groove — you have to pull yourself into it with your hands on its sides, smooth like the walls of a room. There are downsloping holds for your feet. Steve said that I was shaking uncontrollably, but I only remember that I made it, still feeling in control. He nearly soiled his pants when he fell off at the final move while seconding. Somehow we got away with that one.

The Germans were impressed with the accomplishments and adaptability to local ethics of the Americans, although Herbert felt that

> Henry is perhaps still too young (he could easily be my son), or he trusts his ability too much. In any event, he sacrifices safety by not using the necessary precautions. He lays too few slings and climbs on a single strand of nine-milimeter rope, making the climbing go more quickly. But one must remember that Death only looks away into the corner once in awhile.

Leaving was difficult. Henry had led fourteen of the hundred Master routes — and only failed on two; nine more and he would have made the Master quota for the year. He also climbed two unreported routes of Bernd's in three weeks. But more important was the group had made close friends with really good people.

> It's sad that they're never going to escape. I had many good times with Herbert, his wife Karin, and their kids. When Herbert said goodbye to us at the train station, he brought me these leather anklets and bought us a couple of beers. I was about to cry at the thought that I might not ever see them again. These people have nothing, compared to Americans. It takes six to eight years to get a car. But they have more fun than most Americans. Otherwise, the people in these Communist countries are solemn and quiet. The climbers have a common interest that's very intense and which draws them together, much more so than in the free countries.

"It's all very simple," says Herbert.

> I have gotten acquainted with many fellows who have climbed difficult routes — but with only a few with heart. My hope is always alive that I'll see them again, climbing on our beautiful cliffs.

Word came one night that Herbert's son Thomas had been gone for the entire day. While the other guests continued dinner, Herbert got up immediately to search, silently accompanied by Henry. The pair toiled up and down the hills for hours in the dark. "That was the gesture of a comrade who it always pleases me to think about," Herbert warmly recalls.

Henry did return, in 1979, to climb for ten days with Bernd and Herbert, and to make a film of Dresden climbing with Ruedi Homberger, a Swiss filmmaker with whom he worked on Mount Johnson in Alaska. While in 1976 he had climbed the hardest routes with the use of chalk, and introduced its use to Dresden climbers (who later banned it), on his second visit he climbed without it and furthered his efforts to climb at the top standards in other lands and to adopt the *local* style. The first trip, however, had the biggest impact. Henry feels that he "is going to develop as a climber over a period of time much the same way that climbing in Dresden has developed." He has seen into the future.

There is a difference, and possibly a conflict, between Bernd's sustained drive in a tightly constrained pastoral universe and Henry's expansiveness and need to be different, though Henry feels he is moving more in Bernd's direction now.

> I understand what Bernd is doing, but could never be content with it. My world is bigger than his world. If Bernd were living my life, he might look at it and decide that it was undesirable, and begin to do other things outside of climbing. He is making the best of what he's got. There's nothing you can read into it: it's just simple and pure.

As a parting shot in their initiation into Dresden climbing, the three returned to the Rost Kunte, a Master route that Henry had previously tried and failed on. It remains one of his most prominent nemeses. The climb was done in 1924 and has had fewer than five ascents in the original style. Climbers usually set up a toprope from a tower behind the route. In this way, when the leader falls on the Rost Kunte, he swings wildly backward through space in a twelve-meter pendulum and crashes into the tower behind him. If attempting the climb in the style of the first ascent, without a toprope, he would definitely suffer a ground fall.

Henry considers the route "the most amazing free climb" that he's ever seen. The route ascends an overhanging wall covered with downsloping pockets. Starting on this wall, one must climb out to an arete as sharp as the corner of a brick building. Broken boulders are scattered beneath the completely unprotected first pitch, which ends at a ring about twenty meters up. On his first try, Henry

> never even got to the hard part. I did about two 5.10 moves and downclimbed. I don't think that there's any route around that's as serious as this one.

Henry and Bernd in 1979/Reudi Homberger

In one of those acts people feel strangely compelled to perform, Henry returned to the foot of the Rost Kunte. The trip was over. The rain, the desperate daily acts, the oppressiveness of the country had taken their toll. Ric cautiously set up a belay away from the face, and prepared to pay out the rope, there being no protection to warrant a belay. It was their finale in Dresden.

Henry tentatively tested the first moves, came down, and then went back up and beyond. He eased up higher on the pegboard of sloping holes, constantly glancing at Ric standing below him in the boulders. A light wind swayed the pines, which seemed to be watching; no words were spoken. Barber worked up a little higher than the first time, and studied the two perspectives — ahead along the sharp arete, down to the ground.

Suddenly, he says, "I blurted out, 'Ric, I'm going to live.' I came down and that was it."

6

Celluloid Heroes

*H*ENRY HAD ALWAYS envisioned himself being filmed. From the time he first emerged as a powerful and graceful climber, he desired a way to step back and see himself move. He felt good about letting others appreciate his "subtle flow on the rock." Increasingly conscious of his abilities, he carefully strove to present an aura of grace, competence, and control to those around him.

With the AMC group around Boston, Henry had put on informal slide shows during drinking sessions, trading shots of weekends past and banter about those coming up. About the time of his first trip to England, he began to give slide shows for schools and clubs. At Deerfield Academy, he gave his very first paid lecture for twenty-five dollars. The school was a two-hour drive from his home in Sherborn, which meant he lost money due to the cost of travel. He found it rewarding, though; he discovered that he could, indeed, teach a subject well, and he found that a large group of people did not make him nervous, mainly because he knew that no one else knew anything about the subject. Later on, as he began to lecture more frequently, he realized that no one in his audiences had been to all of the areas he had, although he was usually far younger than the majority of his listeners. He says,

> Already, in the first part of my lecturing career, I was beginning to become somewhat controversial. Right from the start, people had definite opinions about me. Getting into the public eye was a natural progression. I never felt that I had to work at it, or wanted to, for that matter. I just felt that I had something to offer.

One summer at Telluride, the crew for an "American Sportsman" TV show segment materialized. Dave Farny's good word got Henry a position as a boatman for a filmed descent of the Delores River. The concept of the show, viewed weekly by millions on Saturday afternoons, is built around placing a celebrity in one field in an unusual outdoor sports situation; in this case, skier Spider Sabich and actress Claudine Longet were to run the Delores, although they were eventually not involved in the filming. Henry got along well with director Scott Ransom, an independent filmmaker in his early thirties, despite the highly theatrical nature of film crew interaction.

In 1975, the National Geographic Society decided to produce an hour-long documentary on mountaineering, and sent Yvon Chouinard and other climbers with director Charles Grosbech to the Baltoro region in northern Pakistan. While the setting was remote and fantastic, the footage obtained was uninspiring because of bad weather, personality conflicts, and organizational problems. In an effort to salvage more of a chronicle of mountaineering, Grosbech, Chouinard, and crew headed to Ben Nevis in Scotland, site of Britain's fiercest storms and ice climbing, in March of the following year. Yvon was to climb with the local master, Johnny Cunningham, in a fictional film they were producing at the same time for their own use, and he asked Henry to come along as a climber in the Geographic film.

From the earliest days of the filming, director Grosbech and his crew of technicians and climbers were at odds. Henry, in particular, had his differences with the director, who sidelined him for much of the climbing footage.

> Grosbech would tell me to do this or that and I would simply tell him to shut up or screw off. I was always angry with him for something. He didn't like people talking back to him.

There were problems with the Scottish film aside from personalities. The schedule was often thrown off by inefficiencies and inadequate planning. The cameramen were flown by helicopter each day to the filming site, and the helicopter often

Hamish MacInnes filming John Cunningham's crampon placement during the National Geographic Society's filming in Scotland/Henry Barber Collection

Jeff Lowe being filmed by Bob Carmichael and soundman Peter Pilafian during an ice-screw placement/Henry Barber Collection

arrived late, missing the best light for filming. Once the winter winds blew down the tents at base camp, and another time knocked over and incapacitated two $20,000 cameras left at the shooting site overnight. The filming took six weeks instead of the proposed twenty days. Chouinard was avalanched 400 meters down an ice slope; in addition Henry was hit by a slide triggered by the film crew while he was soloing and trying to take out an ice screw placed so that Cunningham could be filmed being inundated by a small slide. The film was never completed or shown.

The Life and Climbs of Henry Barber

Among the coterie of Scottish and English climbers assisting in the production was a Boston-area acquaintance named Rob Taylor, whom Henry had on occasion met while bouldering. Rob had spent most of the previous year in Scotland's mountains, working with Hamish MacInnes — known as the Fox of Glencoe for his inventiveness and entrepreneurial talents — and his celebrated mountain rescue team. Rob had become a part of the local ice climbing and rescue scene, acquired a bit of a Scottish accent, and was recognized as one of the better technicians in the area on hard ice. Although they had met before, the Boston pair spent little time together, since Henry was playing the role of visiting star and Rob that of a local on home territory. They would meet again, though, and share two bold adventures that forcefully intertwined their lives.

By 1976 Henry Barber was, in a certain sense, famous. His lecture tours had made a wide international audience aware of his climbs. For several years he had been accustomed to being recognized on sight at many different climbing areas, and was used to the silent crowds of onlookers at the bases of routes he was leading. The recognition, Henry maintains, sometimes depressed him. In reaction to the adulation he developed an aloof, even cold, manner; he pretended that the crowds were not there and kept his distance, especially when spoken to by strangers. In his mind this was the only way to keep his own climbing private, to maintain its artistic integrity.

A critic might well argue that Henry's 1976 solos on Welsh sea cliffs for an American TV show prostituted that integrity. Henry strenuously denies the allegation.

> I would have felt I was prostituting myself if the film had been poorly done. If it had been only fifteen minutes instead of thirty-five, it would not have been a good job. What the movie does is to show impeccable movement, like ballet on a tilted stage.

Yet, in the next breath he sounds ambivalent.

> It was a business film. I went over to Britain to climb, to do

some routes that I hadn't done before. When I got there the film turned into just business. I knew it was something I could use occasionally on my lecture tour. I worked closely with the director. It turned out to be a very successful thing.

After arriving in Zurich following three weeks in Dresden in the spring of 1976, Henry received a message to call Scott Ransom in New York. The outcome was that Henry flew to his home in Boston, talked with ABC-TV, and ten days later flew to London to meet the film crew for an "American Sportsman" show entitled *Sea-Cliff Climbing*.

Most of the crew were friends of Barber's from past trips to England. Henry, Al Harris, Ray Lassman from Australia, and Pete Minks were to spend long hours renegotiating their friendships in the pubs around Wales. Ken Wilson of *Mountain* and Harris had scouted potential sites and had recommended Barber to Ransom.

The shooting took place on the sea-cliffs of Wales, a spectacular setting of rock, fog, and booming surf. Scott Ransom, in a somewhat unorthodox procedure, handed most of the technicalities of the filming over to the climbers. To a large extent, Henry decided where the camera should be positioned and how the forty-minute climb could best be filmed.

Climbers are not professional actors, and they need the appropriate atmosphere to get in the mood to create without inhibition. The "Sportsman" film had few problems, though, due primarily to the amiability and talent of Ransom, who had the final word in all of the filming. The work went smoothly and a well-made documentary resulted. For the first climb of the film, Henry and his old pal Al Harris were going to do A Dream of White Horses, a majestically located Very Severe climb (in the British adjectival rating system, equal to about 5.8 in the American).

For the climb the pair were fitted out with synchronized-sound transmitters. The cameras were positioned far away, equipped with sensitive receivers to pick up the slightest sound. Immediately Al and Henry started clowning, although they whispered to avoid detection.

141

"Al, how's your wife?" Henry asked in a whisper.

Al bolted upright, yelling, "I'm not going to tell you about me wife!"

Henry whispered back, "Oh, come on, Al."

"But she's me wife!"

Somewhat stage-struck, Al tried to emulate a Hollywood film star. He was dressed for the role in bright red pants and an electric blue cagoule. Leading the first pitch, he went off route. Way out beyond his last protection, he hammed it up: "Oh maan! Now ah'm gripped!" He lost whatever stage fright he might have had then and launched into a monologue about the horror of his position. Finally, he reached a positive, well-protected section of holds and yelled, "Hooray!"

When a film take is about to be made, the sound must be synchronized with the film. This is normally done by sharply clapping a slate to activate the tape. Henry and Al, however, had to improvise by clapping their hands together from their frequently precarious stances. To the horror of the cameramen, Henry, on small holds above a long fall, would let go with both hands to clap — then grab his holds just before he was about to fall off.

One of the cameramen, John Cleare, an experienced climber, filmmaker, and mountain photographer and writer, was not amused by the constant bantering. He wanted something different to come across in the film. Says Henry,

> He loves the seriousness of it all. He loves those character-istically British gripping shots of guys with nuts hanging all over the place and one sleeve rolled up, one sock up and one sock down, blood dribbling from the knee, EB's with holes in them, and really slimy rock.

In his jaunty white cap, with his copyrighted nonchalance, Henry hardly fit the bill, and he knew it.

> We didn't feel like we were going to work the next day. We knew we had a job to do, but we knew that we could do it without a lot of tension because we wouldn't be climbing

Henry Barber and Al Harris during a break in the filming of Sea-Cliff
Climbing/*John Cleare/Mountain Camera*

5.10. There wasn't anything to get uptight about. The
cameras were far away, and we just had a good laugh.

After the completion of the climb, Ransom asked Henry if
he would repeat the route, solo. Henry agreed, after being
promised that the shooting would be uninterrupted throughout. The climb was only 5.8. Henry never dreamed that he was
about to undergo one of his closest brushes with death. Cameraman John Cleare distracted him while he was immersed in
the difficult stemming moves up toward the top of the route,
almost causing the soloist to fall. Henry just barely managed to
recover and finish the climb.

Despite the scary near-accident, Barber agreed to solo a
much harder route as the *piece de resistance* of the show. The
Strand is a 65-meter climb set a full 130 meters above the
ocean. A hand and finger crack splits a vertical slab of intermittently loose rock. The difficulty of the crack is sustained
throughout its entirety. Ransom had talked at length with
Henry about soloing the climb for the cameras, and both
decided that he could be as alone as he needed to be. At 5.10,
the climb would be no more demanding than numerous

others that he solos each year, provided the right atmosphere was created by the film crew. Henry stated his criteria to Ransom:

> I ask only that nobody asks me to do anything, or say anything, and that you are set up and ready to go on schedule.

As it turned out, he arrived at the base of the climb and was told there would be a two-hour wait while the cameras were set up. This delay put him off immediately, and he opted to fill the wait with another climb to restore his mood.

> I soloed a thing called Central Park (H.V.S. or 5.8) in the meantime. I had done the route before, but right at the top a seagull dove at me and took my hat off. I almost went 200 meters, right off the edge. It was a very tense situation. I had incredible butterflies and was pretty freaked out.
>
> I was nervous, but not about Strand, not about the difficulties of the climb. Rather, I was bothered by the question, *Why am I going to do this thing?*

Of course, Barber's reservations had been aggravated by the seagull on Central Park, but other factors contributed to his uneasiness, too: while climbing during the wait, he became reacquainted with the loose rock on the cliff, and near the end he found that the temperature had soared in the bright sun.

By the time two and a half hours had passed, Henry's second thoughts had replaced whatever equilibrium he might have had with a growing tension. The crew was still not ready because they had misjudged the light. They told him to wait another few hours.

So, Henry had lunch. He drank a few beers and finally he was told that he could proceed, a full four hours late. As planned, he would walk to the base of the Strand undisturbed to begin the climb.

Several people had gathered at the base: Al Harris, who acted as a commentator, Pete Minks, Ray Lassman and Kim

Blanch from Australia, the directors and, of course, the cameramen.

> When I got there, everybody was completely solemn. They all looked like they were about to watch somebody's body be cremated. If it hadn't been for all the good times that we'd had, the Strand would not have been a possibility at that point because all of their expressions were so grim. I felt somewhat relaxed at this point, but at the same time I had some worries.

Henry approached the base of the crack, started up, and Paul Ryan, one of the cameramen, asked him to repeat the first few moves.

> He did exactly what I didn't want him to do. He is a professional filmmaker. He doesn't understand anything about the level of commitment necessary. Because of him I had precisely the attitude that I didn't want. All I wanted to do was bag it.

However, he didn't back off and leave the climb. He felt that he could still do it. His sense of pride was possibly the sole motivation for continuing at this point:

> I started to climb and it seemed that everything was working against me. I felt the cameras and all of America watching me. All the people that had enabled me to get to the climb — my family and friends — they were all watching me. All of the people down below obviously believed something was wrong, and it was all too clear in their faces. I realized that the rock was very loose because I had just soloed Central Park, fifteen meters away. The seagulls were still around. The extreme heat was oppressive. I'd had to wait for four hours and consequently was not in the right frame of mind. I just kept thinking, *Man, this is not where I want to be.*

But I thought if my philosophy on solo climbing is as

145

strong as what it seems to be, or is true and not just b.s., then I should be able to put myself in the right frame of mind and overcome all these things. So I started up, and I tried to do nothing but zoom in on the first ten meters or so. It wasn't very hard, only about 5.8, but I was just trying to get myself to be perfectly fluid. I would see two holds, one of them a little bit loose and small, the other bigger but a long reach, and I knew I'd have to stretch way up for it, and that would throw me off. So I would purposely grab the potentially loose and small hold, knowing I would not fall off because of my other footholds. I needed to get that fluidity.

The obstacles had thrown Henry off, however, and he was having trouble maintaining the proper concentration.

I had a lot of thoughts of family and friends. That was okay, as that's often the case, but the problem here was that I couldn't get rid of them. It's one of the only times in solo climbing that I had to do something where I couldn't really concentrate on what I was doing.

Kim Blanch, his closest friend among the group at the base, left shortly after he began, too frightened to watch. She was not the only one affected; the nervous strain told upon everyone during the one-and-a-half hours that Barber spent on the climb. Considering that he had spent only two-and-a-half hours on the Steck-Salathé, which is 550 meters long, the slow time reflects the difficulty of the 65-meter Strand.

The crux section came twenty meters up, where the moves, though not loose, require strenuous laybacking and jamming. Suddenly Henry found himself in the right mood. It was time to "get down to business." Once past the crux, however, his new-found sense of security dwindled rapidly.

Under the circumstances, I realized that I could not downclimb the difficult moves. It's one of the only times in climbing that this has been true. There were just too many things working against me.

146

Barber soloing after crux on The Strand/Edgar Boyles

147

He thought briefly about being rescued. Old nuts filled the crack, making tempting resting points. He considered several options, and decided to go on.

The second half of the route followed the crack up a wall with a slight overhang. The climb continued to be sandy and loose, but the moves were now awkward and strenuous. The heat had also taken its toll. One's feet swell noticeably in tight rock shoes in the heat. Often, the pain can be so bad that the climber may well begin to think only of his feet and not about the climbing, a potentially more dangerous situation than loose rock or the severity of the climbing.

The nervous strain and resulting exhaustion, precipitated by the pain in his feet, had a visible effect on Henry as he moved away from the crux section. In the movie one sees him take too high a step, shudder noticeably, and come down from the move. Henry rarely shakes. It indicates that he's "off," that there's something to worry about. And there was — the whole process had become a calculated risk with every move being initiated by what Barber calls a conscious effort.

That perfect mood, though, was always just one move ahead. Of course, I started thinking about my parents, my friends, the film, and the people who would be seeing the film — Am I really doing this for myself? Am I doing Strand because I think it's a challenge, or am I doing it because I've committed myself? I've said I was going to do it. They spent all morning setting it up. Why am I doing it? Today, I cannot answer that question. I would have to say that Strand was not for my enjoyment.

The last section of the climb was the most excruciating. Barber was obviously suffering, but Cleare asked him to repeat the final part where he moved from the cliff onto the meadow above the Strand. Henry was angry and had tears in his eyes. He describes the pain as a pressure inside him, like compressed air in a tank. Once the film was over, he took off his shoes and threw them far across the meadow. He felt no satisfaction, no elation or feeling of accomplishment, only a growing sense of relief that it was done with, that the tension

*The ABC film crew in Wales. Standing left to right: Scott Ransom
(director), unknown, Henry, Al Harris (in truck), Paul Ryan (cameraman), Bruce Perlman (sound), Mary Catherine (coordinator), Edgar
Boyles (cameraman). Sitting left to right: John Cleare (cameraman), Kim
Blanch, Ken Toms, Ray Lassman, and Pete Minks/Scott Ranson*

could begin to dissipate from his body. "I was hot, I was tired,
and I was beaten," he said.

In retrospect, he comments:

> It was an incredible mental challenge for me. But I
> wouldn't do anything like it again because it was too close
> to death. In a way, I felt let down. My judgment could
> have been better. The only thing that got me through was
> my philosophy of solo climbing: doing it on-sight, with no
> previous knowledge of the route, and being able to re-
> lease myself from all inhibitions in order to do the crux
> moves. At that point in time, once I'd done the crux, I
> could have jumped off, and I still would have won my
> battle. All I had wanted to do was to rid myself of all these
> thoughts that I was having. I managed to do that on the
> upper part of the climb.

The solo effort would inevitably earn the film success, as
Henry saw it, because

> never before has there been a film which portrayed such
> difficulty of moves and intensity of life and death as was
> shown in the footage of the Strand.

149

The crew moved on to Cornwall to shoot a combination climb called Dream and Liberator, on which Henry would be joined by the noted English cragsman Pete Livesey. They met in Wales, Henry and Al Harris a bit stiff from a hard night at the pubs. This did not prevent them from downing their fill right before the climb, but Livesey had only a few sips.

Pete and Henry had already developed a competitive relationship on his first trip to England years before, when they had struggled with each other on climbs in the Cheddar and Avon gorges. The antagonism surfaced openly on Dream and Liberator and became central to that segment of the film.

Prior to shooting, Livesey appeared anxious. Henry thought this was due to the fact that his solo of the Strand rated as one of the most noteworthy accomplishments in British rock climbing. Livesey often enjoyed the spotlight in his country, and resented this outsider's success and the corresponding media attention. Henry recalls,

> We didn't really talk much on the climb. It was a very intense situation. I think that in his mind, the cameras documenting him and Henry Barber climbing together really put him off. The fact is that we were just at grips with each other. Because of his attitude, I responded with competitiveness.

The voice of the film's narrator is immediately familiar. It tells about the setting and sets up the action to come by noting that "underneath the laughter and the cheer, a fierce competition rages." The theme is clearly stated: the constant testing of your companion. The voice belongs to Curt Gowdy, series host of "American Sportsman." He introduces Pete Livesey by saying he is an ardent athlete, and a first-class caver and kayaker. The soundtrack is then dominated by Livesey, who describes the route as a "fantastic arete of yellow rock, which the climb hugs as close as possible." Pete bluntly broaches the psychology of the event.

> The biggest obstacle is not the climb at all, but a leap across a four-foot-wide trench that drops thirty feet to the

Pete Livesey and Henry Barber before the start of Dream and Liberator/
John Cleare/Mountain Camera

sea. The ledge one has to land on is only two feet wide and
covered in a slippery sea slime. The rock has a nasty glaze.
Of course, Henry won't admit it's difficult — that's where
the competition comes in. He'll always say it is easy, no
matter how hard it was, and, of course, I always say that
my pitch is easy as well. It's a pity that I won't be able to see
him leading up there once he goes around the corner, as
he goes up the final groove to the first stance. It's a pity, as
I won't be able to see him struggle up. It's always good to
watch someone else struggle. That gives you back your
confidence for the next pitch.

The two were trying a climb that had not gone free yet.
Livesey had eliminated most of the aid on an earlier attempt,
but one point remained under a roof on the second pitch,
which was to be Livesey's lead. Pete explains in the soundtrack
that if he can do it without the use of the peg as a handhold,
then he will have won, but if he uses the peg and Henry follows
him without it, then he will feel that Henry has won. After
climbing up to the overhang to look the situation over and clip
a sling for protection into the peg, Livesey gives in quickly,
grabs the sling, and pulls up on it to make the move, knowing
full well that Henry will definitely have to do it free now, to

151

Henry free climbing aid maneuver on the roof of Dream/John Cleare/ Mountain Camera

zero in on the kill. Pete stands on the belay ledge above and watches with obvious consternation as Henry powers over the edge after working out the moves, even though the holds are covered with Livesey's sweat and caked with chalk, Barber then flies swiftly up the groove to Livesey's feet.

Henry's voice in the film is younger, higher pitched, more naive, without the deep, booming authority of today. He seems just like any other twenty-three-year-old talking about something he loves. He talks little on the soundtrack about the politics involved, as if he were oblivious to it (though that was certainly not the case), and instead concentrates on the *art* of climbing, a peculiarly American predilection. He continues with a very clinical explanation of technique. As the sound-track deftly switches back and forth between the two very different voices, young exuberance and older, deeper prag-matism, it appears that they are not even addressing the same subject.

In looking back at the climb, Henry feels that Pete had

gone up and felt rushed, probably because of the cam-eras. He shouldn't have felt that way. We had the time. He should have sat there and figured it out. So it didn't really matter if I made the move or not, except that I had told Scott Ransom that he should not document the climb if the move was not freed by one of us. When I reached the belay ledge after making it, Pete was a bit uneasy. He was pretty down. But that's his problem. He knew damn well that he could have worked it out. If he had different ethics in climbing, he probably would have successfully done the crux free.

On the final pitch, Henry spent a good deal of time hanging awkwardly under a roof looking for a crack in which to place protection. In the soundtrack, Livesey remarks that he knows there is a good spot just a little higher but that he won't tell Henry, since he seems to want to hang there under the overhang. That comment summarizes their teamwork.

Livesey had recently been "burned" by criticism in *Moun-tain* of his practice of "gardening" (cleaning holds and cracks)

Henry leading and Pete belaying on the last pitch of Liberator/John Cleare/Mountain Camera

and inspecting routes on rappel before attempting their first free ascents. He rebutted the charges, but the touchiness of the issue may have contributed to the unpleasant rivalry on Dream and Liberator. In the completed film, the competitive natures of two fine climbers surface in an already hostile atmosphere. An unbiased viewer might conclude that Livesey clutched. Henry was more used to the pressure of people and cameras and rivalry.

After the Dream and Liberator segment was shot, the filming took on a much lighter air, with a frolicsome girdle traverse of rocks right at sea level. Al Harris, Pete Minks, Ray Lassman, and Henry each hit the water at least once. There were parties most nights, including a filmed night at the pub, "when the competition moves indoors," as Curt Gowdy put it.

The last adventure actually occurred after all the filming had ended. Ray Lassman was soloing to the top of one of the routes near Dream and Liberator. He could not finish the climb and begged a friend to throw him a rope from the top. Ray grabbed the rope as it came down, but while hand-over-handing up it, he lost his strength and slipped off the end into space. Falling close to twenty meters to the deck, he landed on his chest and face on a flat slab of rock with only a single shallow groove breaking its otherwise uniform surface. Somehow Lassman's head landed right in the groove. Miraculously he walked away unharmed, except for a six-stitch cut in his head. The obligatory celebration took place at a nearby pub.

Shortly thereafter, the film crew disbanded. Henry flew home to Boston, and two days later was on his way to Moscow with the American exchange group of mountaineers. The crew had run up a very expensive segment bill for the all-night partying, and was thoroughly amused when the film shared the hour-long "Sportsman" slot with footage of comedian Red Foxx shooting pheasant.

In watching the film now, Henry sinks into the mood it creates with prominent headlands drifting in and out of the coastal fog, seagulls sweeping overhead, and foghorns rumbling deeply and mysteriously in the background. Two thoughts always predominate. On the one hand, when he sees the Dream of White Horses solo sequence, he wonders why he has to work and cannot climb like that all the time. The totally free and uninhibited set of moves "is not just climbing — it's the life." On the other hand, watching the Strand solo makes him wonder if he can ever climb at that level again, soloing things that difficult. "But I also hope I never *have* to perform climbing that hard in front of people to feel good about myself."

Yet, the Strand climb in particular was clearly a success, both in terms of popular recognition and in Henry's own inner world.

> If I had gone up ten meters and had not been able to get my rhythm together, or wasn't able to do the moves in the crux section, and had come down, then that would have been a success. But if I had just walked away from the whole thing, then I would probably make a mistake in a climb later on just because I didn't have the guts to live my own lifestyle. That's the way I live. To turn away from one solo climb because of something that I couldn't face would have been absurd. I knew that I'd be encountering similar sorts of problems at some point in my career. There was little choice for me but to face the difficulties at that particular time, on the Strand.

In Britain, as well as on the continent in France and Germany and Italy, media interest in mountaineering in the decades following World War II had elevated it to a very public sport, although one still acted out in remote settings. Media personalities had emerged from the sport to an extent unknown in the U.S. Joe Brown, Christian Bonnington, Don Whillans, Tom Patey: all were familiar faces and characters to British audiences, ones who had built public personae through their understanding of the power of the camera. So when Henry made his first real film debut in Britain and learned the rules of the game — in part from the film achievements of the masters — he was participating in an established tradition. He was one of the best and brightest young stars, who simply happened to be American.

Not that other climbers in the U.S. had not tried the media route to immortality. Paul Petzoldt and rival Teton climber Jack Durrance had briefly been in the public eye in 1941 when a stunt parachutist jumped onto the isolated top of Devil's Tower in Wyoming and could not get down to the ground. The pair combined for a rescue ascent of the peak and faced hundreds of radio and print journalists upon bringing the chutist to safety.

Warren Harding and Dean Caldwell mesmerized radio, print, and TV reporters with their twenty-seven-day ascent of the Dawn Wall of El Capitan following near-rescue in 1970. Harding used the event to propel himself to fame and TV talk shows, but disappeared from prominence soon thereafter.

Jim Whittaker, the first American to climb Everest (in 1963), went on from that extravaganza to do the first ascent of Mount Kennedy in the Yukon, with Robert Kennedy, for a film; he later got involved in other media projects. Jeff Lowe of Colorado has been highly visible in sports films on climbing and on TV in recent years, and George Willig (who climbed the World Trade Tower in New York) has appeared on several TV specials.

But climbing as a profession in America is a frontier. As John Bragg observes,

Henry's biggest contribution was as the first American professional climber. He sought more publicity, more actively, than anyone else, although he seldom wrote articles for or sent accounts of first ascents into magazines. He wanted to be famous more than anyone else in the American climbing scene, and was the only one of us not guilty about using the media toward that end. Chouinard and others were very reluctant about using it.

Bragg and others his age, some four or five years older than Henry, grew up at a time in the late 1960's when the goal was to drop out of the system, to become involved in radical politics and spend the summers in the idyllic surroundings of the west, going climbing when things got boring.

Henry saw climbing as athletics — not as an alternative lifestyle. His flamboyant personality constantly drew attention. As a result, he developed a very polished and controlled climbing style, since he had created an image and a place for himself in which he could not afford to flounder or fail. Barber has a need to communicate using his climbing style,

Bragg speculates, because of his lack of interest in verbal communication with strangers, and his rather formal, impersonal lectures. Bragg observes,

> I don't feel that Henry's a very good communicator. He never expresses his concern for other people's climbing. Yet once he had fame, it has been very hard for Henry to abandon public attention, as any star needs it to sustain him.

In 1976, the year of the sea-cliff climbing film, the trip to Dresden, and the Soviet exchange expedition, Henry incorporated his nascent slide lecture and photography business as Mountain Ventures, Inc. For two years he took losses and worked largely as a sales representative for climbing equipment manufacturers. Finally the money began to flow in. His photographs began to be published more regularly (including a continuing series of photo essays in *Climbing* magazine that began in 1977), and he managed to repay the hanging debt created by repeated borrowing from his college account to finance trips abroad. He never had an apartment, living instead on the road, with friends and sometimes with his parents, until one day he spontaneously decided to buy a house. Henry's father, the usual source of prudent business and legal advice, immediately calmed him down long enough to explain the complexities of the process. But after a period of incredibly hard work, Henry scraped together the ten percent down payment and bought an eight-year-old two-story house with cottages high on a hill outside of Conway, New Hampshire, looking north to Mount Washington.

> This changed my whole lifestyle. I flipped into overdrive then, and started to do both climbing and business with the same intensity. The more involved I became in business, the more I liked my lifestyle and the wider range of things I appreciated. Joe Brown likes to fly fish, and now goes to wild places like Walter Bonatti did — the Sahara, Karakorum, and so on — because of his notoriety. Those

trips keep him meeting interesting people so he doesn't get bored and become an alcoholic.

At that time it became clear to Henry that if he wanted more material goods, another Windsurfer or surfboard, then he had to work more.

My house is nice and in fine shape, but my car's a piece of junk. So I separated life on the road and at home: when I'm on the road, I enjoy the people, but when I'm at home, I live comfortably. I knew I couldn't stay in mainstream climbing, and didn't past about 1977.

By the mid-1970's, as Henry became increasingly well known through his exploits abroad, ideas for general-audience films on climbing began to be funded more regularly. Independent mountain filmmakers were coming of age in America. In an era that celebrated personal exploration and fulfillment, the market for climbing and other adventure films expanded rapidly, especially the television market.

Barber's initial attraction to film was as a medium for seeing and sharing his own special movement, in a further manifestation of his intense self-awareness as an aspiring star. But after the sea-cliff film with Scott Ransom, Henry was gradually drawn into the business of filmmaking. Although he had always envisioned himself on film, even after his supporting role in the Ben Nevis film fiasco, "never in my wildest dreams did I think that I'd be doing films for *National Geographic* or 'American Sportsman.' " He had little interest in becoming a director or producer of big-budget films on climbing. Filmmaking on that scale requires too much capital, too many sensitive egos out on the set, too many cocktail parties and trips to New York or Los Angeles, too many compromises, and a finished product bearing too little of one's personal stamp. Instead, Henry has sought to transfer the dedication he invests in his slide shows and work one step further – to 8mm film. He has starred in and helped create a series of short subjects for use in his speaking engagements.

The Life and Climbs of Henry Barber

One of the talented, fun-loving crew that boldly attempted Mount Johnson in Alaska in 1979 was a Swiss photographer and filmmaker named Ruedi Homberger, whom Chouinard had met in Europe. Ruedi turned out to be "one of the craziest people I know" for Henry, and they got along famously. The pair had climbed together in the Dolomites of Italy and in Switzerland before Henry and Ric Hatch visited Dresden with Fritz Wiessner in 1976. Ruedi came to the States the next summer for a transcontinental climbing tour with Henry. In the course of it, they made a short film of Henry soloing a steep 5.9 wall called Directissima at the Gunks, one of the principal reasons for Ruedi's visit.

The film was shot in one full day. The three-pitch climb ascends a slightly overhanging white quartzite wall, which Henry slid up smoothly, with complete confidence, arrogantly hanging off one hand to chalk up on the crux, and continuing with the elegance, precision, and deliberate movement that characterizes his style. Since Ruedi was the only cameraman, Henry had to hang in place for up to ten minutes at a time while Homberger scrambled down to the ground or up to the top to produce lyrical distance shots from positions on adjacent climbs. The idea for the film had germinated in the fall of 1975 during one of Henry's ascents of the route, well before his involvement in *Sea-Cliff Climbing*. It had grown in importance ever since, and had become almost an obsession — a summary of his climbing, perhaps. The film is unpretentious and yet bold, and has been given the pure, direct name of the climb itself.

As yet, *Directissima* is unfinished. It is a personal commitment to complete expression, since the idea, performance, and editing are all the work of a climber venturing cautiously into filmmaking for the first time. While the usual cut ratio in a film of this sort is about ten minutes of rough footage to one of final product, because of cost and logistics *Directissima* is being reduced from twelve minutes rough to an eight-minute film. In four years, about half the work has been done, a little at a time. Most recently, the creative energies of film editor Fred Padula, responsible for editing the brilliant *El Capitan* film shot by Glen Denny ten years ago but only released in 1980, have been enlisted during Henry's frequent business trips to the west coast. Unlike the other collaborative efforts with Homberger, which do not have soundtracks and are narrated by Henry, a solo piano score has been added as the project has slowly evolved.

A return trip to Alaska's Mount Johnson in 1978 provided the opportunity for Ruedi to convey the essence of extreme alpinism on film. The wolf's jaw rigorousness of the Ruth Gorge peaks, the creamy expanse of untrodden glaciers, the desperate rock climbing in fog and darkness and falling ice, the grotesque torture of bivouacs on broken ledges, the frustration of another failure — all combine to fashion a searing vision of expedition climbing. The film is rarely shown, however, since there is little demand for it on Henry's lecture circuit, and because a several-hundred-dollar lecture fee is required to compensate for the wear on his single copy.

Back in Eastern Europe in 1979, Ruedi made a pair of films of Henry climbing with the local hard men. It was Henry's second visit to the austere world of Dresden climbing, and he approached it in a far different manner. The intensity and intimidation of the scene had far less emotional impact than on the first visit three years earlier, and Henry brought with him a refined, matured notion of the politics of exporting American style and ethics to the rest of the world. Personal perspectives on style were not simply imposed by an outsider, as in Britain and Australia. Instead, Henry relinquished his chalk bag (which he had used on his hardest climbs in 1976 and had introduced to Dresden) and climbed largely without shoes, absorbing himself in the local traditions of the sport. He had become more a student of their mastery, less a missionary of American ethics. By this time, chalk use in Dresden had been outlawed by the Federation anyway, and the once-innovative practice of leading past several rings on a lead had been adopted by the best local climbers.

Henry stayed at Bernd Arnold's house several nights and became much closer to Bernd and Herbert Richter. By this time, Barber wanted to make a film of climbing in Eastern Europe, and so he supported Ruedi's trip to Dresden and Czechoslovakia. Separate films of each area resulted. In *Elb-*

161

sandstein Ruedi filmed East Germans climbing on difficult routes, with early Master Fritz Wiessner leading Henry gracefully up a steep sandstone tower, largely unprotected, in a climbing team that represented well over fifty years of the Dresden tradition. The filming across the border in Czechoslovakia features Milo Schmidt, Barber, and superb stylists unknown to the west who are currently putting up routes considered to be superior to Dresden standards. The pair had planned to join the annual speed climbing championships in Russia and film them, but Henry was unable to obtain a visa at the last moment, and had been advised as an AAC board member not to participate in those competitive events long opposed by that group's leadership. Ruedi continued on alone and managed to shoot the event.

Every time he leaves Karin and Herbert and Bernd, Henry is deeply depressed by the thought that he may never see them again. At the end of the last visit, he stayed on in Dresden a few extra days to go solo climbing with Bernd, who had very much wanted to do that with him; he then spent the weekend in Czechoslovakia climbing with Herbert. After the filming there, Henry, Ruedi, and another climber drove to the West German border. They were stopped by Czech officials, since they did not have the proper stamps from a hotel for each night of their stay to prove they had spent the necessary amount of money. The border guards eventually accepted their explanation that they were on a climbing exchange, but still insisted they return to the police in the town where they had stayed (and Henry had lectured) the previous night.

The trio was reluctant to do so, since it would have meant at least a three-hour round trip, and as the argument proceeded, the guards rummaged through all of their playthings in the car. When they found a bright skateboard, they were puzzled and wary, and the situation looked glum. However, their climbing companion casually took it and began to do tricks for the guards on the pavement in front of the crossing station. He would go up a slight hill and then speed down toward them, executing wild high-performance maneuvers right at their feet. Ruedi played with the board too, since he routinely skates downhill the dozen or more kilometers from his home in Arosa, Switzerland to the adjoining town. The Czech guards were very curious about this behavior and the eccentric trio, and watched carefully as the climber hiked back up the incline a second time, sped down toward them, and suddenly veered off across the border into West Germany and safety!

As yet, it is too early in the U.S. for fictional films on climbing subjects, Henry feels, and so he remains committed to the notion of creating quality documentaries. The American audience does not understand who climbers are and why they immerse themselves in alpinism. The European and British publics have long been exposed to the life of the mountain guide, rescues, and major climbs, and consequently continental filmmakers are producing dramatic material in this area. Reenactments of historical ascents draw upon published accounts of significant climbs, and fictional works are being produced in France and Britain from short stories by mountain writers. The American mountain aesthetic is still contemplative, personal, and present-oriented; it has yet to move into the realm of invention and history.

And so Henry occasionally returns to work on *Directissima*, thinking about the soundtrack, editing footage, and slowly evolving a filmic equivalent of his dream of a perfect solo experience. He talks about the film often, about the details of how best to present to others his own way of movement and to record the grace and style for posterity. Like soloing, climbing for the camera illustrates the paradox of the inner game — the tension between personal realization and public expression, and how each nurtures the other. Barber's sensitivity to the history of major climbing achievements and to the personalities of top-ranked climbers helps contribute to the gradual shaping of a visual representation of his personal efforts at unifying self and the route, mind and body.

In a way, Barber has always been producer and director of the story of his deeds. He has always thought of himself as being in a movie, standing back to watch himself climb. Through magazines, lectures, slide shows, and the force of his personality, Henry has creatively shaped the way the world thinks about what he does and who he is. He has chosen the images to be published, fashioned the kinetic sculpture of his movement on the screen, created illusions of flawlessness. He has shared this with others, and in the process has become his own historian.

7

Beauty and Death

S OLOING IS AN OPIATE: addicting and dangerously
beautiful. It contains both the essence of intimacy, of
private movement, and the promise of a dazzling performance. The paradox — for self, or for others — is bold and
strongly drawn.

Sometimes the mind races away. Sometimes the body
moves so gracefully that the mind is pulled along in its wake,
and succumbs to the euphoria of the moment. When free
soloing, without a rope or protection of any kind, the stakes
are ultimate, and the consequences of success or failure are
exhilarating and very real.

For the "American Sportsman" sea-cliff climbing film, the
same one for which Barber soloed Strand, he also soloed A
Dream of White Horses. He had climbed it on-camera already
with Al Harris. When Scott Ransom, the director, asked him to
repeat it free-solo for the film, Henry readily agreed. It was a
perfect climb.

> Euphoria is something that is realized only when you
> suddenly comprehend that you are not in control of your
> mental faculties. You are operating in a wholly physical
> mode and your mind is left behind. Only a reflex action
> will bring it back. On A Dream of White Horses, the
> euphoria was not recognized until high up on the route.

The climb began auspiciously. Down by the water at the
base, there was a sense of peace and solitude that put Henry in
the right mood. The cameras were hundreds of meters away.
He covered the first hundred meters of the climb in a matter

of minutes — smooth and easy climbing all the way up to a complex system of corners and grooves near the top.

The last section is difficult because of the tendency to be thrown out of rhythm by the deviousness of the climbing, even though the technical difficulty never exceeds a moderate 5.7.

There are a lot of intricate moves, upclimbing a corner and then downclimbing a slab, making it hard to get a good rhythm, but it comes out very well in the film because of the perfect mood I was in.

My mental balance was great. I had overcome the obtrusiveness of cameras, the uncertainty of loose rock, and the fact that I wasn't soloing this route on sight, which made me uneasy. In accepting and then ignoring all of these things, I developed a balance and euphoria.

Toward the end of the climb, John Cleare came rappelling down with his camera, swinging from a rope anchored at the top. I was totally ignoring him, having no problems whatsoever, until I came around into a groove, and he moved his rope over about a meter to get a clear shot. It caught me the wrong way. I could feel that somebody was there, that somebody was filming me, and it was crucial to that moment. My inner and outer balance were thrown off when I started paying attention to the foreign presence of Cleare.

I went up into the groove, and was doing some stemming moves, pushing with both hands against the sides of the groove. I pushed just a little too hard and my left shoulder bumped the wall, so that I started to fall. Adrenaline shot from my toes right up to my head. My mind came back instantly. In the movie, you can't actually tell that I flinched at all. You can see my shoulder hit the wall, but you can't see me push with my fingers to keep myself in the groove, or sense that I had started to fall, that I was off and headed down. But the balance and flow of all the movement that had gone on until that point carried me through, keeping me on the rock and still moving. The shock was absorbed so well that the near-fatal mistake can't be seen on film.

The style of climbing in Dresden, as Henry found some years later, was so immaculately clean and simple that the only possible advance beyond it was free soloing. Fifteen or twenty years ago, soloing without a rope and self-belaying system was virtually unheard of in the United States. It was an era that emphasized a dogmatic, equipment-oriented approach to safety. Guidebooks equated solo climbing, if they acknowledged it at all, with suicide. The purism of Dresden, had it been widely known to outsiders, might have been severely criticized as recklessness.

But in the 1970's, climbers in America began to push the possibilities of ropeless soloing. Many of the more severe roped climbs that appeared each season involved the possibility of dangerous falls, where a soloing perspective is necessary in order even to explore the route. Precise psychological control was fast becoming mandatory for many of these routes as the inner game of hard climbing matured. Soloing became another kind of challenge — competition and self-definition. And no American climber had more to do with the development of soloing difficult rock climbs than Henry Barber.

Even in his first years, when he was quietly doing a lot of solo climbs at the Shawangunks, Henry was aware of the deeds of people in the west like Steve Wunsch and Jim Erickson, who operated at the upper limits of both roped and solo climbing. Erickson especially had demonstrated his innovative stamp by making the first free ascents of several 5.9 and 5.10 climbs solo. The year before Henry's second visit to Yosemite, Erickson soloed the first free ascent of the awesome Sooberb, an aid climb near Boulder put in in 1965 and dominated by a prominent roof. His strict and highly evolved sense of ethics and his stunning performances had a marked influence on the younger Henry, and still guide Barber in his thinking about ethical issues. Years later, Henry and Jim soloed 5.9 climbs together around Boulder, something Henry found "incredibly satisfying." They joyously mocked standard leader-belayer parlance by excitedly yelling to each other while soloing: "Watch my ass! Catch me! Don't let go!"

Henry's second visit to Yosemite in the spring of 1973 was marked by brilliant and fast climbing on established classics

Sentinel Rock in Yosemite. The line of Barber's 2-1/2 hour solo ascent follows the sunlight and shadow/Henry Barber Collection

and desperate new lines, as well as first ascents of his own routes. He was acting like a Valley regular now, shorn of innocence and awe. He put up the hardest thin crack climb yet done in the Valley with Butterballs, and climbed the Nose on El Capitan in record time. But his solo of the Steck-Salathé route on Sentinel Rock was the deed that aroused the greatest response and assured him prominence.

The 550-meter route, regarded by many as one imbued with a sense of evil, has been the scene of numerous accidents. Henry had lost his close friend Roger Parks on the route the year before, when Parks had taken a fatal fall on the next-to-last pitch.

In the third week of his stay in the Valley, Henry decided to attempt the first free solo of the route. Sentinel lords it over the Valley from on high, like some mausoleum of the gods in an early American landscape painting. It is impossible to ignore. Henry had been contemplating the idea for days. His confidence in the venture increased through talks with Steve Wunsch, who felt that the solo was feasible. Wunsch even said that he would come looking for Henry if he did not return in normal time. The basis for the soloing idea, Henry ardently insists, "lay in the fact that I couldn't find anyone else who wanted to do the climb."

The Steck-Salathé fit the bill as a good climb to solo. Barber had not done the climb and so had no preconceptions about what was involved. It was during this period that he was exploring the notion that on-sight soloing was safer than soloing a route one had previously done. If one did not know just how difficult a route was, there would be little chance, he felt, that the mind could overstep the body's limitations. One would not be apt to lapse into false confidence. The capacity to solo difficult routes is entirely dependent on confidence in one's ability to downclimb out of even the most outrageous situations. Thus, it was partially technical skill and partly a question of having "the right stuff" to survive, through self-control. "Even at the top of the Steck-Salathé," Henry maintains, "I could have reversed every move to get back to the ground."

Another point which made the climb appear safe to Henry was that the climbing was varied: from large cracks to small finger cracks, to the crux of the route, a section of thin face climbing. If the climb had involved just one or two techniques, such as friction climbing, he felt, there would have been more room for error. The repetition and subsequent monotony would not have evoked the extreme concentration required.

A further key to the climb, Henry believed, was the knowledge that he was not soloing the route for anyone except himself. Whenever pressure from other people intrudes, the soloing mood dissipates. Despite the considerable impact the climb had on the mountaineering world once it became known — launching a strong local and regional performer to international prominence, Barber steadfastly maintains that no calculation of such an effect entered into his planning. Despite his fastidious list-making and propensity for collecting, he appears to have been relatively spontaneous in his major ascents, at least until he recognized the potential for travel and celebrity after his trips to Britain and Australia.

He started the route in the early morning, after a restless night's sleep, and felt at first that he was moving slowly on the lower pitches. Actually, the pace had accelerated beyond that achieved by any roped pair. Early in the climb he was plagued with second thoughts about the difficult face climbing high on the route.

There are places around the Wilson Overhang, on the fourth pitch, where you would definitely have to do some tricky reversing, lots of jamming in off-width cracks that are hard and weird. This is a negative way to climb — thinking about reversing all the time — but it's also a source of positive reinforcement. It almost lulls you into a false sense of security. The whole time I was on the climb, I knew that I could downclimb everything, though there would have been a few moves that would have been damn hard.

During the fifth pitch, a desperate squeeze chimney, I began to think that I probably wasn't going to be able to do the climbing up higher. For the next six pitches, it kept recurring that if the climbing down below wasn't as hard as the crux, I didn't stand a chance up higher. I did know, though, that I could reverse the whole thing.

The climbing went smoothly until he reached a section called the Flying Buttress, where he was unsure whether to move right or left. More than one party had chosen the wrong direction.

He opted for the left, and was soon relieved to see the slab section mentioned in the guidebook. This part, Henry later decided, had the hardest climbing on the route.

The climbing started to get varied, and that put me in a really good mood for the crux up higher. I was in a nice rhythm, doing all these different techniques, and all of a sudden, I had to make an incredibly desperate face-climbing move to get established on this slab. I was thinking that this was the 5.7 move I'd been told about. If this was as delicate as it seemed, then I knew that there was no way that I was going to be able to do the 5.9 up higher. Jim Erickson had fallen off that section a couple of years earlier. I was having more than just a few doubts. And of course, the more I started worrying, the harder all the moves became, and the more I was psyching myself out.

After awhile, I was really gripped. But up just a little higher, there was some beautiful 5.7 climbing that really got my mood back. At the hard moves — they were obvious — I didn't really think much about it. I sat down on a big hold, looked at my book and ate a candy bar, and got myself sorted out for about five minutes, maybe more. I figured out a complicated entry move which put me in a better position to look ahead and allowed me to learn how to reverse the difficulties there, and went right across. It was a piece of cake.

A section called the Narrows followed, a large chimney system in which one disappears far into the back of a gigantic crack. The climbing was secure, Henry declares, but once he slipped a meter or so and found himself in a horizontal position, held only by an armlock in the narrowest portion of the crack.

I was absolutely stuck. I couldn't move up or down. I was there for about fifteen minutes, hanging half upside down, trying to figure out what to do. Eventually, I wiggled out of the hole, but the climbing above was so tight that I was sure that it was going to happen again. I just knew that I was in the wrong place at the wrong time. I was thinking about when other people had done the route, about a climbing friend of mine, Beverly Johnson, and how she could never have gotten her ample bust through these places.

Once through the Narrows, Henry moved quickly as the difficulty began to ease. He was on top only two and a half hours after starting the climb. It was still early in the day. Smooth, rounded boulders competed with a few twisted trees for space at the crest of the peak.

I stayed by the edge and just looked down at where Roger had fallen. There was a kind of morbid fascination — me doing the route and him being killed there, but that certainly wasn't the main reason for doing the climb. While I was sitting there, I was flashing back on some times that I'd had with him. I felt like a kid who's walking through the park and has some dirty old man come up to him and expose himself. The little kid just doesn't know what to do or say. There was this fascination in looking down at the place where Roger had fallen, but I couldn't pinpoint what it was.

After thinking about Roger, I had absolutely zero feelings. I sat down and looked around, just because that's what you're supposed to do. I got up and walked away from it and didn't think anything more about it.

The descent was miserable. Henry found himself slipping constantly in his smooth-soled climbing shoes. He recalls his thoughts being "fuzzy," that he "couldn't believe" what he'd done. He began reflecting on the climb and what it had meant to him, coming more and more to the conclusion that the climb had left him partially uneasy.

It seemed, in a way, bad to me to have done the route that quickly. That's not why I climb. I started getting more feelings of having cheated myself or a good friend out of a partnership on the route. That I'd in some way cheated myself of the mountaineering experience by doing the climb in the style that I had. There was no exhilaration in the completion of the climb, no thrill in having knocked off something that no one had ever done before. It never occurred to me that the climb had meant a huge step forward. I was thinking about Royal Robbins and Tom Frost's ascent in four and a half hours. That's teamwork and harmony. It's what the whole thing's about.

Robbins himself, however, was impressed by Henry's ascent. In *Mountain,* he described the solo of the Steck-Salathé as "an act of vision."

Henry told only a few people about the solo. It did not occur to him to flaunt his success, but in the tight-knit group of climbers in Camp 4, word was out before he even arrived back at his tent. He had run into two acquaintances at the post office when he picked up his mail at eleven that morning. Yes, he replied, he had indeed done that particular route on Sentinel. Back at camp, Henry and Steve Wunsch talked over the details of the climb so that the latter could verify the completion of the route.

Only days later did Henry feel a sense of accomplishment.

It wasn't that I felt that I'd achieved something great. The only thing that I had done was once again successfully complete a struggle to get mind and body in harmony with the object at hand, which in this case happened to be a very long route.

The Steck-Salthé was the first of four major solo climbs Henry performed in as many years, along with several score minor ones. It was followed, successively, by the Strand, a route on a Welsh sea-cliff; an ascent of a 1,300-meter ice route on Korea Peak in the Soviet Pamirs; and a long 5.10 route called Hollywood and Vine on Devil's Tower in eastern Wyoming. The boldness of these solos was intensified by the fact that each one was done on-sight, with little or no previous knowledge of their quirks and difficulties.

Paradoxically, Barber has always thought that on-sight soloing is safer for him.

I first started soloing at the Shawangunks in the rain. I was worried about the wasps, and because it was wet and slippery, I had to be very cautious. I couldn't take anything for granted. It made me start to realize that if you have no preconceptions about the route, you have little chance of getting heady. I'll usually solo a route that I've done before only if it seemed difficult when I did it with a rope. This way, I virtually never go up on a route saying to myself how easy it's going to be because with protection right at my waist, it was easy last time. It's a matter of having your guard up.

The Strand was an altogether different experience from the Steck-Salathé, and not one to be repeated. Since he had been asked to do the route for a network TV show, it was a job, a performance for a fee as well as prestige. The presence of cameras and the pressure of climbing for an audience combined to destroy the deeply harmonious mood normally required for a serious solo. Henry reflects that

it wasn't at all a safe thing for me to do. But it was an ultimate challenge just because of the outside forces. The only thing that could have been worse was if the millions of viewers had been right there at the base. I wouldn't have been able to make it if I hadn't had all the soloing experience I've accrued over the years. I had to draw on my idealism to get rid of the extraneous factors and get down to the job at hand.

As such, the Strand crisply portrayed the central paradox of his hard soloing: the pursuit of inner knowledge versus the quest for public appreciation. The two overlap in a cloud of gray.

The exploratory intimacy of hard soloing breeds privacy. The number and quality of climbs soloed which the public does not know about far outweighs those with which they are familiar. Especially in the deserts of the southwest — around Lake Powell, in northwest Colorado on the Green and Yampa

175

rivers, on small crags and two- or three-hundred-meter soft sandstone cliffs — Henry has played and investigated. The events are not shared with others, like Henry's early confidences for Ric Hatch alone.

For Barber, the notion of very hard free soloing is closely tied to his concept of the essence of climbing — that it requires fine-tuning of mind and physical prowess, as well as penetratingly deep personal understanding of the inner game of control. Highly committing and intimidating leads far above protection are the definition of true climbing skill for Henry, exemplified in the purity and seriousness of the mature, evolved climbing in Dresden. Scary, unprotected 5.10 and 5.11 leading is what excites him, since

> that involves real climbing to me, not weird gymnastics. You have to rely on your mind a lot more, not on equipment, to prevent fear and maintain control.

Soloing is the ultimate extension of this belief, a direct encounter with the vagaries of *control.*

Naturally, the failure rate on solos is very high — Henry guesses it's 60 percent for him. Everything must be perfect. A wasp, a crowd, thoughts of a friend — anything can disrupt the clarity.

The land's end of the southwestern peninsula of England is a bleak sweep of moor roughened with granite. Bosigran Face looks sternly out to the North Atlantic, and is the scene of the finest climbing in the region. Two intricate lines laced through overhangs, Suicide Wall and Bow Wall, are among the very first discovered on the cliff, yet they remain preeminent among dozens of equally challenging ones since their discovery in the mid-1950's.

Bow Wall's crux was put in by Joe Brown, so it was natural for Henry to be attracted to it on an early one of his nine trips to Britain. On a typically misty, gray day, Barber straightforwardly soloed up two short pitches to the crux overhang. Once established there, it was necessary to step up onto a precarious hold, tug on an insecure fist-jam in a groove, and throw oneself over the lip and onto a thin slab. Henry studied the moves, absorbed the sea reaching into the cove far below, tested the jam. It felt questionable. The ground well displayed between his feet was composed of rubble and blocks. A collection of climbers, until then intent on other lines, gathered and gawked. The fog twisted around itself in a knot of indecision and hung in the cove.

As the crowd grew and gazed, Henry felt that they "put undue pressure on me." He would have come down much sooner from the crux, but the presence below forced him to weigh the moves more seriously and longer, such that he could never feel secure about making them. He would be assessing and doing them for ulterior motives. Finally he came down, to the obvious relief of the crowd. They figured he must be a regular flesh-and-blood human after all.

Henry feels that he does not subconsciously accept the idea of death. Yet, at the same time, "death is the unknown," and it is intriguing. Early in his career, he soloed the notorious MF, rated 5.9, at the Shawangunks. Moments later, a hiker, inspired by the climbers all around him, climbed alone and without protection on the rocks near the Gill Boulder he fell, hitting his head. Attracted by the faller's scream Henry ran up behind the boulder and found him, a pool of blood radiating from his battered head. In a vain effort to keep him alive, Henry dug the man's tongue out of his mangled mouth to clear an airspace — and then helplessly watched as the man died in his arms. It was "very sobering, something to think about," he says but the implications were never really pursued.

Not long afterward, following a solo of Birdie Party several weeks before, Henry returned to the route to climb it with Ric Hatch. While near the crux, Barber wandered off-route because he was too confident and so, careless; he took a ten-meter leader fall. The two boys laughed uproariously, but later, a realization struck: *I had just soloed it, alone, without a rope.*

Henry is willing to confront the possibility of self-destructive impulses in himself.

I suppose I have suicidal tendencies, but everyone does. How many times have you been driving along the road and said to yourself, "What would it be like if I steered

Brush Off at Helsby near Liverpool, England/Ian Campbell

into the trees over there?" You're wondering about dying, what it would be like to be somewhere else. I've thought about taking my life thousands of times. In climbing, it's so easy because you're in such a vulnerable position. This isn't to say, though, that I've put the mental processes of taking my life into motion. It's just an interest, and I think that everyone has these thoughts, whether they realize it or not.

That struggle is there every time I solo something.

Once I get that balance, which I do in every solo that I finish, then the thought of *what would happen if I let go here?* is only an academic question, because my body is already into the next move, along with the momentum that's in my mind. Letting go is not even a possibility if I've made the decision to be up there in the first place.

I'm not afraid of dying. I think about it a lot, and the only thing that I ever come up with is suffering. If I were to be afraid of dying, it would be difficult to achieve the things that I do. I *do* worry about suffering, so I worry about falling. Every time I solo, I have to overcome thoughts like these: that there must be better ways to spend my time and my life, things that must be more rewarding than soloing difficult climbs. Often I think that I would feel better about what I was doing here if I'd thought about my girlfriend more, or, I would feel better about what I was doing here if I'd taught at the Telluride Mountaineering School for the summer instead of climbing on my own. Once I can't get rid of thoughts like these, it's time to go down.

Henry describes the fear of falling and suffering as sometimes overwhelming.

I would hate to fall a long way and not be killed. I wouldn't mind breaking a leg, something minor like that, which is the reason that I push myself so hard at a gritstone crag where the landing is good — very little chance that you're going to get killed.

An added element of danger in recent years comes from the frequent shoulder dislocations to which Henry is prone. His right shoulder has gone out five times, his left, six. At least three times, the dislocations have occurred in situations that are decidedly awkward — leading the imposing 5.10 Diving Board in Colorado, while ice climbing in a remote valley of the Sierra Nevada, and while bouldering seven meters off the ground. The problem, however, hasn't curtailed Henry's soloing at all.

Ironically, one thing that scares him badly is to watch other people solo.

> I don't know them as well as myself. I can't tell how good their mental strategy is for dealing with the situation. I look at my friends soloing, and I see life — all of the vivaciousness that goes into their way of living — and I see the struggle that goes on in me every time that I solo. They should not have to go through that sort of thing, when they could be doing something else.

Henry's worst solo experience came on a 5.9 climb in Colorado called Gorilla's Delight. He had mistakenly thought that the climbing would be on large holds, but the crux was slippery friction far off the ground. It was 1973, and he did not have the fund of experience that eventually developed through exposure to a vast assortment of rock types and moves. He found himself committed to the insecure moves without having amply considered them.

> I was absolutely terrified, just barely making it. I was way out of control, and once you're scared, the whole game starts to become very dangerous.

Fear approaching panic, as on Gorilla's Delight, has thankfully only happened to Henry a few times.

> In those situations there are quick subliminal flashes that are trying to grip you up, make you hold on tighter with your hands, things that make you all the more scared if you're scared already.
>
> I went back to Gorilla's Delight one time and went to pieces. I was with an old girlfriend, and I was having a very good time with her. I had just dislocated my shoulder on a climb called Kloberdanz, and we were watching Ric Hatch and Ajax Greene climbing Gorilla's Delight. Tears just came to my eyes. I couldn't handle it. The value of my existence never hits me while I am actually soloing. It's always afterward.

Intimate relationships have changed his views about climbing, and about soloing in particular. Throughout his career and life, women have always been an outlet for Henry's deepest emotions, especially about close calls on solos and failures, since their "level of awareness is so high, and there were few male friends I could confide in." As reservoirs of trust and faith and the world outside of competitive climbing, women have always been critical factors in Henry's ability to keep up the pace and climb hard; they have also been the source of essential emotional support for recovery.

This was starkly manifested all at once when he was up on the northwest ridge of Capitol Peak in Colorado. Henry had gone to the Elk Range to be alone with his girlfriend, but now, while she waited in the meadow below, he was soloing.

> On about the third pitch I got into some rotten rock. I was thinking that it would be exciting to be down in those meadows, spending the day just with her. Well, the climb was only going to take me an hour-and-a-half anyway, so I had plenty of time. But it seemed such a waste to be up here screwing around on this loose rock that was soaking wet when there was something much more rewarding down below.

Sometimes in the middle of a solo, the face of a lover or friend flashes through his mind. The effect is disruptive.

> But the movement of my body is powerful enough so that I'm carried past the kind of crisis that may dictate going down. The mind has to recognize when an inhibiting thought comes through and deal with it rationally. The mind has to be able to say 'look, body, we're not quite as attuned as we should be here; otherwise, that face would not have flashed.' The body, at this point, is likely to be saying, 'screw you, mind. This movement is so good that we're just going to keep stroking it out here.' While this little confrontation is going on, the mind has to have the capability of bringing back that initial thought and giving it a chance either to develop into something that should

be dealt with and sorted out before continuing, or to be recognized and discarded instantly because its only purpose is to inhibit the movement that is going on.

Climbing, especially soloing, brings Henry closest to a sense of himself and to his personal, nonclimbing relationships.

After a solo climb, I feel so much more attuned to the people I'm involved with. My senses are much more keen and aware, and I appreciate very little things. It's not because I've courted death, but rather because I've already opened myself up completely to my own feelings while climbing. This type of energy is transferred into everything that goes on after I've finished the climb.

It all runs in a circle. Henry solos to be attuned more fully to the relationships going on around him, to become centered. At the same time, however, he feels that in order to be safe, he must rid himself of all ties while on a given climb. The two directions appear mutually exclusive, but in soloing, self-preservation wins.

The chance to do a new long ice route on Korea Peak came in the middle of an international expedition sponsored by the U.S.S.R. in 1976. When Henry managed to climb the ice face, he had very little familiarity with alpine climbing; his forte for years had been pure rock work. He had never done even 300 meters of ice, let alone four times that. Nevertheless, he took it in stride. Today, his strongest memory of the ascent is of the flowers on the way down.

What made the meadow flowers particularly beautiful was that the climb had produced so many vibrations in me I was able to feel everything more deeply.

Henry maintains that he does not solo to get away from other people. He does, however, have a strong instinct to be alone, where the decisions he makes will affect no one else. Soloing fulfills this urge, which he traces back to childhood. In elementary school he was a loner who felt "in the dark," afraid

Soloing Double Column Central in the Organ Pipes, Mount Wellington, Tasmania/Peter Jackson

to ask questions in the classroom "because I was worried that my personal feelings might be squelched by kids tittering over what I asked."

The drive to solo stems for Henry from a need to be different from others.

> I'm not trying to impress anybody. What I'm trying to do is turn a nonadventurous thing into an adventurous one. Soloing can't be goal-oriented. I do it to get the maximum sense of movement, the best harmony between mind, body, and object — the rock.

In his view, soloing requires standing above competitiveness.

> As long as I can do things that are unique, I'll be happy. There's no threat from anybody else because inwardly, and maybe egotistically, I think I'm better. Competitiveness will get you hurt. To be driven to push yourself beyond normal limits by soloing is incredibly dangerous.
>
> I identify with Icarus. I'm never conscious of pushing a limit. I'm always expanding my vision. I never think about Icarus's fate, however, or for that matter about anyone else's fate. There's a mechanism in me that allows me to save myself.

The great Italian alpinist Walter Bonatti stopped climbing abruptly after his finest achievement: a new solo route on the north face of the Matterhorn in winter. He gave as his reason the certainty that sooner or later his luck was destined to give out. Henry rejects this depleted-luck theory of soloing. To him the key is not luck but control, which arrives as a by product of a certain physical rhythm.

> It begins with flashes in my mind of where my body is. It may be ten meters, stop, ten meters, stop. It might be thirty meters or just two moves. As the rhythm develops, it carries me out of the doubts that might make me stop and say, "What am I doing here? This is crazy."

The rhythm lulls the soloist into a meditative, trance-like state. Henry likens it to nitrogen narcosis, the rapture of the deep experienced by divers. It feels euphoric and threatens to carry the mind beyond rationality.

At this point it's critical to have some distance on the situation, so that you can stop and say, "I should not be doing this. I've got to get a grip on myself and work out this situation." And your mind has to be able to recall instantly any climbing situation you've been through before. If a certain bridging move comes up, your mind has to recognize as familiar the particular feel of that move. Soloing is safer for someone like me who has climbed all over the place than for someone who has spent time at just a few areas. The larger repertoire of moves, with more experience, provides confidence.

Henry continues to solo, more now than ever. He constantly searches for those theoretical climbs he terms "ultimate:" perfect solo ascents of 5.10 difficulty or better. One, of course, will be a *ne plus ultra*. Certain stipulations are placed on this climb: it must be an on-sight first ascent using no shoes or chalk. The climb should encompass three feelings — adventure, beauty, and harmony — in oneself. For Henry,

the adventure is that it hasn't been done before. The beauty of it is that it is untouched and you are solo. Being alone automatically makes me more perceptive. It is a time without distractions, when you can only look deeply inside yourself. The harmony occurs when you have to break through the beauty and adventure to gain the balance of mind and body needed to solo difficult routes.

He has done numerous climbs that approach the conditions for an ultimate climb, but something is always present to make them fall short. "I haven't done my ultimate climb yet," he says. "But I have come damn close." This climb will never appear in any sort of media. It will be a climb that has nothing to do with anyone else.

8

Mountains Like Brave Fellows

*I*N THE BEGINNING, THERE WAS 1976. That was the
year that a casual itinerant and avid climber became an
international-class mountaineer and young businessman, and
learned the ways of the world, of where he might go. It was a
year of maps and plans and movement.

Henry Barber spent January at home in Sherborn, Massachusetts climbing constantly before leaving for a national
sporting goods convention in Chicago, after which Yvon
Chouinard joined him in the northeast for a series of ice
climbing seminars and ascents which lasted for a fortnight or
so. Henry and Ric Hatch then drove down to North Carolina
to climb and lecture. The spring saw four separate trips to
Europe. In March Henry joined Chouinard, John Cunningham, and a host of luminaries in the world of British climbing
in an effort to make a TV film for the National Geographic
Society, an attempt that was abandoned following bad weather
and equally poor management while on location on Ben Nevis
in Scotland. After three weeks at home, Barber, Hatch, and
Steve Wunsch went off to Dresden with Fritz Wiessner, climbing en route in the south of France, Switzerland, Italy, and
Czechoslovakia. Henry returned home for nine days, went to
England for ten days to star in the "American Sportsman" film
on sea-cliff climbing, came home for four days, and then flew
to Russia for six weeks as the leader of a team of American
climbers on an exchange. He was then home for nine days,
went out west for a month, and came back to work for eight or
nine weeks. Afterward he flew to spend time with his friend,
Kim Blanch, visiting from Australia. A trip "into the deepest,
darkest wilds of Mexico" followed. Barber arrived home two

days before Christmas — that was 1976. "It was one of the best years of my life" he later said. It was full, every bit of it.

In 1974, the American Alpine Club (AAC) and the Mountaineering Federation of the U.S.S.R. instituted an exchange program in which one of the countries would host a team of visiting climbers from the other country each year. In the summer of 1975, six Soviets came to the U.S. From east to west, they climbed in the Shawangunks, the Tetons of Wyoming, the Pacific Northwest, and Yosemite. They thought their stay at the long cliff line of the Shawangunks futile, because in the Soviet Union, as in Dresden and other Communist countries, an ascent is successful only if one reaches the summit. There are no summits in the 'Gunks.

The following spring, the AAC chose six climbers, based on their "ability and compatibility," to represent the U.S. in a six-week exchange trip to Russia; they were George Lowe, Alex Bertulis, Craig Martinson, Mike Warburton, Chris Jones, and Henry Barber, as leader of the expedition.

The group left only a few days after Henry returned from filming for TV in Britain. Since he was out of the country, Bertulis, Warburton — who had done the Salathé wall on El Capitan with Sergei Bershov and Valentin Grekovich during the previous exchange — and Lowe did all of the planning and legwork. Some team members felt that perhaps one of them should have been designated leader as a result. Barber, still an AAC board member, had simply been appointed to choose five other people for the journey. Apparently there was one reason or another that the board did not want to select each of the other potential trip members as leader. Henry, on the other hand, while an old hand at complex logistics for personal ventures overseas (and recently returned from a trip to Communist East Germany), had some reservations of his own about his ability to handle the intricate diplomacy and group politics demanded by a venture of this sort. Also, he had no real alpine climbing experience so, as he remembers it,

> I sat everybody down in the hotel in Moscow and told them there really was no leader, that I'd make final decisions, representing the group, but with a lot of input from

Samarkand/Henry Barber Collection

everyone else. . . .Our arrival in Moscow then could have been a tense scene because one of the guys who was helping us get our visas, Christopher Wren, a *New York Times* correspondent, was accused of espionage three weeks before we left on the trip. We got the visas about two days before boarding the plane.

All of this was somewhat unnerving, especially since they had to talk through interpreters, who would often alter the content of conversation to suit a variety of personal and Russian needs. Luckily, Bertulis (who is of Lithuanian descent) and Lowe knew some Russian, so they could catch wind of the subtle games of interpretation that were always being played.

After the requisite tours to highlights like the Kremlin, the National Gallery, and Lenin's Tomb, the team flew south to Samarkand, the exotic Central Asian caravan route town famous for its Islamic architecture and culture, where they met their Soviet counterparts. Vladimir Shatayev and Slava Onischenko had both toured the U.S. during the exchange the previous summer. They now escorted the Americans to their first camp.

The Americans, according to Barber, were slightly awed during the initial meetings with the Soviets.

Slava and Vladimir — the leader of the Soviet team — had thighs as big as six watermelons and looked like they could hike uphill forever carrying granite boulders under each arm. Once we were shown a picture of the south face of Pik Communism, the highest peak in the U.S.S.R., that Slava had climbed. We all said that it looked like a real nice line until we noticed another photo of the whole gigantic peak. The entire face lies under a 200-meter hanging glacier, and every one of those suicide routes had to go through it. Then, of course, you would see a Russian climbing in boots that weigh almost eight kilograms, carrying a pack approaching forty-five kilos. You automatically get intimidated.

For their part, the Russians raised a few eyebrows and even inquired about the fact that Henry, one of the younger members, was the leader of the Americans. In their administrations of expeditions and bureaucracy, leader selection is done strictly on the basis of seniority and experience. They were reassured when told that Henry would do just fine.

The Americans soon left Samarkand for the Fansky Gory, a mountain range north of the well-known Pamirs in the much broader Alay group. Westerners had, of course, climbed on many occasions in Russia, beginning with the explorations and routes of the famed English alpinist Whymper and of the Duke of Abruzzi from Italy, among others, before the turn of the century. The British and Scottish had journeyed to the Pamirs in the early 1960's, and only two years prior to this visit, a team of Americans had joined a spectacular international climbing meet and successfully ascended many of the largest peaks in the country. It was, however, a summer of accidents and death; the group lost Gary Ullin to an avalanche. The theory of this trip was different, since it was conceived as a full exchange in which mixed Soviet-American teams would attempt to concentrate not on the heavily trodden giants but instead on smaller 5,500-meter (17,000-foot) peaks offering more demanding climbing and opportunities for first ascents.

Ten to twenty thousand Russian climbers go into the mountains for three weeks each summer to one of about twenty-five permanent mountaineering camps (owned by a sports federation of the state). They pay the equivalent of about forty dollars (the rest is subsidized), and receive room and board, the use of rental equipment, and instruction. Since it is nearly impossible for most climbers to purchase ropes and hardware because of their cost and unavailability, one must attend the camps in order to climb. Virtually all modern nylon materials and the proper alloy bar stock and machinery necessary to make hardware are controlled by the state as well, so there is a complete monopoly on climbing rules, instruction, and route choice. Some fifty to eighty climbers per camp live in rows of cabins or canvas tents, eat in common dining halls, and move up on schedule to advance base camps in alpine meadows high above to begin their orchestrated climbs.

Instructors volunteer their time and are usually successful, older doctors or other older professionals whose presence helps keep technique conservative and students unmotivated. The result is an estimated 80 percent dropout rate. The beginner must progress tenaciously through a set series of classes and graded climbs for many years before being allowed to test his mettle on a difficult climb, whereas in the west it is not unheard-of for someone with considerable talent to be leading routes near the top of the standards after only a year or two. Each summer, the progression up through the grades must be repeated before even the best climbers are free to contemplate routes equal to their abilities, and then only if all the proper documents are in order. As Chris Jones heard one student, frustrated at having made only two climbs in a twenty-day stay at a high hut, succinctly summarize the situation, "Many papers, few summits."

The first thing the weary Americans noticed upon finally arriving at camp was a brightly painted banner strung across the pathway that read: "Mountains like brave fellows. You are welcome in our camp." — written in English. Henry recalls, "We were all thinking, 'Jesus, we don't want to be brave. We just want to climb.' We all joked about getting back on the bus." Almost immediately, they embarked on a "training" hike with the Russian team, to work up through the grades. The mighty-thighed Soviets easily outdistanced their visitors, who were loathe to train and so were caught unawares.

Drastic differences in style surfaced on the peaks. Chris Jones and George Lowe joined with Misha Ovchenikov and doctor of sports medicine Slava Onischenko to attempt an unclimbed direct route on the north face of Pik Mirali (5,200 meters). Slava had the physique of a bodybuilder, and was very capable on technical ground. His strongly chiseled features and meticulous grooming belied a gentle soul, equally masked by his complete inability to utter English words. Ovchenikov, however, was neither as strong nor as skilled.

On what was probably some of the hardest ice climbing yet done in the Soviet Union, Ovchenikov struggled to cope with the steep ice and darkness. He grabbed the rope leading to Jones, belaying above on a tiny stance, and began hauling himself up hand-over-hand, much to his belayer's astonishment. Not only was this considered unsporting and poor technique by the Americans, but it was also very dangerous, for until he stopped and allowed the rope to be pulled up tight again, he simply increased the distance he would fall. Eventually he arrived at the stance, and as Jones was urging him to clip into the anchors, Onischenko slipped off and fell seven meters, tugging on the two climbers at the stance and Lowe leading above, out of sight. Jones later wrote in *Mariah* magazine that all this was madness:

> We were on 75 degree ice with someone who'd never been on such stuff. However, the angle eased off just ahead, and Ovchenikov appeared remarkably unconcerned.

191

Misha with typical Soviet equipment/Henry Barber Collection

Henry, in the midst of continual diplomatic and organizational chores as team leader, still got off climbing right away,
and was impressed with the Soviets' ability in alpine conditions
of mixed ice and rock. He immediately teamed up with noted
speed-climbing champion Sergei Bershov, a strikingly handsome star with the lean, hard appearance of a dedicated marathon runner. Henry eagerly sought the experience of climbing with Bershov, but spent the evening before departure in
animated debate with him over the style and equipment for
the climb. The Russian wanted to cart along a lot of gear, but

Sergei Bershov low down on the first route with Barber on Mount Rodaki. Whereas the four-thousand-foot ascent had many previous ascents in two or three days, this team managed it in 6 hours/Henry Barber Collection

the American refused to bivouac on the route, even though all previous ascents had required at least three days. When Sergei put a heavy salami the length of his arm into his pack, Henry stealthily removed it, cut it in half, and replaced it with the uncut end sticking out.

After a bivouac at the base of the climb,

> We soloed up a good ways, then put on a rope and climbed together for a long time. There were no communication hassles. I'd just say things like 'okay' most of the time when I wanted to give him some call like 'off belay' or 'climb.' If I couldn't find a belay, I'd just yell down *vimesti*, which means 'together' in Russian, and we'd climb together without belaying for another 200 meters.

The reason things went so well was that he was flawless, effortless. There was never any wasted motion, no hesitation or backing down. It was as instinctual as walking for him.

We topped out on this thing early in the afternoon. It was such a good climb that I decided to go to the summit with him, as it is very important in Russia for everyone in the party to reach the summit. Normally, I don't care, but this time I really wanted to go. When we got down from the climb, it was like coming to the sidelines after you'd made a crucial touchdown in the Superbowl. They couldn't believe that we'd actually pulled it off in only eight hours, and their reception showed a real feeling of camaraderie.

The second stop for the Americans was a camp in the Tien Shan ("Celestial Mountains" in Chinese), a range northeast of the Pamirs in greater Turkestan (now the soviet of Kirghizstan) featuring high, glaciated peaks rising to 5,800 meters, with solid rock and ice faces similar to the western Alps around Chamonix, France. The visitors were getting used to

Women returning from climb and being received in the Tien Shan/Henry Barber Collection

the Soviet system of mountaineering and so were not overly surprised to witness a scene resembling a Boy Scout jamboree, with tents stretching out in row upon row. Early the first morning, cheerful, energetic music poured through the camp from the public address system, and all of its Russian inhabitants reported for group calisthenics, while the Americans stood on the balcony of the main lodge to view the proceedings in amusement.

The climbers had begun fraternizing regularly with their counterparts and came to be much freer with each other. As in any collection of individualistic climbers, debates raged over equipment and tactics. Henry recalls bickering with Misha Ovchenikov, who spoke fluent English, over the list of pitons they would bring for one of the climbs. Misha would lay out thirty of his lightweight pins to take along. Henry would whittle these down to ten, then subtract seven and substitute hard chrome-molly Chouinard pitons of his own, instead of the malleable Russian titanium pins. They alternately went back and forth like this for some time, until an exasperated Henry blurted out, "Look, this is the way it's going to be!" and threw down his gear.

Ovchenikov countered, "But why? Mine are good!"

"Because we're going to take these chocks and pins of mine, and that's the way it's going to be!" Henry retorted.

"But these pitons are very fine," Misha protested.

Finally, Henry grabbed one of his pins, holding it aloft in a paroxysm of frustration and screaming, "You see this?" Then he began to beat the daylights out of it on the cement with his heavy alpine hammer. Nothing happened to it. He then grabbed one of Misha's pitons and started smashing it, until it rolled up into a little ball of titanium; he also broke one of the Russian's large-angle bongs right in half. He took one of his own bongs and beat it as hard as he could without effect, yelling, "You see this?" He scattered Russian pitons in every direction, but Misha managed to spirit them into the pack when the pair finally left for the climb.

Choosing appropriate objectives for the mixed parties was equally difficult. Henry had identified a potential new route on Corona Peak. Lowe and several others expressed interest in doing some ice routes across the way from Corona, but the Soviets were not quite up to them. They switched their plans and indicated that they wanted to do the same route as Henry, who thought it his rightfull option to have first crack at it.

They finally compromised and went up on it as a party of five to the base of the line, where they observed the situation first hand. Henry, seldom enthusiastic about alpine climbing in any situation, decided right then that because of the expected slow pace, large group, and concomitant danger of stonefall he would retreat and let the others continue in two pairs. The party spent three days on the climb, which was highlighted by Misha's serious ten-meter leader fall while wearing "this GI Joe plastic army helmet, the kind kids play in with the little rubber string that goes under your chin."

Barber came down and played two days' worth of cards with Shatayev's handsome wife, all the time looking up at Korea Peak, which had come out of the clouds in breaking weather. Earlier George Lowe had asked Henry about the possibility of soloing a prominent couloir on the face, but Henry had dismissed the notion by telling George the Soviets would never allow it. Vladimir Shatayev came down from a climb late on the second day. Henry told the Soviet leader that he was interested in a particular new route, and that he would meet him for a climb together the following day. Was it all right to do Korea Peak? Shatayev said fine. Then was it okay to do a new route on it? Sure. Solo? Well, okay, Shatayev answered, and then asked which route? Henry pointed casually to the same frightening central ice couloir, unbroken for a thousand meters.

Vladimir gazed at the glistening face, and then slowly asked, "Solo?" and frowned, no doubt remembering his Federation's total prohibition on soloing in any form. Then he asked, pointedly, "Do you do this sort of thing all the time?"

Henry replied, yes," slyly, he did it all the time. Actually, the Pik Rodaki climb earlier had been his first major alpine route, despite his trip to Alaska; he had never completed an alpine climb with a glacier approach and mixed climbing. Of himself, Barber says,

I always look for some uniqueness whenever I climb. I make things up in my head, something to keep the drive up. One time it was doing all six desperate routes on the McCarthy Wall in the Shawangunks in a day; another time it might be the first free ascent of a route by a visiting climber and in bad weather. Motivation is not a game — it's something you have to have, or you're not much of a person.

So Henry told Vladimir, yes, he did this all the time, referring to solo climbing, not alpinism. What the hell, he felt, his first major rock face had been the first solo of the 600-meter Steck-Salathé in Yosemite.

The couloir was the most spectacular line on the face, and Henry felt it must be comparable to the fabled routes on Les Courtes and Les Droites in Chamonix, which he had never visited. It was a bold venture, considering virtually no major alpine routes like it had been soloed on their first ascent, with only a few very notable exceptions.

Vladimir asked me how long this would take: two, three, four days? I was trying to speak Russian to say four. He finally got what I was saying and thought four days. I said, no, not four days, but four *hours*. He was pretty startled.

Henry went to bed that night after telling the others he would see them for lunch tomorrow, at which they scoffed. He only slept "for about five minutes because I was so gripped;" instead he actively invented numerous excuses to avoid departure as he readied himself at 2 A.M. He searched the camp on his way out for a light still glowing, so he could spend the rest of the night sanely drinking tea with some other insomniac, but no alibi presented itself to him.

While he believes alpine routes can be unbelievably difficult at times, Henry does not find alpine climbing on mixed terrain of ice and rock very hard, because the rules are so flexible: it is considered fair to pull up on slings, use occasional artificial aid, and cut steps in ice since the conditions are so

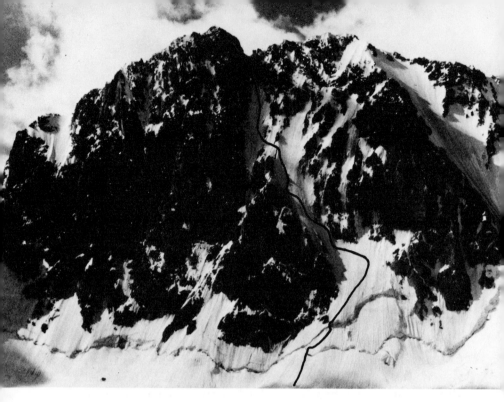

Korea Peak. The central couloir is the one taken by Barber on his nighttime ascent/Henry Barber Collection

atrocious. Anything goes, and the purer ethics and rules fiercely upheld at small crags at home are forgotten. Alpine routes change rapidly, since ice and snow freeze or melt or disappear. One can wait for optimal conditions, or do a climb in more challenging times to increase the level of technical difficulty and adventure. While it is possible to impose pure, personal style in alpine climbing, "that has never caught on," according to Barber. Alpinists do not follow ethically pure innovations as much as they aspire to difficulty, and instead of improving their ability or technique, Henry feels that they adjust their equipment or style as necessary to get up routes. He has done so himself at times.

Crossing the glacier alone only made him more reluctant. While on his way back to camp from Pik Corona earlier, he had at 2 A.M. fallen in several hidden crevasses up to his armpits. Fear of crevasses mounted into sheer terror, as he hesitantly placed each foot forward, gingerly put weight on it, and jumped back sweating and out of control whenever his boot sank into the snow even slightly more than usual. Finally he was halfway across in the darkness, and it was as foolish or safe to continue as it was to retreat. By sheer luck, since he was traveling in the dark, he ended up close to the face at the proper spot; here he dangled from an overhanging berg-schrund (a huge crevasse where a slope steepens at the bottom of an ice face) from his two ice tools, without wrist loops on for support, his hands slipping down the shafts and himself slid-ing toward the dark depths below. Finally, with fading compo-sure, he hauled himself up on the route. Giving in to what was standard practive for most ice climbers, he fashioned a hasty wrist loop for one of his axes, ending his years of purism in exchange for some slight reassurance.

> I had this headlamp which created my ten-meter world in the darkness. I could never see past the light to the base of the climb once I started up it. If I had fallen, I would have fallen forever into that other world. I was well on my way into a deep sort of euphoria.

Higher in the couloir, after surmounting a small band of rock barring his progress, Henry ascended toward higher cliffs above where he hoped to gain protection from rockfall, but he went too far right and began zigzagging up the broad 700-meter ice face. Graceful French technique using only one axe allowed rapid movement up soft snow-ice névé, with patches of harder water ice, until a crampon began to come off.

The weather was beautiful and he enjoyed the pure move-ment of climbing on a massive face of rock and ice in darkness, alone, unroped. Two hard sections on steep rock allowed him to become fascinated with the idea of *difficulty* for a half-hour; here he consciously engaged in his rock climbing technique, before the first hints of dawn revealed his incredible exposure above the bergschrund far below.

Hard water ice shattered into glossy plates by the axe went skipping off into the void, and Barber started to take more precautions, changing over to the more secure front pointing technique as the slope steepened to sixty degrees. At another band of rock, covered by ice only three centimeters thick,

Henry pulled out his light rope and put in three mediocre pitons for a rough self-belay. He tied the rope into them and led off, but he soon fouled the rope at the crux; cursing it as he realized the tenuousness of his life at that point, he finally just let it trail out behind him in the narrow couloir above. It was frustrating to be so close to the summit a few hundred meters above, and yet be ensnarled in a rope on a few centimeters of ice smeared on near-vertical rock, a position demanding exacting attention.

Much of the natural flow of the climbing was lost in the upper part of this gully, where the ice steepened again. Second thoughts about the project and its outcome came more frequently. The rockfall gradually intensified. Once, the rope jammed and he was forced to set an anchor and gingerly rappel down and untangle it, wasting time and threatening his composure.

Eventually the couloir merged into a sky that was fully light and flecked with color. Henry relaxed a moment and saw, far below, the movement of people and tiny lights in a camp that was just awakening to the day. Looking across the summit ridge at the horizontal dimension once again, he was amazed to see Mike Warburton standing within shouting distance.

"What time is it?" Henry screamed to Mike.

Mike asked someone in his party below him, and yelled back to Henry, "7:30!" Bertulis or Jones calmly retorted, "Mike, we're all right here with you. You don't have to yell. It's okay."

"No, there's some guy down there who wants to know what time it is," Mike replied.

"But he's Russian, Mike. What are you screaming English at him for?"

"But he's not Russian. . . ."

Suddenly, everyone comprended the situation. They were amazed and chagrined that Henry had just pulled off a solo first ascent in four-and-a-half hours of a route adjacent to one that they had spent two-and-a-half days ascending.

On the way down, I was walking through fields of flowers. Whenever I do a solo it always seems that if I am alone afterward, I am much more intensely aware of the beauty around me. When soloing, your focus of attention is so acute for so long that the mood carries on with its own natural momentum, well after the climbing. Instead of concentrating on an ice axe and points, you are intently absorbing the delicacy and colors of a wave of flowers, the rock, the fickle clouds, and the sun. Your senses suddenly let go, are free to explore all the things withheld from them during the solo.

Yet at the same time, sometimes you subconsciously feel that it was a stupid thing to do, unnecessary, potentially final. Ideally, you meet someone you care about deeply, to share the high.

The long walk down an alpine valley was trying; what Henry desired was instant relief from the weight of the endeavor. As the camp appeared in the distance, he heard the lunch call over the loudspeaker system, and quickened his pace. With a sense of timing and theatrics borrowed from a John Ford western movie, Henry strolled into the massive hall.

> All at once, all of the utensils fell onto the plates. Everyone sprang up spontaneously and mobbed me at the door. It was like I was the pitcher who'd thrown the winning pitch at the World Series.

Everybody shouted congratulations at once in Russian; the sentiments were clear. The outburst of tears and emotions was partly a result of a fine climb done in impeccable style, and partly because the Russians realized it was something they could never do within their own system. Until that time, the Soviets were unsure of the Americans' capabilities. They began to comprehend that the Soviet way had limitations, and that other philosophies of climbing could produce spectacular results. They were simultaneously sad and ecstatic.

As if trying to keep up the pace, George Lowe returned from the Corona Peak climb that Henry had abandoned, jokingly acknowledged the artful gamesmanship that had gotten Barber the central route, managed a few hours' sleep, and then went up on Korea Peak himself. He had reserved some strength for a personal climb of this kind, and operated without jealousy or competitiveness. He soloed another new ice route in a lower-angled couloir to the right of Henry's route. Since the weather had deteriorated, George completed his route in storm and snowfall, also impressing the Russians.

As usual, Henry retreated into the sensual life after the intensity of his climb. He had met a tall, strong Soviet woman climber named Ludmila in camp, and now he hiked for half a day into another valley to see her. She ran out and picked him up high in the air in delight at both his feat and his arrival, all the while calling him *aspichka*, her sparrow, a term meaning "free spirit" in Russian. They drank and sang and partied nonstop, forgetting the mountains for a while, but the intimacy was tinged with sadness over the distance that geography and politics would soon put between them. She would return to her native Sverdlovsk, and they would write, but for the moment they wanted to forget that; the hard climbing was over, and there was time for sharing.

Meanwhile the Americans rested and caught up on each others' exploits. While lying around the tents that day, sunbathing amid debauched squalor, they noticed fifty people returning from their first climb. Russian custom dictates an initiation ceremony after one's first real climb of a mountain. The smiling initiates filed through a receiving line of instructors, who kissed them on each cheek. Their faces were stamped with paint, which was smeared into crude aboriginal designs during a group dance. A heroic and somewhat self-mocking skit was performed while everyone stood at attention, saluted, and roared out collective yells of frenzy before breaking out of a huddle. To the individualistic Americans, it was a bit too much like the classic locker room scene after a homecoming victory in the Big Game.

As a result of the solos on Korea Peak, the Soviets were anxious to learn about the techniques involved. Henry conducted an ice climbing seminar, in which he spoke of the new technical ice gear as the fundamental vehicle for difficult ice climbing. It was an ironic moment for a true believer in the primacy of personal technique, not equipment, and one who had only days earlier relinquished a purist attitude about the use of mechanical devices in climbing. The exercise was self-defeating, however, since the Soviets would never have the opportunity to possess or practice with such gear.

The Americans had a chance to see another unusual facet of Soviet climbing one afternoon after one of Henry's seminars. Two teams went climbing on short cliffs nearby. Lowe shot up a twenty-meter pitch in about seven minutes, while Sergei Bershov, then the Soviet champion speed climber, did the same pitch in less than a minute, almost as fast as the rope could be coiled.

Speed climbing contests in the Crimea each year bring mountaineering into the public eye in Russia, recruiting climbers for the camps and international competition, and causing the government to allot more money to the Mountaineering Federation. There are two varieties of speed climbing. The first involves a race up a hundred-meter wall by two climbers side by side, who then switch routes and are timed again. The other type is team climbing, in which Bershov excels. The contestants tell the judges exactly which route on a multi-pitch face they will lead. The leader always has a toprope for safety. Contestants are judged on speed, rope handling, and style. Medals are also awarded for first ascents of a high-altitude climb or a major alpine face. All of this is taken quite seriously. When Bershov trains, he climbs 1,000 meters of reasonably difficult rock every day, and so is able to race up 100 meters of hard rock in about eight or nine minutes. Henry was intrigued by all of this, and two years later attempted to join in and make a film of the competition in the Crimea, but he was denied a visa at the last minute.

Sergei was in training and lived a temperate life, but the other Soviets took it upon themselves to show the Americans the social customs surrounding mountaineering. They did not sip liquor; toasts were thrown down speedily, to brotherhood or nationality, to future routes, and to the Tien Shan or a dozen other ranges. Eight people easily went through beer, seven bottles of vodka, some thick and fruity Georgian wine, and the ever-present champagne at one sitting. When there was nothing left, they would head for the medical kits and pull

Barber giving climbing demonstration in the Tien Shan with interpreter in the background/Henry Barber Collection

out syringes to empty sterilizing alcohol into a glass or to mix it with a murky disinfectant that looked like pine tar and throw this concoction down as well. Meanwhile everyone ate cucumbers, onions, and caviar incessantly, singing songs about Soviet mountaineers returning from the war all the while. The next day it felt like they had been embalmed.

By the time the teams moved to their last climbing in the Caucasus, the climbers were telling each other their life stories. A Russian climber named Misha Konkov told about the six falls he had taken since beginning climbing — about when he had gone sixty meters to the end of his rope, bounced down and hit a ledge, and was knocked out; about the time he fell many meters down a couloir. They spent entire days in alpine meadows eating and telling stories. Back in the resort town of Dombay, there was more champagne, and even more exorbitant hotel bills, paid in crisp American dollars. Henry observed:

> The Soviets are much closer to capitalism than to the Marxist-Leninist communism one reads about. Most often you can get what you want through some financial or material considerations.

At Uzonkil, the final camp, while the others were on the beautiful Yosemite-like granite of the classic Stepanov route on Pik Dolar, Mike Warburton and Valentin Grekovich decided to repeat their teamwork on El Capitan and went off to do a new route on the north face. They were on it for seven days. Just one day before the Americans were scheduled to leave for Moscow to attend banquets and the Russian circus, and after the pair had been soaked in dense cloud for six days, Warburton was leading a pitch just below the summit, struggling to top out and head back. He fell forty meters, suffering concussions, contusions, and severely bruised legs.

Up to that time, Henry had been having intense ethical discussions with the Soviets about why they used radios. He had maintained that climbers become overconfident because they know they can call and summon help, and that if someone misses a call, everyone becomes overly worried. Upon hearing of the accident, Henry had to spend the duration of the rescue on the radio, doing exactly what he had been fighting against all along.

Barber remembers that the rescue was really impressive.

> Out of a hundred and thirty or forty people in this camp,

about a hundred and twenty participated in the rescue. All of these people carried a ton of equipment up to the peak. The doctor who was in charge was awake for two and a half days straight. He'd just gotten down off a climb and went all the way back up there. Sergei and a few others were climbing to them all through the night. These people got to him at about two or three in the morning and got back down to camp at about six. It was probably the best thing that happened on the trip because of the sense of camaraderie that we all felt. But at the same time, it was a miserable way to end the trip.

Warburton was hallucinating, saying things like Grekovich had fallen, not him. Well, it turned out that Grekovich *had* fallen, but on the second day. He had gone twenty-five meters and broken his foot, then climbed the next four days with a broken bone, rescued Mike, and then went to another camp in the Caucasus and, sixteen days after his own accident, found out that his foot was indeed broken. That's a typical tough Russian right there.

The incident has haunted Henry ever since. Mike Warburton was littered off the mountain, still delirious and unmanageable, and then taken away in a truck to an airstrip with Bertulis, Barber, and a doctor in attendance — but Henry and the others never saw Warburton again in Russia.

Mike was immediately readied to fly to a hospital in Moscow, but while Henry tried numerous times to get on the plane to accompany Warburton (who was in shock and suffered from amnesia for a month), he was forced off the plane while it was on the runway, then allowed back, then bumped again for a Russian couple. The situation left Henry exasperated, and he wisely agreed to let Bertulis go with Mike to the hospital. Anything could have happened there. Henry felt he had to go with Mike, and he felt severely compromised that he could not. Bertulis sat next to Mike — who was raving off and on, strapped in his litter in the plane's narrow aisle, and led the way through twelve hours of bureaucratic delays before reaching the hospital in Moscow. Henry — busy with organizational

details of the group's departure for eighteen hours straight —
never made it to the hospital, nor did anyone else on the team
besides Bertulis.

> Four of us left without ever seeing him in the hospital. At
> that time, we didn't know that his back and legs weren't
> broken, but still no one went to see him. We believed we
> had gotten him to the best hospital in the Soviet Union
> with the help of our friends the Soviet climbing doctors.

Bertulis later came back with a report on Warburton's condition, having ascertained that he would recover. "But the au-
thorities would not let us visit or stay on beyond our scheduled
flights," Barber said.

In leaving the injured man the team broke a cardinal rule
of expeditions and ropemates, which is that climbers always
take the utmost risks to bring back a teammate in danger and
see him to safety. Everyone left the country with only sketchy
and secondhand knowledge of Mike's condition. It was a personal and collective lapse that still torments Henry, and that
proved to be a precedent for an even darker and more serious
incident two years later, deep in East Africa on Mount Kilimanjaro — an accident that drastically altered the way he looks
at the world.

9

Frozen Faces

*H*ENRY HAS GIVEN UP ice climbing three times since he took up the sport in 1969. He sold all of his equipment once, after he had come to believe that the objective dangers and the necessary reliance on breakable equipment created a situation in which he was unable to control fully the events on a given climb.

When Henry began ice climbing, he remembers being "obsessed." Living at home in the exclusive community of Sherborn, Massachusetts, he would hike for thirty minutes through the woods virtually every day to a secret set of very short ice bulges, and "go up and down them until I wanted to scream." Sometimes he would go to the Quincy Quarries, climbing short rock routes when the temperature was well below freezing. On the weekends, he and others in the Appalachian Mountain Club would drive north to New Hampshire to try the standard beginning ice climbs in the White Mountains. They had epic adventures straightaway at places like Willey's Slide, a 200-meter slab of low-angle ice flowing down a mountainside in the wilds of Crawford Notch.

For added warmth, Henry climbed in nylon overboots designed to fit over mountain boots twice his shoe size. Once toothed metal crampons were attached to the overboots, he felt as if he were climbing in "bowling balls." Each ice climb was more than just a grueling experience.

> I felt as though I just could not cope with it because it was all so miserable. It was a major epic when I got to anything that was over about sixty degrees in steepness. I was climbing with a very long ninety-five-centimeter axe and

John Bouchard on the crux of the Black Dike on the first winter ascent following his first solo ascent/Henry Barber Collection

Barber on Black Dike/Rick Wilcox

crampons that came loose a lot, so it was sort of like swinging a fly rod with a two-kilo weight on the end. I'd just about go over backwards.

The first major ice climb for Barber came during the 1970 season, in a 600-meter gully in Crawford Notch with twelve other climbers from the AMC. Despite the fact that Henry had walking pneumonia, he went on the climb, which dragged on well into the night, as the group struggled up very slowly and then descended through the wooded snowpack in the dark, falling over unseen ice bulges, hitting heads on tree limbs, their headlights flickering out. As soon as Barber was late for dinner, his parents called every authority they could think of, including the state police, but to no avail. The crew finally staggered back to Boston at about 4 A.M.

At that time, few climbers had turned their attention to the steep ice that cascaded over rock crags around the North Conway area; instead they saw Pinnacle Gully, set high in Huntington Ravine on Mount Washington, as the ultimate ice route in New England. Climbers since the 1930's, when Everest veteran Noel Odell and others first climbed the gullies, had

Left to right: Wilcox, Barber, and Bouchard after the first winter ascent of the Ghost on Cannon Mountain/Rick Wilcox

always cut steps up the whole three or four rope lengths of Pinnacle, whose hard, blue, water ice averaged sixty degrees in steepness at the bottom. Jim McCarthy, in the 1969–70 season, led a party including Rick Wilcox and others on the first stepless ascent of the gully, made possible by the new, very secure, curved Chouinard axes and hammers, and opening the way for exploration of other extreme ice routes in the North Country.

The equipment that climbers learned with in the late 1960's became antiquated within two or three years. The radically drooped pick designs and rigid crampons that Yvon Chouinard and Tom Frost introduced at this time created a revolution in ice climbing. The nature of the sport changed as swiftly as the design of equipment progressed, with each season revealing innovative new tools and ascents. So, ice climbing, which was once tormented, tedious practice for summer trips to alpine peaks, was transformed into a type of winter crag climbing on short but brutally steep waterfalls. Suddenly everyone was doing it, as an end in itself.

211

The year following the Crawford epic, Henry left the ice flows to his hardier brethren.

It was just too cold and miserable. That was the year I met Bob Anderson. We were climbing on the walls around MIT, doing bizarre things in the weight room there, and starting to go to the Waban Arches. I had no desire at all to go ice climbing.

The next winter, though, found him out again. He was adamant this time, and had ambitions. After one or two climbs, he went with John Bouchard, John Bragg, and Rick Wilcox to do the first official winter ascent of the dreaded Black Dike on Cannon Mountain, an hour from North Conway. Bouchard had soloed the much-coveted route during the previous winter, to the complete amazement of the climbing community, but many were hesitant to give him credit for the climb, since he had done it two days before winter officially began in December and under marginal ice conditions.

The fierce White Mountains offered their very finest dead-winter extreme cold and wind during the ascent. Three or four pitches of thin yellow ice were smeared like drool on the near-vertical black dike of rotten stone cut deeply into the 300-meter cliff. The dike rises from a talus slope of enormous boulders piled another 300 meters above the road through Franconia Notch, and is fully exposed to wind and storm. Upon reaching the base of their intimidating route, beneath huge icicles hanging over a hundred meters higher, the group hesitated. When they finally arrived at the foot of the crux traverse to the left on mixed rock and thin ice, Bouchard started across, stopped, and then shuffled back to the belay, saying to the others that he had already led it once. Bragg stepped in and led the pitch and the other hard lead. Although they had planned to climb in two pairs, Henry had to follow third or last on a lightweight seven-millimeter rope intended for use in rappelling. No one else wanted to lead the traverse, so they all roped together. It was his first hard ice route and he was awed by the setting and climbing. A certain amount of hesitant exploration on each lead was necessary before the route was finally completed. Henry recalls "counting on Bragg and Bouchard to pull through," to get them off the climb. It was the opening salvo in Henry's hard ice work, and the beginning of a fine season for Bragg, who went on to do the first winter ascent of the famed Repentence route with Wilcox a few months later, setting the pace for all New England ice climbing that year.

During that season, Henry began to develop his own sense of ethics in the sport, which paralled the beliefs of some other skilled climbers throughout the country. He refused to use wrist loops on his axes, feeling that his climbing would be purer if he was not hanging by his wrists off the tools like everyone else, and he climbed with the classic Chouinard wooden tools even when shorter, more sophisticated designs appeared. It was a signature, a statement of intent and individuality.

> We were just holding onto our axes while everyone else was frigging with a lot of gadgets. Unfortunately, technology is often more fascinating to people than technique.

In 1973, with Bouchard and Wilcox, Henry managed the first winter ascent of the Ghost on Cannon, the first winter grade IV wall climb on the cliff. The ascent of the 400-meter route required two full days (without a bivouac since four pitches were fixed the first day), and was marked by highly "interesting" mixed climbing on both rock and ice. A great deal of complicated direct aid was engineered in high winds and deep cold. Each climber was forced to rely on the skill of the others in numerous places. Bouchard was the most confident on ice, and Henry on rock.

> We developed a real bond between us. It was extremely cold while we were on the route, very miserable. Through it, though, we worked together and pushed something that nobody had done before. It did not feel like the strength in numbers that we had on the Black Dike. That makes a very big difference in a route of that caliber.

The notion of what was possible on ice in winter was redefined for New Englanders by the climb.

During that winter season, Henry spent much of his time in New Hampshire, climbing with many of the locals. He came to know his partners in a different light; the times were more relaxed and personable than in the summer. Ice attracted far fewer adherents and involved continual epic adventures, and so took on a more exploratory, less competitive nature than the rock scene. Local climbers would gather, after most days, in a back corner of the Eastern Mountain Sports store to discuss their adventures.

Bouchard sticks out in my mind because he was driven. We'd go cross-country skiing, and he'd ski ten kilometers, and I'd ski three. He was obsessive in the way that he had to go out and climb.

He was a part of this hero-corner that we had in EMS. At that time, I was drinking almost a case of beer a day. People would come in and talk with me. It was a real hero thing. But we'd all be sitting there sometimes, and Bouchard would bolt out of his chair and say, "Gotta go climbing now." And he'd be off to solo something. Once, he grabbed Wilcox. They went off and did Pinnacle Gully in four or five hours, round-trip from North Conway. That would take most people a full day. Bouchard had such energy and drive that occasionally he was hard to deal with, but he was also the only person besides Bragg you could really count on to push it out and get you up some of these difficult routes.

The statistics compiled during that season illuminate a many-sided scramble to knock off the most desperate routes in the region in the best possible style. Consequently, Henry made a trip to Mount Katahdin in far northern Maine towards the end of the season. He was the leader of an AMC trip to the remote, alpine-like peak, and climbed primarily with Dave Cilley, a manager at EMS. They put in a prominent ice route, 650 meters long and straight to the summit, that became one of Henry's earliest skirmishes with disaster.

Because of the length, the two of them figured on a bivouac somewhere on the descent. However, Henry remembers that

> there was no chance of our being able to survive the night. We got up there in typical Maine cold and were climbing in down parkas under our wind parkas. Then it warmed and we got soaking wet immediately. The route turned into frightening climbing on very thin ice.
>
> Finally we ended up just soloing, except that we were roped together, up fifty-degree ice for a hundred meters or so. We hit this twenty-meter section of vertical ice. I used almost all of my ice screws getting over the top. At the belay, cold and exhausted, I placed a very bad screw that only went in about a couple of centimeters. I backed that up by placing my axes and ice hammer and tied them off, then belayed. Well, as Dave came over the top, flailing wildly, he broke off the end of his axe; he had broken a crampon and his alpine hammer the previous day. As he fell off, he pulled me off my step in the ice and ripped out one of my axes. I was just sitting there on the ice hanging from the screw, screaming at him to get back on the ice, watching the screw in back of me bending outwards. He was yelling, "I can't do anything! I can't do anything!" And I was yelling at him. It didn't really matter what the other was saying. We were both gripped out of our minds. I knew that we were going to die. It was bad, but we finally settled down and got him back on.

They wandered down the back side of the mountain in the dark, scared and with the adrenaline flowing but flushed with the knowledge that they had pulled off a coup.

Later that winter, Henry again gave up ice climbing, he claims.

> Every time that I went out, I was terrified, either about the conditions or my tools. There was always something. But I felt like a pioneer, so I kept coming back. This carried me through into the next rock season, with all of

the new climbing I was doing in Yosemite. Ice climbing transferred nicely into my rock climbing. It taught me how to climb on rotten rock, and vice versa. You have to know where every part of your body is in case the rock or ice breaks away and leaves you hanging from one or two points. You have to know how to compensate immediately.

Back then I never felt at home on steep ice, though. It wasn't so much the gear breaking, but that it was in some way mechanical; tools were foreign objects attached to my body, I'm terrified of machinery in general. I hate cars, and I won't even consider using a power lawnmower. It's mostly that machines are forever breaking. If I could, I'd have nothing to do with them. I don't feel any different now. It's just that I've developed the technique of climbing ice as if it were rock. I'm trying to use my tools as infrequently as possible, unless it's eighty to ninety degrees and smooth. Then, there's little left to do but go for it. So, as a result of distrust, I began climbing without wrist loops. I didn't think anything about oneupsmanship, as there was nobody better than Bragg, Bouchard, and myself. It was only for my personal satisfaction.

In 1975, Henry accepted Yvon Chouinard's offer of a venture to the Sierras for long ice and mixed routes. Chouinard is recognized as the foremost American practitioner of the difficult, balance-oriented French technique on ice, which he learned under the tutelage of French master alpinists. It was an opportunity for Henry to serve a brief apprenticeship in order to become highly proficient and a skilled instructor in his own right.

Together, Chouinard and Barber taught several ice climbing seminars on Mount Hood in Oregon and in New England. After a class in North Conway, the two managed the third ascent of Repentence on Cathedral Ledge. The route remains one of the classic ice routes in the east. In not using wrist loops on the climb, vertical for most of its hundred and forty meters, Henry felt the experience embodied all that he and Yvon were attempting to teach.

Yvon Chouinard leading the last pitch of Repentance in New Hampshire on an early ascent/Henry Barber Collection

I was climbing a very thin band of ice at one point and chopped through the rope. That's an instance where you have to be collected in your thoughts. So what if I chopped through the rope? As long as you keep your head together, you're fine. You do that by having as many different facets of your personality to rely on as possible.

After the schedule of seminars, both flew to Scotland to take part in the National Geographic Society film shot on Ben Nevis. Henry eventually left the set, but still praises climbing on the Ben as the

finest anywhere in the world, the best training ground. You have weather, route finding problems on every route, long approaches, solitude, and incredible variance in techniques required on the climbs.

Jeff Lowe in Point Five gully of the Ben Nevis in Scotland/Henry Barber Collection

It's a bad place to make a mistake. Chouinard was avalanched there. It happens all the time. Jeff Lowe completed a very impressive solo climb, came down, and the same day went up and soloed another route, then spent ten hours trying to get back down in a snowstorm, walking down the back side by compass through the night. This type of incident makes you think a little more than you'd have to on, say, an ice route just off the road in the States. Ben Nevis is one place where the tools aren't going to get you up. The experience means more, and makes the place into a feeling, an adventure, not just a name or an accomplishment, the way much modern climbing has become.

Ice climbing's evolution, is a reflection of modern society. They'll take the tools to their highest point of capability and way beyond, until the equipment fails.

Then it's not the climber who failed. It's the machinery, that piece of technology. It's always "the tool was too weak and it didn't swing right in the first place." Or, "we didn't have the right bivouac sack," or "our gear got wet." Tell all that to Fritz Wiessner on K-2 for a week in 1939 in a wool coat at 27,000 feet. His gear didn't fail. He had the worst gear you could ever imagine, so he didn't have that problem. I'm pretty pessimistic about the trends in the sport. Only a very few climbers in this country rely on confidence in themselves rather than on their gear.

Rumors had been circulating among British climbers for years about the very pure ethics and unimaginable ice potential of waterfall climbing in Norway, with its deep granite fjords, big walls, and arctic conditions. While in Scotland, Chouinard and then Henry had heard about it from Johnny Cunningham and Hamish MacInnes. They had seen summer photographs of the Mardalsfossen — the third highest waterfall in the world, and the highest that might freeze over — in Tony Howard's British climbing guide to the Romsdal Valley. They were amazed at the prospect. "Can you imagine? Can you *imagine*? Going there and climbing Bridalveil Falls six times in a row!" Barber exclaims.

Plans began to unfold, and the winter following the filming on the Ben, the pair began seriously to consider the venture. Yvon, through his business trips to the continent and the annual sports show in Germany, knew Thomas Carlstrom, a Norwegian climber and mountain gear retailer, who was to be their contact and host. At the last minute, when it was apparent that Chouinard might not get free, Henry asked Rob Taylor (then a student and employee of MacInnes and a close friend of Yvon's as well) to join them. The younger pair — Henry was 24 and Rob 23 — finally left Boston in February of 1977 for a three-week stay in "fossen-land," as they called it.

Ice climbing was Taylor's forte. While he had grown up around Boston and had climbed locally, he had just spent several years learning about mountaineering in Scotland, the home of his ancestors. "Rob climbs steep ice as well as anyone in the world," said Henry, "a brilliant ice climber, although he

219

doesn't really do any rock climbing at all," which is curiously atypical for a mountaineer. Henry had encountered Rob again during the Ben Nevis filming, where he thought of him as a classic film gopher, helping arrange the setting, carrying loads, climbing with the camera crew, while Barber was supposed to be one of the three stars.

Norwegian climbers seldom reported their new routes, in a radical departure from most of the rest of the world, because they wanted to dampen competition and allow each party in turn to experience the full flavor of a first ascent. Very few outsiders had climbed on these "fossens," as they are known locally. Henry and Rob both saw an excellent opportunity to climb one of the two highest fossens in the country — both are over 400 meters — if one had the right partner. Even given Norway's lackadaisical system of reporting, Henry surmised that neither of the climbs could have had an ascent. It was the first time he had really thought about how winter conditions might create entirely new climbs, not just iced-over versions of summer rock routes.

When the Americans arrived, the Carlstroms — Thomas and his wife Cecil — treated them royally. The pair felt at home, beyond the competitive pressures common in most climbing areas. The Norwegians they met were mostly older and solid but not brilliant climbers, more like the AMC group Henry had started with than the aspiring "19-year-old rock jocks" who inhabit crags today. They enjoyed the rolling, pristine countryside and the friendships, the things that had drawn both of them into climbing in the first place, but they almost immediately began to go aggressively after the relatively untouched big climbs.

For a month prior to his departure on the trip, Henry had sojourned in the pubs and on the frozen waterfalls of Telluride, Colorado. Most important to the climbing he would find in Norway was his ascent of Bridalveil Falls with Chip Lee, a fellow guide at the climbing school there. As the cascade freefalls for 200 meters, it creates overhanging formations and thick icicles grouped together, one of the few falls in the U.S. to freeze in this way. A considerable amount of intricate rock technique up delicate formations, like hand-jamming

Barber with Chip Lee on Bridalveil Falls/Greg Davis

between or laybacking off of pillars, is necessary. Bridalveil was, unknown to Henry, the ideal warm-up climb for his trip to Norway.

In somewhat atypical conditions, Barber led all five pitches in what was probably the fifth ascent of the Bridalveil route. The sun had struck the snowfield above, causing a large amount of water to run onto the climb, where the temperature was well below freezing in the shade. Both climbers were bordering on hypothermia from the moment they walked outside. Due to the pillar formations and fenestrations — like classical architectural motifs — on the second pitch, Henry was able to climb it virtually without using his tools.

Leading the climb was a stepping stone. Henry felt that few people had the capability of pulling it off in those conditions.

221

View of the Vettifossen/Henry Barber Collection

I'd never climbed anything that long before, or that weird-looking. I had always had a Bouchard, a Chouinard, or a Jeff Lowe to rely on in the past. I was pretty gripped because there was no one there to bail me out, like Chouinard, who I relied on psychologically when we did Repentence. When I got into the middle of the first pitch, I honestly was beginning to wonder whether I was going to be able to do the route. I just didn't know how good I was going to be at this very specialized type of climbing.

Several years later Henry returned to the climb as part of a filmed recreation of the first ascent for ABC-TV. Jeff Lowe and Mike Weiss, who had originally done the route, starred in the production. Colorado filmmakers Greg Lowe and Bob Carmichael had approached the network about the project and had elicited its interest. Just as the filming was about to get under way, Henry caught wind of it and contacted ABC, saying that he had proposed a similar ice-climbing film to them much earlier, following the success of *Sea-Cliff Climbing*. As a result, at a sports show in Chicago that all were attending as equipment representatives and manufacturers, the group sat down and decided that Henry would be included.

Due to threatening avalanche conditions, the whole crew cross-country skied and partied for a week while awaiting the proper moment to go up on the climb. Under pressure to begin shooting, the trio of climbers felt endangered and considered going on strike, a time-honored acting tradition. They insisted that a helicopter be called in to drop dynamite on the hanging snowfield in an attempt to avalanche it off, but to no avail. Jeff, Mike, their lady friends, and Henry all went out to dinner at a Chinese restaurant one night at the height of the negotiations, trying to decide whether or not to acquiesce and attempt the route. After a long, pensive, and well-lubricated Asian repast, a plate of fortune cookies came with the check. This aroused considerable interest. One by one, each diner selected a cookie, opened it, and shared it with the others, reading out loud: "Sing 'Lover come back to me' and you will receive a surprise;" "We make a living by what we get, but make a life by what we give;" "Great hopes make great men;" "Advice comes too late when a thing is done;" and finally, the last portent of the future, "Great restraint is called for." That settled it.

Soon thereafter the producer succumbed to their demand and ordered the helicopter in, but the explosives had no effect on the snow, so they filmed the climb. Jeff was the real star and led the first and fourth pitches, while Henry and Mike led one rope length each. With the high-speed cameras and three climbers involved it was a complicated filming. A lot of film could be wasted just waiting for a camera to warm up to shoot somebody's foot kicking into the ice, and then one had to make sure the foot matched the appearance of who ever was leading at the time. Due to technical errors, Henry's lead was not recorded properly and was left out of the film, much to his chagrin. The final product remains an impressive record of creative vertical waterfall climbing of the first order, though.

Buoyed by the confidence and experience he had gained on Bridalveil from his original ascent, Henry was primarily interested in new routes upon arrival in Norway, as was Rob Taylor. But they found that their views on such matters changed, once they were exposed to the Norwegian perpetual first ascent philosophy. The array of potential motivations was confusing: for achievement, notoriety, self, fun, and friendship, as well as for fine-quality climbing in a beautiful place. Nonetheless they recognized theirs as a "pioneering situation," and they were hoping

> to capitalize on a place that essentially only a very few people had been to before. It was less from the standpoint of achieving something, and more from the point of doing something no one has done before, for the adventure of it all — getting there while it's easy to do first ascents. I don't want to go somewhere and have to walk fifty kilometers to do something new.

A major obstacle right away was Henry's bad shoulder, which had dislocated again in late January, two weeks before the trip, while he was bouldering in Colorado. The injury was the worst yet, but the shoulder began healing when he slipped off his crampon points during an early climb "and once and for all relocated the thing when the well-placed tools yanked the arm back in."

Norway was another trip that had "to look good on paper." To do this, Henry had to retain his reputation by completing often-dangerous routes, ones that others had not finished, or climbs others were unwilling to explore. In Norway, this could take the form of climbing a type of waterfall that had not been done, by pushing the existing style to its limits.

The Norwegians could not understand the Americans' preoccupation with firsts. Their hosts simply asked them,

"Why do you want to do new routes? What difference does it make if you do new routes or any other routes? It doesn't matter because no one here will know anyway what routes you do." We freaked out a little bit because that was an attitude that we had not seen before. This was something new.

These were certainly admirable thoughts, they mused, but the drive to be first still came above such codes. On the first day out, Barber and Taylor managed "two first ascents that were fairly difficult in their steepness."

The Carlstroms were exemplary hosts. Their home in Hemsedal, in the central valley of Norway, was often a long drive from many of the climbs the visitors were interested in, but the couple were always eager to make the trips. They owned and operated a sports equipment store, importing their gear from the U.S. and Britain. They lived comfortably, as do most Norwegians.

Far more than his companion Henry was ready and willing to enter into local life — to drink with his hosts and, on rest days, to go skiing with the family. He recalls,

Skiing was the best thing we did there. In all the trips that I've taken, climbing is just an excuse to go somewhere and to see new people and cultures. The actual climbing is minor compared to the rest of the experience.

Despite all of the talk about the experience as a whole, Henry does remember that he and Rob were hyperactive in their scheming for new routes. On the third day they went to climb the Hindesfossen, a 240-meter wall of ice. This was originally planned as a "warm-up" for the Mardälsfossen, a 400-meter waterfall. Upon completing a 1,000-kilometer journey to get to the route, Barber was surprised to learn that the Romsdal power project had drained the fossen of all its water. Their ultimate ice climb no longer even existed. The

Hindesfossen would have to provide training for some other climb, one they would have to discover.

They spent two days speculating on whether the climb could be completed in a day. Henry always has to have the conditions of a particular venture exactly to his liking, and he wanted to do the route in a day. Rob is by nature a cautious person, on the other hand, often "worrisome, too paranoid to be in the mountains," according to Henry, and as a result, was reluctant to attempt the climb in a day's push. Henry felt confident.

> I'd climbed Bridalviel, and I knew that we had it in the bag. Rob was saying the ice was too brittle. I knew that we could even walk to it and get off in a day, although it was a little longer and harder than Bridalveil.
> We went up there and bivouacked at the base. Cold as hell. The morning was beautiful, though. I got up and promptly told Rob that I was going down. All of the speculating had gotten me down. I don't like to talk about climbing. I like to climb. It didn't take much to talk him out of it, as I don't think his confidence was up to it. I just wouldn't go up on it if we were planning to spend two days on it.

An internal paradox had arisen, one that neither of them had fully anticipated. Rob was clearly the more experienced ice expert and general mountaineer. He had some questions about Henry's abilities on difficult ice and his risky climbing style in true mountain settings, which Henry could not control through will, with the attendant decisions about weather, commitment, and retreat. Yet at the same time, Rob was concerned about his own ability to pull off big climbs, and had deeply ingrained personal doubts about his performance in international-class climbing. It was something he had aspired to for some time, and was just beginning to explore with this bold sortie to Norway.

In many ways, mountains were just oversized rock crags to Henry, who routinely applied his crag precepts to bigger problems, contributing to his great success. Mountains presented significant challenges, abounding with dangerous situations to ignore or control as much as possible through blazing speed and daring, and yet at the same time they were a source of perpetual comfort, respite, and beauty. For Rob, mountains were instead opportunities for personal discovery and exploration and challenge, and were not to be taken lightly. They operated by their own laws, over which man had negligible influence; he felt he must bend to their power and might. As a result, Rob was more inclined to study their composition and await the proper moment to attempt an ascent.

Henry recognized that Rob needed a strong personality to rely on, to make the decisions and provide focused drive. At the same time, Rob did not always feel comfortable with the assertive decisions made by strong partners, and sought more egalitarian relationships founded on mutual respect. There was a lingering competition between them as a result of this motivational discrepancy. Rob did not fully trust his partner's judgment in alpine situations, since Henry had a very carefree, spontaneous, and somewhat disorganized approach to climbing, compared to Rob's own more studied perspective, based on his formal mountain training in rescue and avalanches. Taylor's stationery indicates his field as "Orography," the study of mountains, and he proudly tells the story of his struggle with the University of Massachusetts to receive an extension service independent study degree in that somewhat self-invented field. Perhaps as a result of their dissimilarities, they made a strong team: Henry's brashness and confidence, Rob's alpine knowledge and concern about dangers and conditions. Unlike Henry, Rob had also had his share of mishaps in the mountains, including being avalanched 130 meters down a slope in Scotland just days after he first arrived there, breaking an ankle and tearing ligaments and tendons. It had made him wary.

In a coffee-table book on Norway, the pair discovered a photograph of the Vettisfossen, a 300-meter freefalling waterfall near the town of Ardal. The idea of ascending this highest fossen was ambitious, and yet both climbers felt that no more than two days would be needed for the climb. Henry again maintained that only one would be necessary, although this time, he admitted he could be wrong.

We went prepared for a bivouac, carrying a sleeping bag and water. There were very few places to spend the night, though, because about halfway up, all of the platforms and pedestals ended, leaving much of the upper half with gently overhanging ice. A bivouac would have been very serious.

The day and night beforehand were as anxious and full of excitement as those before any major climb. Rob recalls that he managed to sleep a bit, but was too wound up in anticipation of the climb to taste his breakfast.

Both were apprehensive about the route. Neither was certain that the route was indeed possible, since from the ground they could see the numerous looming overhangs halfway up, and again at the top, protecting the finish. As Henry describes it,

Where the base of the route meets the channel — the main flow of water coming from the top — there's an overhang that's literally fifteen meters away from the wall, with twenty-meter icicles dripping off of it, hanging like the body of a semi-trailer truck.

While Carlstrom and Hakon Gammelsaether climbed an equally immense though far less steep and difficult fossen nearby, the two began their ascent with the usual hesitation. Rob, according to Henry, insisted on carrying the pack, rather than hauling it. Consequently he tired quickly. The first five pitches were straightforward enough, just steep and intricate ice meandering through several overlaps, but culminating in a mixed rock and ice traverse to the left, the first hard section, which was led elegantly by Rob.

Taylor, hardly a newcomer to the medium, was duly impressed with the type of climbing they had discovered, and also with the creative and innovative technique displayed by

Taylor on the initial pitches of the Vettifossen/Henry Barber Collection

his partner. In an article for *Climbing* magazine after the trip, Rob wrote,

> I wasn't long in Norway (in fact, the first day) before I realized something was radically different about this Nordic ice which completely altered my preconceived notions of waterfalls. What, no ice bashing here? . . . . These fossen presented the most diverse and delicate ice I'd ever come across: hellenic columns, off-width cracks, bombay chimneys, ballroom caves, shattered pillars, por-

celain pedestals, mirror-like slabs, and even deep blue twisting tunnels — all capped possibly by an immense ice parosol dripping crystalline eighty-foot stalactites. The possibilities in a single pitch were incredible, never mind an entire climb . . . . Normal ice-climbing techniques allow one to make his route where he chooses, necessitating that he only string together a series of duplicate 5.6 face moves one after another . . . . 'Bloody desperate,' I thought, and desperate situations generally call for drastic measures which fortunately Henry obliged to supply. In this type of climbing, as I soon found out, finesse, not strength, was the key ingredient . . . . Henry amazed me as he effortlessly drifted up the most fragile, unlikely looking ice: stemming, bridging, jamming, pinch gripping, laybacking and chimneying, employing every rock climbing technique I'd ever seen and a few new ones . . . . Countless times in a single pitch he would alter his style to suit his needs, often leading out the better part of a rope length without a single placement, his axes safely stowed away in their holsters. The advantages of this technique were immediately obvious.

On the fifth pitch, Rob and Henry encountered the ominous overhangs, with seemingly no way around them. By the grace of the fates, a ramp appeared that led around the overlap and on into the channel. During this pitch, Henry recalls that the climb took on an added seriousness.

We came out of a cave on the fifth pitch, onto a vertical column that was streaming with water. It didn't matter what you were wearing. You still got soaked to the skin. At this point, Rob was getting very freaked. We knew that if we wanted to rappel off, we'd better do it quick. A bivouac would have been dodgy because there were very few ledges up in the channel, and most of our gear was wet. To top things off, our water bottle had leaked all over everything.

We reached these huge overhangs on that pitch. The thing that scared us was that they were only connected by

*Taylor leading mixed ground to circumvent the ice roof/Henry Barber
Collection*

a meter or so of ice. A semi-trailer hanging off the wall, connected by something as big as an armchair. We traversed around right to get by the thing — we'd decided to commit ourselves after some discussion — and I was laybacking up a thick icicle. My head touched a huge block. It fell right onto my forehead. I got a few short cuts on my head, and blood was everywhere. I felt faint but kept climbing and made it to a two-meter-square stance that was connected by about a half-meter of ice. That really terrified us. It was about 2 P.M., and we had essentially committed ourselves, as we had bypassed these huge overhangs.

Rob recalls Henry's injury as something of "a blow" to the confidence that he felt was necessary for the completion of the climb.

I think that his injury was much worse for me because I had to go around that corner and begin moving up, seeing all of these red blotches all over the ice. Then I get up to the belay stance, and here's this person with blood streaming down his face and all over his clothes. That was rather shocking for me. I began suggesting that maybe it would be better if we went down because he'd nearly fainted. Henry was much better at the type of climbing that we found on the Vettisfossen, so I put a lot of confidence in him when we decided to go on.

The ice became extremely steep for the remaining six pitches. Barber says of his battered condition that

it had hurt me, but I wasn't out of it by any means; I couldn't be because Rob didn't really want to go on. He'd never climbed anything like this before. I had all of the experience gained on Bridalveil, and knew there had to be a way off.

During the hundred meters between the fifth and eighth pitches, there was grave concern as to whether there was, in fact, a way off. On the ninth pitch, they again encountered an overhang too large and delicate to climb. This overlap ran the width of the icefall, but in the back they found a chimney leading through to the vertical ice above. Rob remembers he had to take off his small pack to fit through the hole they climbed. They both agree that the chimney was "the key to making the climb." It was late in the afternoon, and the sun sank rapidly. Both were tired and wondering if another obstacle might remain — one that they might not be able to circumvent. Henry was moving "flat out, just praying that we'd make it."

Both climbers' nerves were on edge, and dusk was fast approaching.

It seemed to us that we were very close, but the trees on top of the route still looked very small from the top of the ninth pitch. Rob was exhausted from carrying the pack, and he wasn't up to leading any more of the climb. We were both psyched-out because we simply did not know what was up there.

After two more pitches, Henry pulled over the top bulges just as darkness came to the hanging tangle of white ice. He remembers looking through the thin ice at the top. The main force of the enormous waterfall was pulsing less than a meter beneath him. Its movement was humbling. He watched the source of the Vettisfossen's power briefly, through the fragile and uncertain veneer of its surface, and then rushed on.

Taylor began climbing the last pitch after the light had left the climb, but providentially the moon rose. He fell several frightening times, snapping the rope taut in the darkness. Exhausted, he finished the last section by climbing up the rope on Jumars; in confusion, he dropped one of them 300 meters to the ground. It was 8 P.M., eleven pitches and thirteen hours after the beginning of the ordeal.

To Henry the route was "the best ice climbing adventure I've ever had," while Rob felt that "nothing's impossible after that particular ice climb." Both assessments echo pronouncements made by Lowe and Weiss after their first ascent of

Barber leading on the steep pillar/Tomas Carlstrom

Bridalveil three years earlier. In the years since the Vettisfossen, though, an insidious historical revisionism has surfaced in their accounts, the way ascendant barons or presidents rework their humble origins or their people's pasts to fit their current perspective. Today, because of events that transpired in Africa a year later, Henry and Rob remember little details of the trip that might have otherwise been lost or discarded. They burnish their remembrances and squeeze meaning out of every action or statement, to show how each of them should have known what was to come. Henry recalls Rob's lack of interest in driving seven hundred kilometers in two days to see the famous Troll Wall, "but I never thought that it would translate into Rob's not going rock climbing when we sat around Nairobi for eight days." And Rob now looks at Henry's forcefulness in going on in spite of his bleeding head injury and dizziness in a far different light, viewed with hindsight after Africa.

Very difficult ice routes have been climbed in Norway by both locals and foreigners since Barber and Taylor's climb. At the time, Henry maintains, "there were only five or six real ice climbers in Norway," but the foreign alpine press has carried accounts of much action in successive seasons following their venture. The Poles and Czechs were always on climbs of the huge Troll Wall, and the British climbed on everything else that was steep and frozen. Rob has remarked that "our climbing there was to the Norwegians the greatest thing since the explorations of C. C. Slingsby," the British exploratory climber active after the turn of the century. True to local ethics, few details of their climbs were disclosed in print. Yet a noted Yosemite climber commented, a year after the ascent, "It took them eighteen hours to climb that? Awfully slow, wasn't it?" A product advertisement had mistakenly given that figure. Whether they acknowledge the pressure to perform or not, "professional" climbers are well aware that their economic well-being, as well as their pride, is dependent on doing routes like the Vettisfossen. Things have to look good.

The business side of the venture was ascendant later, back at home. There were the usual slide shows and articles. Henry was representing Bannana climbing equipment at the time. Rob, who seldom had a regular job outside of the family summer camp business, was always freelancing and had some contacts at W. L. Gore in Maryland, makers of a revolutionary new breathable yet waterproof material called Gore-Tex. Rob set up a meeting with Gore to discuss use of Henry's photos of Rob's Gore-Tex suit in action in Norway. When they arrived, Henry took over the meeting. He looked the Gore executives in the eye, and proceeded to tell them how he could help them in marketing and advertising. Henry asserts,

> I had the ideas and he didn't. I said to Rob before the meeting, "Rob, if you have anything to interject, do so; if you have a plan, speak up."

Rob had relatively little to say in the face of Henry's bold move and solid business acumen.

As a result of his constant contact with British climbing, Henry

> was going on what Doug Scott and others had done in Britain: it's all consumer product association. It doesn't matter if a guy is going to climb Mount Everest or not; if he knows a suit went to the top with Scott, he's going to buy that suit.

In a series of discussions, Henry sat down with the Gore people and outlined several potential ad campaigns and slide shows. The only idea they eventually used in the U.S., though their European campaign benefitted from the full range of promotional observations, was a full-page color photographic ad for magazines featuring a small shot of the frozen Vettisfossen, and Rob in his one-piece Gore-Tex suit (actually shot on a very impressive 200-meter climb behind Carlstrom's house). Henry was well paid for the shot, which was later misplaced, and he and Rob received Gore-Tex products to take on a proposed major climb in Africa. Barber admits that he probably did upstage Rob then.

> But I don't feel badly about it. I had the plan and the ideas, and he didn't get it together. He's not forceful, that's his problem. What am I to do? Go fly all the way to Philadelphia and then sit there? No way, Jose. It's not me.

The trip to Norway had been near-perfect. It had all the right ingredients roughly in the proper ratios. The climbs were visually bold for slide shows and business; there was no pressure, no local scene to contend with, but there was plenty of opportunity for great skiing and good times. However, Henry, who felt himself liberated from motivation stemming from others, suffered a rude awakening towards the end of his stay in Norway. He borrowed the Carlstroms' car in order to drive south to the Romsdal region, to take pictures of the countryside and study the Troll Wall (one of the largest in the world) for possibilities of a first free ascent on an existing route. He decided to stop and see a man named Arne Randers Heen, a veteran climber at the age of seventy. In 1958, Randers Heen managed a new route on the Troll Wall in the time of fourteen hours. In 1968, he repeated the route when he was close to seventy, this time taking twelve hours to reach the top. No one else had done the route in less than a day, without at least one bivouac.

Barber went to Heen's home in Andalsnes, a town near the massive cliff. He ended up in a situation very unlike what he is accustomed to in climbing circles.

I was hoping to talk with him about his routes on the Troll Wall, and maybe take a hike with him out to see the Mardalsfossen. Usually, when I go to a new climbing area, I get the feeling that everybody wants to meet me and talk with me, and that they're impressed with what I've done. But this guy had never heard of me and treated me like a two-year-old hoping to go climbing with a great hero. I was upset with him. He was an old guy, and that probably had a lot to do with it. But at the same time, it felt good to be in a place where nobody had any knowledge of my reputation.

It wasn't hero worship that drew me to see him. The whole visit, though, was extremely awkward. He didn't treat me with respect. He just nonchalantly showed me a few tourist photos to get me on my way. He thought that I was in the Troll Wall area to climb. No matter how much I tried to explain to him, I couldn't make him understand that I was just there to look, and that I was climbing elsewhere in Norway. He couldn't fathom that there was climbing outside of this region, and that I was ice climbing on waterfalls — that there was something else to this sport he was involved in on the Troll Wall. It was great, though, because this guy wasn't trying to curry favor with me.

Henry had finally managed to travel outside the circumference of his fame.

10

The Dream of Kilimanjaro

*T*HE OPPRESSIVE TROPICAL HEAT, crawling all over them with its insistent humidity, hit the duo immediately upon disembarking from the two-day-long BOAC flight. Nairobi, Africa, Kilimanjaro — it had all seemed abstract until now.

As soon as they managed to locate their host, an expatriot Englishman named Iain Allen, whom Henry had met in Yosemite, Barber insisted on heading out to the local crag — to something active and familiar. With Ian Howell, Allen's regular climbing partner and another of the best in East Africa, Henry and Iain headed out to the Lukenia crag not far from town to try a new start to a climb known as the Owl. Rob had broken his toe only months before while playing squash, and was unable to force his foot into tight-fitting rock shoes. He went along to take photographs and to be with Howell again, whom he had met briefly in Scotland.

Lukenia was frequented by some very gymnastic baboons. Henry was told about the visit to the area of the English big wall climber and Himalayan veteran Doug Scott.

On one route, Scott pulled over a bulge on these huge pockets, and there were five baboons sitting on this ledge. He screamed and nearly jumped off forty meters to the ground. The baboons climb all over the slabs on the cliff. There's slime from their paws all over the place. They don't use chalk, so everything's greasy. I was trying this new start without any protection and a huge two-meter cactus below me. Allen was telling me that he saw a baboon do this start in about twelve seconds one day, and

*Giraffe with Hell's Gate Gorge in background, Great Rift Valley, Kenya/
Henry Barber Collection*

I was believing him. They actually do some slab climbs just like glass that you could never conceive of.

As Henry had imagined, the wildlife was distracting in its abundance. From the top of the crag, he could see giraffes on the plains below. On another route that Allen and he did that afternoon, after failing on the proposed start to the Owl, Henry had to contend with a nest of overly protective birds in the midst of a difficult portion of the route.

It was pretty frightening, especially as I was just off the plane, tired, and had not climbed more than four days during the whole of the previous autumn.

*Two consistent pioneers in East African climbing: Ian Howell (foreground)
and Iain Allen/Henry Barber Collection*

The layoff, unprecedented for Barber, had been due to
his business obligations. Although the main objective of this
trip was the Breach Icicle, Henry had not been out on ice in the
last nine months, and he was not particularly fit. He had a
house to keep up and had made a conscious shift of his primary focus from day-to-day extreme climbing to a wealth of
business opportunities — guiding, consulting, photography,
and big expeditions with demonstrable financial rewards.
Soon after their arrival on December 30, it came out that he
had to be back in Houston for a sports show on the morning of
January 23, although Taylor was planning to spend another
few weeks on the continent. It was the first time Henry had felt
pressure to perform a particular climb within a time con-
straint. He and Taylor had to warm up, knock off a few good
routes, and then go home. It was all clear-cut.

After their success on the Vettisfossen, Henry and Rob had begun scheming on a grand scale. They decided to climb in a continent entirely new to both, and to attempt an unclimbed ice route on Africa's highest mountain, Kilimanjaro. It would involve severe climbing on vertical ice at the top of the route, at an altitude just under 6,000 meters (18,000 feet). The route had been explored once before, but the steep ice repelled the effort. Yvon Chouinard, Johnny Cunningham, and Ian and Iain knew about it, and Doug Scott had been rained off it only months before. Henry felt that they were the ones to climb it. It was a chance to experience a whole new climbing scene, as he had in Australia, and to encounter cultures he had never witnessed before. Like Norway, Africa fitted his criterion of places ungoverned by local competition and relatively devoid of pressure. But above all, the African outing was very much a business proposition. Rob and Henry had convinced equipment makers to donate gear in return for advertising photographs of the items in use, and they lined up potential articles for *Outside* and *National Geographic* magazines. The Breach Wall had not been done before, and everyone in the international class of mountaineers knew it.

Little could Henry have anticipated that the African trip would be the worst of his career, involving a near-fatal accident, desperate rescue efforts, the irrevocable destruction of a friendship, and a lingering controversy the like of which has been seen only a few times in mountaineering history. It is not, even today, the sort of controversy that is likely ever to be resolved.

Things began to go wrong even before Henry left the States. A week prior to his departure, he found that his passport had been lost in the mail, en route from Boston to the Kenyan consulate in New York. Efforts to locate it were continually frustrated, leaving Henry despondent. In the wake of delayed plane flights and large excess baggage costs, the pair finally arrived in Nairobi, already alert to the crossed stars hovering above the journey. The two-week delay meant that Iain Allen, who had taken time off to climb with them, could spend only five days with them.

On their second day in Africa, the Americans were

whisked off by Howell and Allen to Mount Kenya on a standard weekend jaunt for the locals, though blessed in this case by an extra day due to the New Year's holiday. Mount Kenya is the second highest peak in East Africa, a volcanic cone rising high above the surrounding plateau to 5,200 meters (17,000 feet) and only a few hours' drive north and east from Nairobi.

> When we finally made it to Mount Kenya National Park, I had a little trouble adjusting to the environment. We started hiking up towards the peak — it's about a seven-hour hike — and immediately got into the jungle, which kept getting more dense all the time. In some places, you can't see more than a few meters into the jungle from clearings. I was mostly worried about the Cape buffaloes. They're supposed to be mean as hell. The English climber Rusty Baillie once spent fourteen hours in a tree on this hike. We never saw any, though I was always looking for the biggest trees, nevertheless. The snakes in the area, as well as all the other wildlife, had me pretty gripped up.

Here, for the first time, the seeds of dissention between the two friends and partners began to sprout. On the hike in, Rob, in much better shape than Henry, dashed ahead often, and grew impatient with Henry's slow progress, annoyed at his failure to get in top shape. Henry, in turn, felt that Rob's behavior betrayed a certain lack of poise.

> He was getting very apprehensive about the climb, about whether we could do it in one day, whether it was in the right shape for climbing, whether we'd get pulmonary edema . . . .

Pulmonary edema is a rare but potentially fatal condition that can afflict even experienced climbers going suddenly to high altitudes. Their hike ascended forthrightly from 3,600 to 4,400 meters elevation. Barber continued,

> He's a really fine climber, but I think he was too hyped to

*Porters carrying in an unusual style on Mount Kenya/Henry Barber
Collection*

be in the mountains at that time. He was walking like
crazy, almost running up the trail. He tends to worry
quite a bit.

Taylor maintains that "concern" is more descriptive of his
mental state than "worry" — and that concern is a necessary
part of survival in the mountains.

That night Henry was suffering from the altitude at the
high hut. In the morning, Rob "practically ran up to the climb"
— the famous Diamond Ice Couloir, first climbed by the direct
headwall route by Chouinard and Covington a few years
earlier, and considered at the time the hardest ice climb in
Africa. Taylor offered Henry the first lead. After an interesting initial pitch, Henry felt the rest of the climb was "boring."
At 4,800 meters the steep headwall loomed, seventy meters of
columnar ice curtains and mist. It was Rob's lead, and an
opportunity for training on vertical ice at altitude, though 700
meters lower than what they would confront on the Breach
Wall.

Henry was disconcerted by the way Taylor went at it.

We had already climbed four hundred meters from the hut. Rob was tired but got in high gear for the headwall pitch — he's much better at that type of climbing than I am — but I was just beginning to notice, on that pitch, an aggressiveness in his climbing that I'd never seen before. This was it for him: vertical ice climbing at 4,800 meters. To him, I think that this was something that had to be done, not something to be enjoyed. It was the crux of this 500-meter route, and it was important to him to get it done with as quickly as possible. He simply wasn't taking the care that he usually does.

On the summit snowfields, Rob articulated his fears of avalanche danger. He had been caught in a bad slide on Ben Nevis five years earlier, and had worked as a U. S. Forest Service snow ranger. To his way of thinking, Henry was too leisurely and oblivious to the danger. Henry thought Rob worried too much, but he was equally concerned about the dangers and agreed to move up the left side of the open snowfield. They reached the summit about 54 hours after arriving in Africa, and despite that accomplishment, felt terrible. It was New Year's Day and their rush up so high, so fast, had given them brutal headaches and nausea appropriate to the holiday, though accomplished without the aid of any liquor. After a miserable bivouac on the summit, the two descended in strong winds. Neither had been very satisfied with the climb, and the irritations were growing between them. While waiting for Howell and Allen to return from their successful attempt of a hard new route on the Diamond Buttress, the pair was shocked to see the Diamond Couloir let loose in a momentous avalanche, sweeping the entire gully clean of hundreds of tons of snow and ice. They had been lucky, and had gotten away with it.

The party then returned to Nairobi to climb on a nearby crag called Hell's Gate. More problems with travel plans cropped up. Henry was growing disillusioned with the whole continent.

The initial pitch of the Diamond Ice Couloir on Mount Kenya with Barber leading/Rob Taylor

Africans are incredibly hard to deal with. They're all very slow. They don't really take much notice when someone like me or Rob is trying to get somewhere or get something done. If you go into a hospital and say, "My wife's just had a heart attack, please do something," the chance that someone there will react is very slim. They're just calm and cool. They don't care. The more you make a

245

scene, the less they'll do, and the more obstinate they become. It's the most aggravating place I've ever been. Once, when we got back from Mount Kenya, I tried to get a traveler's check cashed. I ended up making a scene because this guy wouldn't do it for me. As soon as I got irate, he just walked away and came back only when I realized that I had to play his game to get this thing cashed. The reason they are this way is that they've had cultures pushed on them from all over the world. Two hundred years of French, English, and American technology thrown at them in about sixty years. It's just blown them away.

Everything was moving slowly, bogged in the inexhaustibly patient pace of a traditional society in the Third World. No individual, no effort of will, could change this. Henry's carefully evolved trip model of blistering hit-and-run climbing tactics, amid bounteous fraternizing and lucrative slide shows, seemed inapplicable here. For the first time, things were happening of their own accord.

They drove out to Hell's Gate the following day. The drive took them through dry thorn plains in which wildlife was abundant. They learned from Allen and Howell the extent to which problems had developed in maintaining the game. Curio shops all over Kenya specialized in bizarre souvenirs: ashtrays made from the paws of lions and lamp-posts made from the legs of giraffes. The discussion went from the academic to the practical at Hell's Gate.

Sure, I've been scared by snakes and other animals before, but not like I was at Hell's Gate. My concern at this crag had to do with snakes and African bees. It took me about five minutes to walk forty meters through the high grass on the way to the cliff. I told Ian that I was going to bring a torch back to the place and burn the daylights out of all this grass. He told me that there used to be cattle that kept the grass short. And I asked him, "Well, why don't they keep them here now?"

"Well," he said, "they were all getting killed by snakes."

First free ascent of Stage Fright/Bob Barton

And these snakes that they have there are in the big time: black mambas and spitting cobras. If you make it by all of them, you still have the bees to deal with. When John Temple was climbing there a few years ago, he got stung by over twelve hundred bees when he was in the middle of a climb. He was in the hospital for about two weeks. Most people simply would have died. I believe Rob's very allergic to bee stings, so he walked around for awhile and then ended up sitting in the car for the whole day, in ninety-five degree heat, with all of the windows rolled up. He was petrified. I wasn't doing much better. On the first pitch that we did, the moderate climbing that I was on seemed like 5.10 with loose rock. Going through all of the bushes that were on the cliff really did it to me, because that's where the bees usually hang out. While we were walking down off the first climb, I whipped around to Ian and said, "Quick! Ian! Look at that African bee right there."

"Don't worry," he said.

"What do you mean, don't worry? Shit, that is an African bee!"

"Yeah, but it's only one of them. Just be worried when it goes away to get its friends." What they do is to go off and get huge swarms of their buddies when they get pissed off at you. Once, on a climb called Vampire, one of them was buzzing up and down my shirt. He went away and two came back. Then three were there in a little while. I was gripped when all of them went away. I got out of the area pretty fast.

Henry did the first free ascent of Stagefright with two Scots just back from Kilimanjaro, then began another route during which he found out more about the objective dangers of the area. Pulling over a ledge halfway through the climb, he found the remains of an antelope, killed and flown to the place by a lammergeier, an eagle-like bird, only bigger. Although the lammergeiers gave the climbers no trouble on that particular climb, the men still had to contend with 5.10 difficulty, and thus were unable to manage the climb before dark. Again, Henry was terrified, this time because of the wild dogs.

I almost walked off the cliff twice because of all the corners at the top. And these wild dogs were really making me quite worried. They're the most insidious killers in Africa. Packs of ten or twelve of them go along and nip at the heels of a zebra, chasing it in circles while another pack of dogs sits and rests, then takes over when the others need a break. Most of the time they just kill for fun. Then there are the hyenas, which are really strong. Stories have it that at night they like to come up while you're sleeping and bite you right in the face.

Another day at Lukenia helped ease the strain of climbing at Hell's Gate. Rob still refrained from climbing. It was all he could do to get on heavy ice boots. While Rob read and took photographs, Henry was fast slipping back into the pace he'd cultivated in Australia, pushing to do as much rock climbing as possible in the short amount of time available. He eliminated the aid from two routes there, and then went back to Hell's Gate and did what he thought to be the "classic rock climb in Africa." This was a route called Andromeda. Henry eliminated the aid on two pitches, making it go all free. Each of the six pitches on the climb was 5.10, except for the last, which involved 5.8 climbing on rock that resembled solidified mud.

It was hot and I was tired. I didn't have the endurance that I used to in going for it all the time. There were so many things in the trip that had already gotten us down — the plane hassles, the disillusionment of the climb on the Diamond Couloir, the breakage of two cameras, and the very little time we had left as a result of the Kenyan embassy losing my passport — that I simply wasn't as energetic for the climb as I could have been.

The crux section came on the fifth pitch. I was trying to figure out how to do a mantle problem to eliminate a point of aid, and I noticed that the whole tower I was stemming off of was rocking back and forth. I started screaming at Ian, calling him a lot of very bad things. I felt like I'd gotten the biggest sandbag ever. After what seemed like two hours, I figured out the move.

With the completion of Andromeda, the six-day period of rock climbing in Kenya ended. Mimicking in miniature his performance in Australia three years earlier, Henry had completed six first free ascents of routes now considered so difficult that the grading system (modeled after Australia's) had to be expanded upwards by several grades. Barber and Taylor had only enough time left to climb the route on Kilimanjaro and go home. More complications developed, however, when the two were scheduled to fly to Arusha, in Tanzania, two hundred kilometers from Nairobi. The border between Kenya and Tanzania had recently closed due to an airline dispute in the area, and they were forced to fly 1,100 kilometers north to Addis Ababa in Ethiopia, then 1,300 kilometers south to Arusha. It was another sign. Their 7 A.M. flight to Addis Ababa left at five in the afternoon. They spent the night in Addis Ababa, with Taylor sure that customs had lost his innoculation

High on the Umbwe approach route/Henry Barber Collection

booklet, which in Africa, he felt, was more important than one's passport. Henry seemed to be uninterested. Rob's fears about his health records were groundless, though, and they were back at the airport well in time for their 11 A.M. flight to Arusha, which left at 6 P.M.

Rob had been worrying a lot the day before about his booklet and about being late — we only had nine days to do Kili. I'd been telling him that there wasn't a thing he could do. But on the second day, I was bullshit. We sat in a lounge with about a hundred Pakistanis for the whole afternoon. The Ethiopians were moving their troops around, getting ready for the invasion of Somalia, by using the commercial airlines.

250

As a result of the inconvenience that they've caused you, the airline gives you a pass for a free cup of coffee. One guy came up to the bar and ran off with another guy's coffee. That guy demanded two coffees, got them, and went back to his seat. Before you knew it, there were about forty Pakistanis up there yelling and screaming and pushing, all wanting two coffees. I couldn't believe how greedy and rude these people were. I wanted to hurt them, badly. When we finally got on a bus that would take us to the plane, I was the last person on. Naturally, I'd be first onto the plane. When I got off the bus, in about five seconds there were over seventy Pakistanis racing in front of me for the plane, all pushing and falling all over the place. It was ugly. Just as I was about to get on the plane, a guy comes up with his kid. The kid sneaks by me. I jammed my hand across the guy's face, blocking his way and said, "Sir, I'd like you to understand one thing. You're going to wait for me to get on this plane. I think that you're rude, that you're an animal and that you're not getting on in front of me." I wanted to kill the guy and throw him over the edge. Rob was astounded. He couldn't believe what animals these people were.

In spite of all obstacles, the climbers finally got to the boundary of Kilimanjaro National Park. They began the hike upward, north towards the peak from the town of Moshi. The walk along the Umbwe route to the southwest-facing Breach Wall is two days through dense jungle. The wall is in as inaccessible a place as the immense mountain has to offer. Topping off a long walk, a scramble up 1,500 meters of the mountain's lower defenses is necessary just to reach the final great ice pillar leading to the summit at 5,895 meters (19,340 feet).

The sky was invisible through the dense tropical trees on the way in. The pair had been told the story of a hang glider pilot who had crashed in the jungle some years before after trying to fly down the Kersten Glacier; he had never been found. There was also a tale of two Dutch boys who had disappeared forever from the Umbwe. The stories brought a touch of foreboding, in part because of their ill luck thus far, and also because they had not signed in with the park officials.

251

The Breach Wall, Mount Kilimanjaro/Henry Barber Collection

They planned to do the route and get out again in six days, yet they knew so little about it that they were unable to feel confident about their plans. The two Scots at Hell's Gate had been on the Heim recently, doing the first ascent of a new variation, and had given the pair information about the trails and landmarks. Henry remembers not being particularly interested in these details, although "Rob was grilling them. It's not in my character to study topo maps and route descriptions," since he likes to go into situations totally experientially. Rob and Iain Allen, on the other hand, recall Henry gleaning route descriptions. In any event, he had not read the excellent local guidebook route writeups when they began their trek.

Rob ran ahead, as always, perhaps because of his hiking style or somewhat in fear of the wildlife and forest, or possibly because Henry was photographing and less keyed up. Barber gets goosebumps even now when he thinks about that hike.

The denseness of the place was disorienting. And, of course, there were the animals. We'd both freeze if we heard anything. Just a bird going through the trees was enough to make me run for Rob.

The most nerve-wracking part of the hike was knowing about a leopard that had its territory right on the trail. Iain Allen and two friends were once camped at a spring

Starting to solo on the second day of the Breach Wall. Several thousand feet of climbing lead across the face of the icicle. An amazingly rapid descent was made of this on the retreat/Henry Barber Collection

where everybody stops. They spent all night keeping this leopard away from their tent, throwing rocks at it and yelling. They were so terrified that they just hiked out the next morning when they saw it on the trail. Leopards are never supposed to be out in the middle of the day. The night we spent near there freaked us out, even though we never saw the animal.

The trail emerged from the jungle and onto a steep, narrow ridge leading from the jungle to the base of the peak. Early on the second day, they arrived at the Barranco Bivouac, and were forced to spend the rest of the day and night there due to rain, cramping the schedule even more. In an attempt to beat the weather, they left early the next morning on the approach to the ice, working through the complicated Heim glacier icefall of jumbled ice blocks and cliffs. The glacier lay below and to the right of a long traverse running to the west above precipitous cliff bands and leading to the culminating icicle. At noon, in thick fog and clouds that enveloped the route, the two reached the Window Buttress and were forced to wait there for the remainder of the day. The heavy mists caused rapid deterioration of the ice and snow, turning hard-packed névé into slush and hollow ice in hours. Henry was still hoping to be on the ice wall the next day, to master it and sprint up to the summit, but Rob was beginning to have reservations.

> We were thinking that the fifth day was going to be the day. We got up and all of the clouds started to disappear. Soloing rapidly across the icefields, Rob was way out in front. He always was from the very beginning of the hike, always running. The last hundred meters or so of travers-ing required a rope, as the slope steepened and the condi-tions deteriorated. We'd gone very fast, about 1,000 me-ters of climbing in about four hours. It wasn't fast enough, though, because the clouds were back in by the time we arrived at the icicle.

At this point, Rob, who had not liked the weather and the variable temperatures because he felt that they might make a difference on the vertical ice hovering above, wanted to biv-ouac and await the early morning, when the ice would be more solidly frozen in place from the night's low temperatures. A long, heated discussion ensued. Rob was "100 percent against going on," but Barber was for it. Henry argued that it was crazy to wait that long after coming so far on a tight schedule, when they could reach the summit by dinnertime. Besides, Henry had to leave in three days, and food and fuel were low.

Henry remembers several options that were discussed: going up on the icicle immediately, bivouacking and waiting until early morning, aiding part of it if necessary, and climbing left and looking at the wall there. It was just starting to get warm, so he felt that an hour and a half could be safely spent working on the ice, to see if it would go. If not then, they would be in a better position to try it on the morrow.

Moving quickly high on the Breach Wall/Henry Barber Collection

It was a dangerous alternative but a reasonable one, and I wanted to go for it. I know myself and when to back off. The ice was really rotten, lots of air in it, not dripping water although the sun was just hitting it. It looked like the ice at the edge of a pond, sugary, real unstable and dangerous. I might have been pushy, to keep my drive up, and because from my experience on the Vettisfossen, Rob was ready to give up sooner. I'm sure he wasn't psyched about it. After examining the possibilities, I asked if he wanted to try it, or if he wanted me to? I didn't care, as it was pretty big and we expected to get a couple of pitches out of it. The sun was taking a lot out of us, both sweaty and dehydrated, and he may have been more tired. If it had been me, I might very well have decided to do the first pitch, rather than lead the second, higher one after hard climbing at altitude.

Few pitches, if any, that technically difficult had been climbed at that altitude at the time, although routes in the Karakorum and in Nepal in the following years matched the standard.

Henry felt it was a relatively controlled situation. They could try it, or go over to the Heim and finish on it if necessary, and still each could reach new personal altitude records and have a great adventure.

> We would have at least learned the lesson of waiting for things to come into shape, and not to underestimate big and unknown mountains.

It was a personal decision, Henry emphasizes, since climbers at that level of skill do not get talked into difficult leads about which they feel compromised.

Rob finally agreed to go on. He climbed cautiously, placing a secure ice screw in good ice not seven meters up. He recalled that "It was really bad up there." Describing the ice as "vertical slush," Taylor later concluded that he should not have forced the climb. He blamed Barber, in part, for not seeing the difference between a major mountain and a shorter, safer climb such as the Vettisfossen.

As Henry reconstructs the next few minutes:

> By now it was warm enough that the ice was very porous and bad. Just like before, Rob was perhaps trying to go too fast. There's no question that he's one of the best, but on that climb, as on the Diamond Couloir, he didn't have the poise that he usually has. He was just too anxious for these routes. His foot would slip, and instead of holding himself with his tools and neatly placing the foot again, he'd scramble a little. I was thinking that we were trying too hard. I called up to him and said that if it was too hard, we'd just aid that section and climb the rest, that he just shouldn't worry about it all that much. I was concerned about him. This climb was seeming to possess him. After he got his first screw in, I just stopped taking pictures. I knew something was wrong.

According to Rob, the screw was "bomb-proof." He climbed only a meter or two higher; then, as he would later recall, an ice pedestal snapped as he attempted a layback maneuver on it and he fell. The fall should have been short and controlled, but Barber was caught unaware, allowing some slippage, and natural stretch in the rope permitted more. Taylor smashed into a ledge below Barber's belay stance. Dangling from the rope, he felt pain in his left leg, and looked down in horror to see, "instead . . . of my red and blue supergator, . . . only the 12 points of my Chouinard crampons and my boot sole, the arch of which was touching my calf."

Bickering and disagreement among climbers are nothing novel, and many successful expeditions have been torn by very deep dissention. Usually, however, an accident pulls the feuding members back together, uniting them in the common cause of rescue, even in the face of great personal risk. What followed Rob Taylor's breaking his ankle on Kilimanjaro depends on the teller of the tale somewhat. After he had reached civilization again, Rob was so bitter about the treatment he felt he had received from Henry during the retreat and afterward that he broke a time-honored agreement among climbers not to air their dirty linen in public. In the July-August 1978 issue of *Climbing,* Rob offered his version of the story in a scathing article called "A Breach of Faith," later reprinted in *Mountain.*

According to Rob, the first thing Henry said was, "Are you sure it's broken?" Henry remembers that

> I just smiled at him and said something like, "Just like everything else on this trip, isn't it?" What could I say? He was in incredible pain and was apologizing to me. I just told him to stop his sniveling or I'd leave him there. I was so pissed, not at him, but just at our trip as a whole. If we'd believed in karma, we'd never have been up there in the first place. There was no remorse, no worry. It was just hitting me that something like this was bound to happen. We'd lost his tools and a screw, so there wasn't much left. I lowered him and climbed over to him. It was amazing he didn't go into shock. He was very lucid, and as soon as I told him to cut the whining or I'd leave him there, he put

on the most courageous performance I've ever seen or heard about in a human being. He knew I was going to do everything I could for him.

Henry next made a surprising suggestion: that he should lead the icicle, with Taylor jumaring up after him. Barber would then go down the tourist route from the summit for help. Taylor replied that he was going "nowhere but down . . . ."

Henry insists that the idea of going up the route was based on calculations about rescue possibilities, and nothing more. It looked to him as though the hardest climbing ended only about ten meters above the point from which Rob had fallen. By going for help, Henry could have rounded up porters to carry Rob off. In the past, pulmonary edema victims had been evacuated off the gentle tourist route in as little as five hours.

Normally a leader would fall only two or three meters with a screw that close. Somehow the rope slid much farther in this case, perhaps due to rope stretch, slippage of the thin, wet nine-millimeter rope, and some normal brief inattentiveness by the belayer, who had been taking a few photographs a bit before the fall.

As they straightened out the ropes and looked at Rob's ankle, Henry reviewed all possible options. Rappelling straight down the Wall was not really feasible, since that direction held 700 meters of unclimbed, loose, and nearly vertical lava and there was not enough rock hardware available. Another option was for Henry to descend with Rob part way and then solo up the Heim, go over the summit, and get help. The final suggestion was to retreat down the way they had come. None of these potential plans now strikes Henry as clearly the one that seemed best to him at the time. Rob prevailed, arguing convincingly that a summit whiteout in mist or storm could last for days, and that the altitude would pose further medical risks.

The break in the ankle was a compound one, leaving the fibula nearly twenty centimeters away from the tibia and sticking out through the skin. In addition, Rob had broken bones in the top of his foot and had torn the rotator cuff. Gamely he started down, belayed by Henry, traversing back the way they had come. He managed to use his left knee "as a substitute foot" and cut steps for it with his axe in the fifty-degree ice slope. The rest of the morning was consumed in reaching an ice ledge less than a hundred meters away, a protected spot where the pair could bivouac and regroup.

Although he wanted to examine his foot, Rob insisted on continuing down right away, regardless of the conditions. He voiced strong concerns about staying at altitude and urged further descent after a brief respite.

After reaching the ledge, they managed to realign the bones to within three millimeters of their proper position, by virtue of Rob's solid medical training. Rob had some strong pain medication along, but heeding warnings about its effect at high altitude, he largely restricted himself to aspirin. For the first time on a major climb he mistakenly had brought along no antibiotics. Rob took command of his situation and made all the medical decisions, while Henry generally led the technical re-treat. As a result of his years of rescue work in Scotland and perhaps because of his temperament, Rob was always very conscious of proper first aid supplies and technique, while Henry, more a crag climber by training, had always been fairly casual about these subjects. With Henry's help, Taylor loosened the laces on his boot, but he refused to take it off for fear he would never be able to replace it.

In the middle of the ghastly effort of realigning the bloody, greasy bones, he began to think that the situation was hopeless, that he would die here 6,000 meters above sea level and 30 kilometers from the nearest hospital. "Long before I could hope to reach any proper medical assistance," he said, "I knew gangrene and infection would take its toll, making me beg for death." Rob resolved to fight on, however, knowing there was a slight chance of getting off alive, while lapsing into shock surely meant instant death.

Taylor wanted to head off again immediately; Henry felt that it was dangerous. The sun had partially melted huge hanging icicles above the proposed descent route. Shortly after the two had set Rob's ankle, boxcar-sized blocks of ice thundered down on that route, forcing them to wait out the afternoon and evening.

Setting off the following morning, they faced 1,200 meters of downward traversing to reach level ground. The ice was moderately steep, about fifty-five degrees. They had only seven ice screws and two ice tools to assist them both, since Rob had lost two tools in the fall. Henry had already taken apart his alpine hammer, as well as one of Rob's crampons, to use for the splint.

Rob on the pillar of the Breach Wall just before his fall/Henry Barber Collection

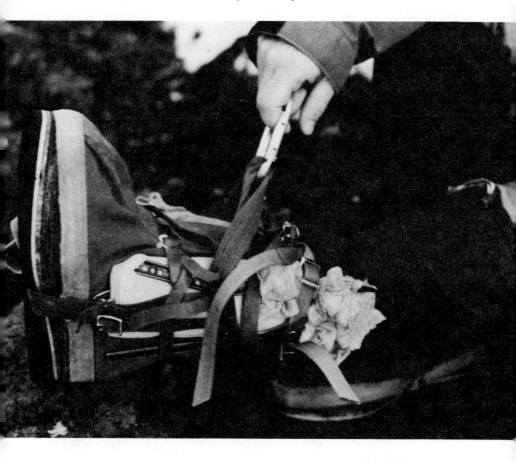

The splint used for Taylor's foot, consisting of foam from their packs and crampon pieces/Henry Barber Collection

Nevertheless, the two were able to reach their bivouac of two days earlier at the Window in five hours, covering about half the distance to the base of the Heim. They arrived there by 11 A.M., but were unable to go any farther because they were once again in dense clouds. Rob was exhausted, having alternately hopped and slid during the rappels, with Henry retrieving each screw afterward and then downclimbing to set up the next anchor. Rob tried every means possible of positioning his body to take the shock, and finally settled on facing headfirst downward and lying on his right side.

261

They descended using linked pendulums. Henry would anchor himself with his axe; Rob would then descend on belay and swing across on the rope on his side in a horizontal traverse. Once Rob was secured to his own axe, Henry would traverse another rope length above and repeat the operation. During one particularly long pendulum, Henry watched in horror as his axe, the only anchor for them both, rotated in the hard snow under the excessive load. Shortly thereafter, Rob's anchor pulled out, forcing him to come on Henry's waist, fifty meters below. This almost threw them both into a void a thousand meters deep. The process was extremely painful to Rob, who frequently questioned his ability to go on and who became somewhat delirious in his exhaustion. Virtually throughout the rest of the ordeal, he remained very lucid, however, and helped make all decisions. Barber praised Taylor's technical control as well: "I was always amazed how well Rob handled the ropes in his state; they never once snagged."

Blood ran onto the snow through Taylor's three pairs of socks, his boot, and his Supergator. Henry's threats of leaving him back at the icicle had spurred Rob on. What has been interpreted as his

> seeming lack of compassion was, I think, my defense mechanism to deal with what was happening. I felt really good and really strong, confident that I could get him out of there.

Vertigo crept up on both of them; they were unable to see, wondering what was below, lost in the thick mist, soft snow, and rumbling icefalls. Both of them began to become very frustrated and short with each other due to the impossibilities of descent in the rapidly changing conditions. Just after setting up their bivouac, they heard massive blocks of ice shattering on the terrain they had crossed just hours before, obliterating the route. The roar continued intermittently throughout the rest of the afternoon and long night. It was very close and very real.

They reached the Heim icefall, where they had begun the

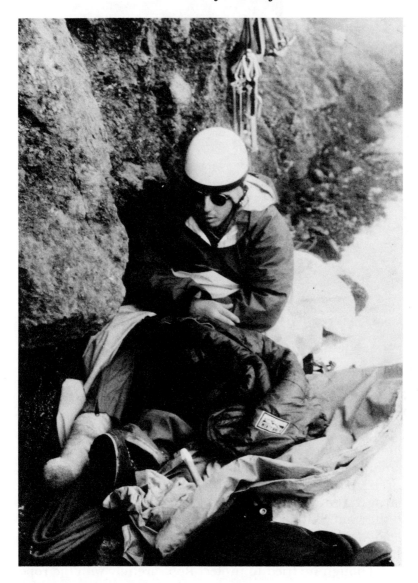

Taylor at the first bivouac after the accident/Henry Barber Collection

technical portion of the ascent, on the second day of the descent. The final screw was placed to allow them to lower over a high ice serac, the last obvious obstacle. From this point,

263

Rob hopping while doing his diagonal rappel on the second day of the descent/Henry Barber Collection

Henry lowered the semi-delirious patient two rope lengths at a time. Occasionally Rob would lose control and be stopped by the rope. Once while Rob was dazed and spinning in space, hanging from the overhanging lip of a serac, Henry was forced to solo downclimb with Rob's full weight tugging at his harness from a hundred meters lower down, stretching Henry to the limit. Barber, scared and exhausted, was feeling light-headed and fearing vertigo, since he had been giving most of the food and water to his partner.

Though he tried to protect Rob carefully with the rope every step of the way, sometimes the buildup of snow in his hands caused the rope to jump, and he would drop his injured companion abruptly for stretches of up to several meters. Finally, weaving through seracs and cliffs of ice, they arrived at the flat rock moraine at the head of the Heim. It was an enormous relief to both to be off technical terrain, once again free to stand and walk without fear.

Henry carried Rob on his back several hundred meters, to an obvious bivouac site beneath a very prominent boulder, so he would be protected from the elements and easy to find. It was near an arch they had seen on the way up, and there was a chance that Odd Eliassen, the renowned Norwegian alpinist who was working as a park official, might know it.

The skill and endurance Henry had shown in getting Rob down were truly remarkable. Responding to later criticism, Henry said,

> Put it this way. I don't think that more than just a handful of American climbers could have helped him more than I did.

Rob agrees with Henry's assessment of his technical performance: " . . .no one could have been more efficient in executing our retreat." And yet, Taylor came to feel that he was nothing but a "burden" to Barber, that nothing but a climbing rope linked them.

Both were exhausted, sapped by altitude, exertion, and uncertainty. It was about 11 A.M. of the third day of retreat, roughly forty-eight hours after the accident. Henry was thinking at the time that he was relieved to be off the ice, and that the descent had gone very well, considering Rob's condition and the lack of equipment. There was relatively little regret on his part that they had not made it to the summit; he remembers, "The only thing I felt burdened with during the descent was facing myself and doing the best job I could."

After making Rob comfortable, the pair discussed strategies for effecting the rescue. They reviewed options for Henry: to traverse and drop down 300 meters to the east to the standard route and its Horombo Hut, staying mostly above treeline; to go down the Umbwe through the jungle (the way they had ascended) to the mission at its base, regardless of the danger from the leopard's den; or, for Henry to bivouac just above the jungle on the Umbwe ridge and sprint through all of the jungle at first light the following day. They agreed that the second option was too dangerous in the face of darkness because the Umbwe was rough and there was the risk of encountering the leopard, about which Rob felt strongly. On the other hand, Henry reflects, Rob was uncomfortable with the third possibility, since it would greatly delay the response time of a rescue team, wasting the entire night. They settled on the Horombo option. From talking with the Scots, Henry recollects,

> we believed that there was a radio, and some "rangers" — they call them rangers, but they're not, just a few local Tanzanian porters — in the hut.

Rob noticed what seemed to him an odd packing job for someone who was expected back in half a day. Henry took most of his personal gear, including two ice tools, some slings and carabiners, sleeping bag, both of their cameras and all the film, and left extra mittens and socks and his pile jacket for Rob, for extra warmth. Henry wanted to take all the valuables, since "small things like film and cameras get lost easily in the confusion of rescues." The two Chouinard Zero ice tools, the ones he had climbed with in Norway and on other critical ascents, were strapped on his pack as well; he felt he

> probably shouldn't have carried them but was glad I did — I just wanted to have *something,* for a weapon or to cut things or to dig a hole.

He felt he would certainly try to return with the rescue team, but was not sure if he was strong enough to do so. What little in the way of raisins, candy, and fuel was left went to Rob. Henry had had very meager rations the day before, and nothing that day at all.

The Scots had said they had made it out to the park gates in one full day from the Heim on a traversing trail marked with red dots, and that the Horombo Hut was about six to eight hours away. Henry recalls that he and Taylor knew little more about the route than that.

As Henry left, Rob recalls, both men knew that help should be back that night or early on the morrow. Barber intended to run most of the way for help, and so would

*The second day of the descent with Rob rappelling on his side/Henry
Barber Collection*

probably not return with the rescue party, but Taylor recalls
him promising to take care of things at the hospital, see him
through surgery, and remain during his recovery.

The first problem was finding the trail in very heavy,
galloping fog; this took perhaps twice the normal time. The
fatigue and emotional drain of the past days and weeks began
to close in on Henry as he contemplated the full weight of the
predicament. He stumbled onto the red-dot trail leading to
the tourist route and the Horombo Hut, one they had followed for awhile on their way up to the Heim. It was, however,

dead luck. When I left Rob he was strong and lucid, but it
wasn't long before I began to wonder. It was raining, we
were both soaked through our Gore-Tex gear, I was

freezing my ass off, and I started thinking the guy's cold, probably running out of fuel, and might go into shock, as I was amazed that he hadn't thus far.

I was really tired and didn't have any idea how long it was taking me. I kept thinking, *This is unbelievable! Why am I not there,* making me feel real guilty that I hadn't made it yet and was going so slowly. I was beginning to get worried that I was going to get done in by leopards, and nobody really knew where we were. I definitely never got lost on this red-dot trail . . . .

In his wretched condition, Henry dragged along in a blur, unaware of the time, subject to gnawing self-doubts about his performance.

Thinking he must be getting close, since the night was setting in, Henry began to get increasingly impatient and

real worried that Rob was going to die. Finally I came to this trail called the Mweka route. I said to myself that I had to go down there, to do *something,* because Rob had said the Scots had hiked from the mountain to the gates of the park in one day.

Taylor contradicts this notion, stating that "it was on the Horombo, not the Mweka route, that this had been possible." Henry — perhaps in his urgency to somehow help out, to perform well, or perhaps in his confusion and fatigue — irrationally decided to head down the Mweka Trail. He says that he

thought that it was sixty-five kilometers out; but Rob had said it should be about six hours walking. I started down this trail, just praying that I was right. I was very tired, thinking all the time I'd screwed it up, that we should have read the guidebook, that we should have done a lot of other things. I was worried about getting hurt in the jungle and not getting back to Rob in time. You have to do a fair bit of climbing on this trail. In my condition, you could easily fall down and screw yourself up. I was slipping and sliding all over the place, doing a lot of stupid things, like putting my foot on a huge hold that I could see was covered with moss. My foot would slip off and I'd hit my knee, making walking all the more difficult.

Finally, I saw these two objects, and I thought they were cars, and started seeing people walking around down there, thinking *there's got to be a road!* I got very excited and started running faster and faster. As I got closer, I saw they were only abandoned tin huts, but I thought maybe someone would be there, maybe with a radio. No one had been there for months. All I found there was a bag of tea and a space blanket. Everything I had was soaked. I couldn't light a fire because my matches were useless. I just desperately crawled into my sleeping bag and shivered all night. The only thing that kept me warm was that space blanket. It had been raining really hard for about ten hours, and up higher I knew that it was snowing, that Rob must be under a lot of snow.

I spent the night there, trying to ponder what I should do. I didn't think that I should continue down through the jungle. I pretty much knew that I should go back up to the split in the trail because the other fork was the one I knew about. I wasn't sure where this one would take me. I was almost in tears thinking about what to do. I was berating myself for not having read the guidebook, but I wouldn't have read about the Mweka route anyway. I would have read about the Breach Wall and the descents off the top. All I could think was that Rob was going to die.

At first light on the following morning, the seventh since they had started the approach to the climb, Henry hiked back up to the junction of the trails. He had slept in his boots and now could not get them off his swollen feet, which hurt horribly. He thought that it would take an hour, and after two he again became worried that he was lost. After several hours, he reached the fork and continued the traverse around the whole of one side of Kilimanjaro, in and out of the valleys that comprise its base.

While contouring around what he figured to be about the eighth valley, Henry stopped short.

> I was hiking down this gully, and I caught sight of a large animal bounding away from me. It began to follow along above me, contouring as well, and was moving very sleekly, with shoulders scrunched, and had an appendage in back. I was trying to think very quickly. I figured it must be an impala or some other big animal, but then I couldn't come up with an animal that moved like that or was that color. There was no animal that could have been up there. Then it stopped and turned sideways, and suddenly I saw all of the spots. I just said out loud, "Fuck." It was one of the only times I talked to myself.

Everyone has something they fear utterly, irrationally, that stalks them whenever they are weak. Henry instantaneously confronted what it was for him, finally encountering a situation that bold confidence and the power of will could not control, the ultimate in uncertainty.

> As slowly as I could, I took off my pack and got my axes out and secured both in my hands with the wrist loops on. Then I was gripping so hard that I could see the whites of my knuckles. I was shivering. I knew that it was the leopard, and that I had to walk towards it to stay on the trail. When I would stop, it would stop and look at me. When I walked in on a contour toward it, it was very close, about seventy meters. Then I went back out on a contour from the valley and it followed along right above me. I felt for so long I wasn't safe, I was so freaking scared. There was heavy mist, a shroud; it was creepy — if a rock fell, I was really petrified, just about in tears. It was so awesome, completely unbelievable, unknown, out of my experience. It was the unknown: completely out of my control.
>   It was totally still. It was that way the whole thirty-eight hours that I was hiking. Not a sound. I was tired, and I was stumbling and crashing through streams. Final-

*Rob in bivouac with mists moving in and the icicle in the background/
Henry Barber Collection*

ly, I got to a road. I was ecstatic, but then it forked. I knew
that I should go left. After convincing myself that I was
right, I felt finally I'd done something right. I felt that up
to then, everything I'd done had been wrong. I was pretty
demoralized. Rob had, by this time, certainly expected
help, and was probably thinking it wasn't coming now.
Thinking of the time element, I knew that the left fork
was right, but that it would be longer. I knew that it went
to the Horombo Hut, because I could see another peak
that gave its location, but the trail seemed to be going the
wrong way. Probably if I'd gone another 500 meters I
would have seen the hut.

Barber took the right fork instead, bypassing the route to

the hut. One of the factors affecting his decision at the time was an outgrowth of all the frustrations in Africa thus far.

> I definitely had the attitude that I couldn't rely on these people, and wanted to be sure it was done right, personally. I figured that I wasn't even going to deal with any Africans in this instance.

He was looking for two Norwegians he expected to find at the park gate — Odd Eliassen and Ulf Prytz. The right fork of the trail headed straight down and away from the mountain; Henry thought it must lead to the gate.

> I just turned around and went back to the righthand path. I wasn't thinking all that straight, and was rationalizing that it was becoming a well-worn trail. It was a jeep track, probably one Odd had used to help build the hut, but shortly it turned into a very rough track that got really deep from water erosion. The grass was getting thicker and several meters high. The trees in the jungle grew up all around me, and I was feeling along a little rib in the grass with my feet, following a swath of greenery where there were no trees. It was denser than the jungle on the Umbwe, and I was scared to death. A big ten-meter moss-laden branch would just give way and go thwoosh! through all the vegetation and hit the deck with a crash, and a bird would make a sound like in Tarzan movies.

Physically Henry was not in very good shape after the ordeal and because of lack of food; as a result he pulled muscles in his legs. He estimates that he went twenty kilometers, half walking, half running on his heels.

> I was thinking totally irrationally. I'd hear a sound and think a leopard's territory was only five square kilometers. So I'd run for what I thought was three miles. Then I'd be safe again.
> Finally I came to a clearing like a woodcutter's camp. A dirt road started up, small at first. Bulldozers were

working there doing something, and the road became four lanes wide. Natives were carrying stuff nearby.

At a small village, a stream ran through a line of houses. Henry remembered about the cholera that was rampant in Tanzania and resisted drinking.

A little old man with an umbrella and wearing sneakers came along. He spoke pidgin English and said he was a guide on the peak, and had been up there fifty times or such, and carried my pack for me, saying we'll go get help. He starts strutting along, walking very fast, while I'm way behind him, hobbling on really painful feet.

The local began strutting with the umbrella, putting it under his arm and sashaying, then reaching out with it to poke it in the soil and gracefully let it pass by like a cane, then whip it back forward with crisp British precision, emulating his old colonial masters. The man led his battered, staggering charge to a mission housing two clergymen from St. Gallen, Switzerland, an eastern city once visited by Henry. Henry guessed there might be a mission in the area, since they had passed one on the way up near Moshi, and he did not think he was near the park gates. They found a beer for him, almost knocking him out, and then arranged to drive him to the park officials a few minutes later, at about 7 P.M. "I was so incredulous it was all happening that I had tears running down my face," he said.

At the gatehouse, Henry

met the blackest man I had ever seen. He was a huge guy, in the same tribe as Idi Amin. He looked to me like he was three-and-a-half meters tall and weighed 300 kilos; he was huge. His skin was very shiny and as dark as black crayon; his eyes were yellow-red.

I stuck out my hand to him and said, "Hi, Henry Barber here." The guy replied, in an incredibly deep voice and very slowly, "Alfred Labumbo here." I asked him if he knew where I could find Odd or Ulf. The guard hesitated, and then slowly replied, "I don't believe you

273

have signed in or signed out," which I was afraid he might bring up. Somebody came by and helped me and called Odd or Ulf.

The two immediately set the rescue in motion, and Henry never saw Odd again. Odd gathered together his African rescue team and drove off west and north to the Shira plateau, to approach Rob — whom they feared was dead — from the west, in continuing rain and snow.

Henry was also in need of medical attention.

By the time I got to Ulf's house, everything had tightened up in my legs, and I couldn't walk. He helped me to the bathroom. I just fell on my knees. I got up and fell down, tried again and then just crawled to the bedroom. I needed a knife to cut off my gaiters. When I took off my boots, the blood hit my feet, and I passed out.

Though normally opposed to painkillers on principle, Henry willingly accepted some medication.

An hour later I was fine. But I went to wash off my feet — they were bleeding from the blisters — and just putting them in the water put me on the floor.

On the following afternoon, the rescue party reached Taylor, who they found "in surprisingly good spirits." They had expected to bury him there, but instead found him warm and dry in his bivouac sack, underneath the snow. A helicopter was supposed to pick them up on the following morning, but was late and missed the good weather. Consequently, Rob was subject to two more days of being carried down through the jungle in the midst of heavy rain. Due to the nature of the trail, he was obliged heroically to resume hopping towards the end of the arduous trek.

Henry spent the day at the house of a Danish couple who spoke little English. Kilimanjaro was perfectly framed out the picture window, days and lives away it seemed, as it repeatedly dissolved into the fog.

Nothing was happening. It was weird, very surreal, like a Fellini movie, and really tense. The helicopter was supposed to land at any time and pick up Ulf and maybe me and get Rob but it never cleared enough. So there was the sound of the helicopter, the waiting, no books or magazines to read, no TV to watch, just the silence. Every so often a meal would materialize out of nowhere, and we'd eat and then nothing.

Ulf remembers that Henry was very disoriented and over-extended, as they talked a great deal about all the climbs he had done in Norway, Australia, and elsewhere. Henry showed some slides of his travels to them that night, returning to something familiar and clearly positive after the uncertainty and self-doubt of the days in the forest. It was a way to share something with the Europeans, some of whom were not climbers but all of whom were equally dismayed at Henry's physical state and Rob's plight. There was nothing else to do, for Odd was driving Rob around the mountain by then, as they learned from radio contact with the rescue party.

The retreat down 1,500 meters of highly technical ice in roughly eight hours of climbing was deemed by Henry "one of the most successful things I had done in climbing." He felt buoyed by that ordeal, and by his trip through the jungle.

Fear springs from uncertainty, and I was jeopardizing my moral fiber and mental stability by going into the jungle. It was a learning experience.

To Henry, the event was a triumph of his technical skills and perseverance; to Rob it was an ordeal of pain and emotional abandonment; to the Europeans in the park it was a confusing mixture of a renowned climber ravaged by the jungle and days on the mountain leaving the area before his wounded companion arrived off the peak. The personality of every participant in the crisis would surface and be remolded anew in the days and months of recovery ahead. Henry would feel pleased with the brilliance of his rescue effort on the peak, and dazed and isolated by the articles and recriminations that followed. Rob would wait in hospitals and relive his years on the heights, watching with bitterness as the carefree innocent days out on the hill with the lads dissolved into a different world full of broken promises, ended careers, and violated codes of professionalism.

Odd's wife, Rotraut, who spoke both Swahili and Maasai, called the U. S. for Henry repeatedly, trying to get through to Rob's mother or his own parents or even to the American embassy in Tanzania, but to no avail. Barber booked a flight to Dar es Salaam, to return to the U. S. in order to keep a raft of business appointments in Houston and California.

> Rob and I had agreed on the mountain that when he was down and I knew that he was safe, that I would leave and get back to all of my appointments. I waited around for two days, expecting to fly on a Friday, but found out at the last minute that I couldn't fly on that day, that I'd have to fly on Thursday night. Consequently, I missed Rob by fifteen minutes, as I had to go to the airport. He was just getting in then.

Rob maintains that he remembers no such conversation on the mountain.

Having gone to the hospital, surveyed the facilities, and spoken with the doctor in charge, Henry felt that he had fulfilled his responsibilities for Rob's safety. Now he had other duties before him, he felt — to report the situation to the Taylor's and his own family, initiate steps for Rob's departure, and return to his professional obligations. Henry feels "that there is no difference between going to see him at the hospital, and knowing that he is there," that there is nothing more he could have done. Others were there to look after Rob. Henry never imagined the horrid hospital conditions Rob would have to endure during the early stages of his recovery.

"My entire foot was gangrenous," says Rob. "The doctors were concerned not about saving my leg, but about saving my life." The hospital in which he spent the next ten days was purportedly the best in Tanzania, yet its operations were inconceivable to its American patient. Rob discovered, on one occasion, that his IV bottle was filled with air; on another, a nurse attempted to give him an injection meant for someone else. His IV bottles were allowed to run empty, so that his own blood began to fill the bottles. Since the hospital had only morphine and aspirin available as pain killers, Rob would regularly receive six injections of morphine each day, after screaming for the narcotic. Such large quantities of the drug make it nearly impossible to have a bowel movement. So, for days he went without meals, since he was told he had to go to the bathroom before he got his breakfast.

As Rob later wrote, "It is not possible to express in words my feeling of total abandonment when I regained consciousness and the full realization hit me that Henry had not even waited to see me." His extraordinary tenacity and will to live undoubtedly had much to do with his pulling through the ordeal as well as he did. Rob was not to see Henry again for two months due to a serious breakdown in communications between the two.

Henry's flight to Paris was alternately delayed, then cancelled. In Dar es Salaam, he had to spend the night. In Paris, he was

> misinformed about when the flights were going to Boston. I was telling this all to a woman behind the counter at the airlines. She finally looked at me and said, "C'est la vie." I grabbed her by her clothes and yelled some pretty terrible things. I wanted to hammer her. I was just about on the verge of an emotional-type breakdown by the time I got in to Boston.

Since he was late in arriving home, Henry had only a tense night in Boston before flying to Houston for a sales convention. He went to visit Mrs. Taylor late on the evening of his arrival, after being sleepless for something like eighty hours, and explained that Rob was in good hands in Africa. He feels he could not have known differently.

Emergency surgery and two weeks of recovery saved Rob's gangrenous left leg from amputation. Restorative surgery and physical therapy in the hospital at home in Concord gradually returned strength to his leg, though he still suffers from a slight limp.

Rob's trip home was extremely trying. The airlines made little concession to his injuries, if any at all. At the airport in London, he recalls, the airlines did everything possible to ignore the fact that he would have to take up more than one seat. If he had not pressed them, he would have found himself with only one seat, forced by regulations to keep his foot on the floor. He had a note from the doctors in Tanzania indicating clearly that he would lose his leg, at best, if the foot were not elevated.

Twenty-four hours after his own return from the trip, Henry was ensconced again in his lifestyle as a salesman, flying among the western states, then returning to the east to spend six weeks in his car, seeing his long list of stores. Finally Henry visited Rob in Emerson Hospital. They had not communicated at all since they parted on the Heim moraine, and a great deal of strain had arisen between the two families due to newspaper accounts of the incident. In a tense and confrontational meeting, Henry broke with the Taylor family over their accusations and judgments. The two have not talked since.

Henry reflects,

It was just life in the fast lane, cruising over there and back, trying to get something accomplished. The original motive behind the trip was the route on Kilimanjaro. After we'd picked it, we figured we'd get involved with the articles, sure that it would be a great story. What finally happened was that the whole financial success of the trip came to depend on the climb. The route became a purely professional concern. We would have weighed things a little more carefully otherwise, because the professional commitments played a large role in pushing us into a bad situation. It's the kind of situation that makes the professional climbing scene undesirable. There simply isn't as much glamour in traveling and living this life as people think.

In a way, it was the end of the dream of how things could

be that Henry had nurtured since his trip to England five years before. On each trip, to Yosemite, Australia, Dresden, Norway, the model of the perfect venture grew in complexity, as Henry learned more and more about the things that were important, that he wanted to experience. New elements were added each time, upping the ante. But the way things worked in Africa was unbusinesslike and unpredictable to Henry, and for the moment his quest for the ultimate adventure, like that for the perfect hard, free, solo, first ascent in a remote setting, was forgotten.

At the intersection of their world views was the ideal of adventure, but Henry and Rob later realized how little they had in common otherwise: Henry the pragmatic professional seeking new technical challenges and grand adventure, and Rob the romantic mountaineer striving to explore the unknown in remote ranges, enhance personal emotional growth, and share the experience with close friends. But that was after the fact. Looking back, Rob remembers he was climbing very hard, dangerous routes and was immersed in a "deathwish." He said that, had he not made the mistake on Kilimanjaro he would probably have died elsewhere. And, had he not fallen, he and Barber would probably have remained friends. "In the end, the basic fault was with me," he said. "Henry was what he was, and the problem was that I didn't recognize that."

Each of them continues to ponder his own personal doubts, nurtured by what transpired in Africa. Will Rob be able to return to the world of hard, world-class mountaineering, and recognize the limitations of his naivete, his natural blessing as a nice guy who is a touch too gullible and is controlled by others? Will Henry ease his quest for control of events and those who make them happen, and freely express his own deep-seated compassion for others in the face of his ardent sense of professionalism and performance?

In the aftermath of their African trip, as Henry started into his frenetic schedule, Reinhold Messner, perhaps the most professional climber today, flew to Africa and patiently waited two weeks for the weather to stabilize. When he was certain that a spell of clear sky was due for a few days, he and Konrad Renzler moved quickly and completed a direct climb of the icicle route on the Breach Wall in twelve hours in perfect hard-ice conditions. *Climbing* wrote that Messner felt it was one of the most difficult routes he had undertaken, and *Mountain* quoted him as saying "it was the most dangerous wall that I've ever climbed."

Upon the publication the next summer of Rob's "A Breach of Faith," the whole climbing world began to buzz with what amounted to scandal. The friendship between the two climbers had come to an abrupt, bitter end. Rob's claims had to do with what most mountaineers would regard as serious ethical issues. The majority of bystanders felt that these allegations damaged Henry's reputation, and some urged him — if they were untrue, as he maintained — to answer them in print. He declined and, out of a distaste for controversy, refused to read Rob's article or the printed comments of other climbers.

Both families became increasingly embittered. Somehow they had known it was all wrong from the beginning. Mrs. Barber had felt that going to Africa was a mistake, that it was a continent of turmoil. Mrs. Taylor called her a day or two before they were due back and indicated that she felt something was wrong. "Where are they?" she asked, before they were even overdue. And, as Henry painfully reiterates,

> Four of us did exactly the same thing with Mike Warburton in Russia — said goodbye to him and they took him away in an airplane from the mountains, and we never saw him again.

For Henry, the real damage was done after Rob returned from Africa and wrote his incendiary articles.

> You know, there was so much of this kind of questioning right away that I never got to think about it all, never got the emotional reward of having saved somebody's life, and never got the emotional reward of having established a wonderful relationship in the first place that I cared about.

As Henry summarized in *Climbing,*

I made a mistake and left Rob in Africa, but only when I knew he was at the hospital . . . . The thing boils down to the fact that I made a wrong decision . . . . I would never do it again, but that doesn't erase the past. I don't feel guilty, though, because of the nature of so many critical decisions I had to make while getting off the thing.

And so ends a tale whose elements appear to be crudely borrowed from the world of intense confrontation with self and the natural world, of a Hemingway short story: Kilimanjaro sailing above the thorn-tree plains; fear, abandonment, gangrene and the smell of the end so near, the harsh realizations forced on partners in a glorious, romanticized struggle, and the blinding immediacy of death's stalking gait. Perhaps Hemingway said it best, after all, in the prelude to "The Snows of Kilimanjaro:"

Kilimanjaro is a snow covered mountain 19,710 feet high, and is said to be the highest mountain in Africa. Its western summit is called by the Masai "Ngaje Ngai," the House of God. Close to the western summit there is the dried and frozen carcass of a leopard. No one has explained what the leopard was seeking at that altitude.

Glossary

*aid or direct aid
climbing* .... Involves the direct use of pitons, slings, or the rope to rest or make progress, as opposed to FREE CLIMBING.

aid elemination .... Eliminating one, several, or all of the previously accepted points of direct aid or support on a climb — in essence, introducing free climbing.

anchor .... General term for any means of attaching rope (and climbers) to the surface being climbed, using natural anchors such as trees or rock flakes or artificial anchors such as nuts, pitons, or ice screws placed by the leader.

arete .... Sharp-edged ridge, often created by glacial action.

belay .... Practice of protecting a climber from a fall by having a securely positioned and anchored partner holding the rope to which the climber is attached.

bergschrund .... Large crevasse at a glacier's upper limit, caused by ice movement downhill, away from the steep slopes above.

bolt .... Metal pin driven into a hole drilled into the rock and fitted with a removable, eyed hanger; used as an anchor or point of protection.

bong .... Piton made of angled metal and larger than standard angles, for wide cracks.

bouldering .... Subspecialty of rock climbing involving the practice of gymnastic climbing techniques on boulders.

carabiner .... Oval aluminum snaplink with a spring-loaded gate; used to connect items of climbing equipment, such as a rope and chock for protection or an anchor. Also called biner or crab.

ceiling .... See *roof*.

centimeter .... Metric measure of distance; about ⅓ of an inch.

chalk .... Chalk dust, borrowed from gymnastics, used on the hands to keep them dry and improve one's purchase on the rock.

chimney .... Crack wide enough to allow the entire body into it; special techniques such as stemming allow chimneys to be climbed.

chock .... Artificial chockstone of soft metal, shaped like a wedge or machine nut and cunningly jammed into place in a crack without force; now used in place of hammer-driven pitons for protection, and preferable because chocks do less damage to the rock.

chockstone .... A natural rock wedged in a crack or chimney, sometimes used for protection and often difficult to climb around.

Glossary

commitment . . . . Degree to which a climber is forced by circumstances — an oncoming storm, for instance, a personal philosophy, or a pitch or more that cannot be safely downclimbed — to continue up a route rather than returning to safer ground.

corner . . . . Angle in a rock face where two walls partially oppose one another, such as in the inside corner of a room or the outside corner of a building; climbed using special techniques like bridging.

couloir . . . . Gully, often ice- or snow-filled, on a mountain; often used for ascent and descent, although prone to be a chute for icefall and rockfall.

crack climbing . . . . Ascending a long, narrow opening in a rock wall, by jamming hands and feet in the crack and using a variety of layback and opposition holds.

crampon . . . . Metal frame, with downward- and forward-pointing spikes, that can be strapped onto mountain boots; permits firm purchase during the ascent of steep snow and ice slopes.

crux . . . . Most difficult move on a pitch; hardest portion of a climb.

desperate . . . . Climber's slang for "dangerous," "threatening," or "extremely difficult."

downclimbing . . . . More difficult than ascending, because it is harder to see the holds; not often practiced, since most climbers hike around or rappel (get lowered on the rope) when descending.

eb's . . . . Special French rock climbing shoes with canvas uppers and very soft, smooth, rubber soles, now considered standard garb.

ethics . . . . In climbing, consideration of and commitment to the principles of one's style of climbing, especially on first ascents; a recent movement toward a 'purer' ethics downplays the use of technology and equipment in favor of the physical and psychological testing of unaided free and solo climbing.

exposure . . . . Clearly observable distance one can fall; a measure of danger and intimidation.

finger crack . . . . Narrow crack wide enough for the climber's fingers to be inserted and twisted so that they jam.

first ascent . . . . First climb of a particular mountain or route.

first free ascent . . . . First ascent of a mountain or route without the use of aid.

first solo ascent . . . . First ascent of a mountain or route by a single unsupported climber.

free climbing . . . . Climbing without the direct support of the rope or artificial equipment, using only holds available on the rock, as opposed to aid climbing; more dangerous, difficult, and commiting than aid climbing the same route.

french technique . . . . Climbing ice using an ice axe and the ten downward-pointing spikes of each crampon; requires considerable balance, skill, and flexible ankles on high-angled slopes.

Glossary

friction climbing . . . . Climbing low-angle slabs using the
(or *slab climbing*)   friction provided by the palms of
the hands and the soles of the feet
on the smooth rock rather than
holds.

front pointing . . . . Ice climbing technique in which the
(or *austrian technique*)   climber ascends steep ice using
only the two front (and forward-
pointing) points on each crampon
(versus the flat-footed French technique) and hand tools.

girdle traverse . . . . A route across the entire horizontal
width of a cliff, parallel to the
ground; popular in Britain.

ground fall . . . . Potentially serious accident in
which a climber falls all the way to
the ground because he is not
caught by the belaying rope or is
soloing without one.

hectare . . . . Metric area measure; equal to
about 2½ acres.

ice axe . . . . Tool carried by ice climbers and
alpine mountaineers; used to cut
steps, as a personal anchor, and as a
safety device to arrest falls.

ice climbing . . . . Subspecialty of mountaineering,
with its own techniques; involves
climbing steep, frozen waterfalls,
iced-over cliffs, and icy sections of
mountains using specialized ice
tools and axes.

ice screw . . . . Equivalent of a piton in rock climbing; used in ice climbing as a
temporary anchor or point of protection; once screwed in, the
threads resist being pulled out,
making a screw more secure than

an ice piton; removed by unscrewing or by its melting out.

jam . . . . Climbing hold in which part of the body — fingers, hand, foot — is wedged into a crack for support.

jumar, to jumar . . . . Metal ascending device used in pairs climber slides them up one at a time and stands in slings attached to them; to use such devices.

kilometer . . . . Metric distance measure; about 3/5 of a mile.

knifeblade piton . . . . Small, very thin piton for use in narrow cracks.

leader . . . . First member of a climbing team to ascend a pitch, as opposed to a second; the decision-maker on an expedition.

leader fall . . . . Potentially dangerous accident in which the lead climber on the rope falls; unless properly belayed and protected, he may fall all the way to the ground, in extreme cases pulling his team down with him.

lie-back, layback . . . . Climbing technique in which the fingers are used to pull on one side of a vertical crack, while the feet press against the other wall.

lock . . . . Climbing hold, such as a jam.

meter . . . . Metric measure of distance; a little more than a yard.

moraine . . . . Terminal line of a glacier, where its rock debris is deposited.

mountaineering . . . . Generic term for the sport of ascending high mountain peaks that require special skills and equipment; usually involves rock, snow and ice climbing, as well as extended exposure to objective hazards such as cold, avalanches, and privations.

névé (or *firn*) .... Zone in a glacier where snow consolidates into ice; also, consolidated glacial snow.

nut .... See *chock.*

off-width crack .... Vertical crack used for climbing, particularly difficult to ascend because it is too wide for secure hand or foot jams, but too narrow to be a chimney.

pin or *peg* .... Slang for piton.

pinch grip .... Climbing hold in which the hand is used to pinch a nubbin or flake of rock

pitch .... Stetch or sequence of climbing by a leader between belay stations, usually measuring less than a rope length, or 45-50 meters (150-165 feet).

piton .... Metal spike with an eye in it driven into a crack with a hammer to anchor or protect a climber; connected to the rope with carabiners and slings.

protection .... Generic term for all kinds of anchoring devices and techniques; involves pitons, nuts, bolts, trees, ice screws, etc.

prusic .... To climb a rope fixed above by means of prusik knots (and slings) wrapped around the rope and tied so that they will slide when pushed up but will jam when pulled down by the climber's weight.

rack . . . . Complement of climbing hardware, such as a sling strung with nuts, pitons, and carabiners, used by the leader for protecting a pitch.

rappel . . . . Means of controlled descent using a rope, usually doubled, that is run through various friction devices and/or wrapped around the body.

rock climbing . . . . Climbing of rock faces on cliffs, pinnacles, or mountains; a subspecialty of mountaineering.

rockfall . . . . Hazard of mountaineering; weathering, wind, and melting snow constantly loosen rock, ice, and other debris, which then slides and bounces down the mountain.

roof or ceiling . . . . Distinct, severely overhanging rock formation protruding from the wall usually very difficult to ascend.

rope length . . . . Usually 45-50 meters (150-165 feet); used interchangeably with pitch (which see).

route . . . . Path of ascent up a particular cliff, mountain, glacier, etc., often described and named in guidebooks.

runner . . . . Sling, usually about a meter long and made of 25-centimeter (one-inch) nylon webbing, used to go over rock horns or around chockstones to provide protection.

run-out . . . . The distance a leader has climbed past his last protection anchor, hence a measure of danger and commitment.

second . . . . Second member of a climbing team, who belays the leader while he is climbing and then follows him up the pitch.

serac . . . . Ice wall or tower in a glacier.

sling . . . . Loop of nylon webbing used to anchor oneself; also used to string climbing gear on.

solo climbing . . . . Climbing alone, either by belaying oneself (roped solo) or without a rope (free solo). More difficult and dangerous than climbing with a partner because of the absence of a belayer.

stemming or bridging . . . . Technique for climbing chimneys in which pressure is applied to the opposing walls to hold the climber up.

stopper . . . . A wedge-shaped nut manufactured in a full range of sizes by Yvon Chouinard.

toproping . . . . Safe technique for attempting or practicing difficult climbs, in which the climber is protected by a rope held from above; the climb is done without a leader.

undercling . . . . Climbing hold in which the hands pull upward while the feet press down.

*yosemite decimal
system* . . . . System for rating the technical difficulty of rock climbs; running from 5.1 to 5.9 initially, with harder ratings such as 5.10, 5.11, and 5.12 added later on as they became necessary.